The Economics of
Governments and Markets:
New Directions in
European Public Policy

Lois Duff

LONGMAN
London and New York

Addison Wesley Longman Limited
Edinburgh Gate, Harlow,
Essex CM20 2JE, England
and Associated Companies throughout the world.

*Published in the United States of America
by Longman Publishing, New York*

First published 1997

ISBN 0582 28984 X

British Library Cataloguing-in-Publication Data

A catalogue record for this book is
available from the British Library

Library of Congress Cataloging-in-Publication Data

Set by 33 in Times

Produced through Longman Malaysia, PP

The Economics of
Governments and Markets

For Jean and David

Contents

Part 4 Environmental themes

List of figures

List of tables

Foreword

It is easy for students of economics to get the impression that the subject has little practical relevance. Economics is often presented as a body of abstract theories, with carefully chosen, highly unrealistic examples used to illustrate them. Too often students are left with the notion that economics is not geared to solving real-world problems, and provides little by way of a guide to policy-makers.

In this highly original book, Lois Duff shows how relatively simple economic concepts can be very powerful in helping to analyse social issues and in providing solutions to a wide range of contemporary problems. The judicious mix of theory, examples and case studies will provide the student of micro-economic policy with a sound foundation for assessing the relative roles of government and the market in dealing with issues such as pollution and waste disposal; the operation of public utilities such as postal services and electricity; and the provision of health care, housing, higher education, roads and railways.

After an introductory part (chapters 1–3), which presents the core theory necessary for understanding the subsequent applications, the book then examines the issues one by one, with a separate chapter devoted to each. Every chapter follows a common pattern: The problem is identified and the current system of allocating resources is described, along with its various strengths and weaknesses; then various options for reforming the system of allocation are considered; there then follow two case studies drawn from around Europe that illustrate different approaches to tackling the problems; finally, there is a discussion section which draws lessons from the case studies.

Students will welcome this book in helping to bring alive a field of economics that can make a powerful contribution to tackling some of the most pressing problems faced by people in all countries as we move into the new millennium. The examples and case studies are all relevant to the student's direct experience of living in a modern industrial society. The uniform structure for each of the chapters in Parts 2–4 will help students navigate their way through the book and show how common themes can be identified in many apparently quite different problem areas.

Tutors will welcome the way that they can tailor the use of the book for their specific courses. The style is straightforward and direct, with theory only used to the extent that it is directly relevant to analysing the issues. This makes the book accessible not only to students of economics but also to those studying sociology, social policy, politics, public administration and business studies, who have had only a basic grounding in economics.

John Sloman

Preface

This book looks at the changing role of government in regulating certain sectors of the economy, emphasizing different approaches adopted in Europe. There has been a change in the way governments see their role in the market economy: many are looking to the market to take an increased role, but under government supervision. This book charts the new approaches being taken by selected western European nations, in their efforts to improve both the efficiency and equity outcomes of their public services, national industries and care of the environment.

This book is written for students who will have, at least, an introductory background in economics, and some of the analysis and economic concepts used go up to intermediate level. It is written for the needs of students of public sector economics, social economics and applied microeconomics. Diagrams have been kept to the absolute minimum because many of the issues discussed can be dealt with adequately without them. Although the book has been written for economics students, it will be of interest to readers in related academic areas, such as social policy, public policy, social administration and political economy, and perhaps to professionals in the fields of education, health and housing.

The book is intended to introduce students to specific key economic concepts, through a framework of analysis, with a strong unifying theme, on a wide range of contemporary economic problems. The aim is to avoid too abstract an approach, but to introduce the relevant theory at the beginning and then apply it in the case studies. As the concepts and theories are explained at the beginning, the book can be used as a textbook; alternatively, it may be used as a supplementary text to provide an understanding of the various approaches adopted by different countries. Each chapter is self-contained and can be read independently of the other chapters. Each chapter contains the relevant economic concepts, questions, and further reading.

The book is by no means comprehensive on the role of the public sector, but rather it focuses on a wide range of sectors where governments have principally adopted market-orientated approaches. This enables students to extract from the morass of detail the essentials of policy decisions and the economic and political considerations at stake. Students often study economics along with other subjects and so an effort has been made to take a multidisciplinary approach. Many textbooks often focus on the theory and offer only brief examination of the policy aspects, whereas this book provides a balance between the two. In addition, the new directions in public policy are set in the context of developments at the EU level, in recognition that the European dimension is becoming increasingly important.

The original contribution of this book is the use of case studies. This has been adopted for a number of reasons. There is a strong argument in favour of teaching economics by the case study method on the grounds that cases can convey information about relationships which principles cannot. Case studies are more than examples: they allow an application of a principle and they can illustrate the complexity of economic decisions which involve trade-offs. In the case of public policy, implementation problems and strengths can be highlighted in a realistic setting. Students can find themselves involved in the middle of a real problem. Realism adds to the setting.

The approach adopted in this book is to use two case studies side by side. This reinforces the learning principles and offers scope for comparing different approaches adopted. More is conveyed in the whole than in the two halves. Also, case studies can motivate: they make us want to learn more about particular nations and the different approaches they have adopted. Finally, the emergence of modularization in higher education presents specific challenges and problems for teachers of economics, in that they often have to teach students with varying backgrounds in economics. One way to overcome this problem is to present the concepts through case studies, thereby creating an unfamiliar environment for those students familiar with the concepts. To this extent the book has some claim to originality. My hope is that other writers will thereby be encouraged to develop the case study approach. If the book achieves this objective, we will all gain.

The early theoretical chapters assume a knowledge up to intermediate microeconomic level. Chapter 1 explains how a market works and sets out the efficiency arguments for allowing a perfectly competitive market to operate. Chapter 2 provides the efficiency rationale for intervention and explains the inequalities which emerge as a result of markets. Chapter 3 introduces the government objectives and various approaches adopted to ensure an efficient allocation of resources. Chapters 4 to 12 introduce the policy analysis. These are divided into three broad themes: social welfare, national industries and environmental themes. All chapters have a common structure. They begin by discussing the factors for change, both within the market and within the current level of government involvement. The economic rationale for government intervention in each particular area is discussed, and this is followed by a description of the possible and actual types of intervention. Alongside discussion of ongoing and possible options for reform, the section ends with a separate reference to developments at EU level. The case studies are then presented back-to-back. Each follows a common set of headings and presents the relevant background and objectives being pursued. Selected approaches are then analysed from the viewpoint of efficiency and, where relevant, equity. The chapters close with a discussion in terms of the costs and benefits of each approach and a comparison between the approaches adopted. The final chapter analyses the new directions of public policy under each theme.

This text is a product of twelve years' teaching, researching and consulting for governments. There is a debt of gratitude to former students, supervisors and colleagues, from whom much has been learned. I would like to thank personally all my present colleagues at the School of Economics, University of the West of England, Bristol, and everyone else who gave assistance and feedback. Thanks to the Centre for Social and Economic Research (CESER) which kindly funded part of the time it took to write this book. I wish to express thanks to Chris Harrison from Longman for the support and encouragement he gave me. Finally, I owe my greatest debt to my family and all my long-suffering friends.

Lois Duff

Part 1

Theory

Chapter 1

The economics of the market

Key words used: equilibrium, quantity demanded, quantity supplied, efficiency, opportunity costs

Society needs to find a way of deciding what, how and for whom to produce. This chapter explains how markets and prices allocate resources between competing uses. Any discussion on the role of markets and governments involves theories of how the market and government potentially operate. A starting point is to describe the market from the point of view of the perfectly competitive model. In reality, all economies are mixed and the divisions between governments and markets are not always clear. Nevertheless, it is still useful to present the material in this way, as it provides a conceptual framework from which it is possible to understand how the free market pricing system should work and how it should allocate resources.

The market mechanism

We are constantly trying to understand the world we live in, and when we provide explanations, we are, in effect, theorizing about it. Scientists try to explain how matter changes, sociologists try to explain how people behave, and economists try to explain how resources are allocated. These people explain the world by constructing simple models about reality. The aim is to try and bring out the important features and to abstract away from the little things. Models can add to our understanding only if they stand detached from the world. A theory helps us to define relationships. Models should be logical, moving from one step to another. They should contain a set of variables and a set of assumptions which link them together. Finally, there should be a deduction or prediction element about what we would actually expect to find in the real world.

Economists have used the model of perfect competition to explain the workings of the capitalist economy. It addresses issues such as demand, supply, resource allocation, price determination and welfare. The perfect competition model is a useful starting point for any discussion of public policy reforms, as many of the reforms rely on the notion of the market when they come to consider issues such as privatization. The market mechanism will be described under a number of key headings:

- Scarcity necessitates rationing.
- Consumer choice and the Law of Demand.
- Producer choice and the Law of Supply.
- Shortages and surpluses.
- Shifts in the demand and supply curves.

Scarcity necessitates rationing

We live in a world where goods and resources are limited in their supply compared to our wants and needs. When goods are scarce there must be a way of rationing them. Rationing in the real world could take many forms. It could be done on the basis of beauty, the most attractive people receiving what they want, or on the basis of the strongest, or on a first come, first served basis, or using a waiting list. Competition is therefore only one way to ration, and it works by rationing goods on the basis of how willing and able people are to pay for the good. Western economies rely heavily on markets and prices to allocate resources among competing uses.

The perfect competition model is based on a number of assumptions:

- The economy consists of many independent producers and consumers: no one is sufficiently powerful to influence market outcomes by their own action and everyone is a price taker.
- Individuals and companies are assumed to be self-interested and rational, and they seek to maximize their levels of satisfaction (utility) or profits. It is assumed that people cannot suffer for others and that their levels of utility are independent of others'.
- Companies are profit maximizing and will always strive to produce at the least cost.
- In each and every market there is a market-clearing price which is determined where quantity demanded equals the quantity supplied.
- There is no government intervention.
- Finally, it is assumed that there is perfect knowledge.

As we shall see throughout this book, in reality, markets are not perfect, consumers are not always rational in their decision making and companies have other goals besides maximizing profits. Moreover, for some goods there is no market demand because it is impossible to state a preference or a willingness to pay.

Consumer choice and the Law of Demand

A market is a set of arrangements by which buyers and sellers are in contact for the exchange of goods or services. With some markets the buyers and sellers meet each other physically, like in a fruit market, while in others someone acts on behalf of a buyer, as in the stock market. Demand is the quantity of a good that consumers wish to purchase at each conceivable price. The demand is not a particular quantity, but a description of how much a buyer will purchase at each and every price. As the price rises, the quantity demanded falls, other things being equal. A number of assumptions are made here. Rational consumers will decide which goods to buy and which to forgo on the basis of achieving the most satisfaction from spending their limited income. This satisfaction is called consumer utility. Prices influence their decision: an increase in the price of a good will increase the opportunity cost of consuming it. In economics we say that the choice to do something is, at the same time, the choice not to do something else. Opportunity costs are the highest value that must be sacrificed when we choose to do something. Generally, the lower the price of the good, the less the cost of consuming it, and hence the higher its consumption. The negative relationship between the price of a good and the amount consumed is called the Law of Demand. It can be graphically presented in Figure 1.1 for the case of lamb.

Let us assume that the average family consumes 1 kg of lamb per week at a price of £4/kg. As the price of lamb increases, the quantity demanded falls, other things being equal. If the price of lamb increases to £6/kg, weekly consumption declines to 0.6 kg. The line through these two points shows the demand for lamb as a function of its price.

The relevance of the Law of Demand to this book is that we are describing

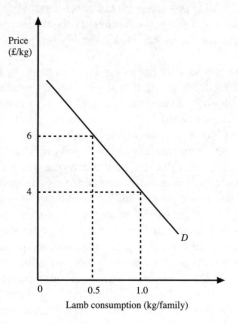

Figure 1.1 The demand for lamb

5

the market process for a private good. There are some goods, provided through the public sector, where it is not possible to express a willingness to pay through the price mechanism, or where the demand for a good cannot make an impact on outcomes because someone else makes the demand decision on our behalf.

Producer choice and the Law of Supply

Supply is the quantity of a good that sellers wish to sell at each conceivable price. Supply is not a particular quantity; it is a description of the quantity a seller would like to sell at each and every price. Goods can rarely be produced for nothing: it takes a certain price before there is any incentive to produce a good, and at higher prices it becomes increasingly profitable to supply a greater quantity. The Law of Supply states that there is a positive relationship between the price of a good and the amount of it that can be supplied.

Equilibrium price balances the conflicting forces of demand and supply. Equilibrium is a state where forces are said to be in balance, where there are no pressures for change. In this case, the decisions of consumers will be consistent with the decisions of producers. Figure 1.2 shows how the market price for lamb brings about an equilibrium. The market price is that price which represents all the consumers' and producers' interests in this particular market. Suppose that prices were temporarily above the equilibrium price P_e, at P_1. Here there is an excess of supply in lamb, excess in relation to consumers' desire to consume. Stocks would build up, and firms would reduce price and cut production. The fall in price would make some producers go out of business, while consumers would increase their purchases of the good. Eventually the price reduction would bring the reduced production into line with the increased consumption at the equilibrium price, P_e.

If the price were temporarily below equilibrium price, at P_2, there would be an excess demand for lamb in relation to the amount producers are willing to supply. The large number of consumers would bid up the price, and producers would raise their prices toward P_e. As the price rises and production expands, consumers will cut down on their consumption, until equilibrium price is reached and consumers' demand is consistent with producers' supply.

In this model, the market decides how much of a good should be produced by finding the price at which quantity demanded equals quantity supplied. The market tells us for whom the good is produced: the good is produced for all those consumers willing to pay for it. The market also tells us who is producing: all those willing to supply at the equilibrium price. The relevance of this process to public policy is that, through the price mechanism, people will engage in activities only when they get paid for it or receive a level of satisfaction. For some goods and services, however, it is not appropriate to use the price mechanism, and the price of the good is zero at the point of consumption. This may arise when a good or service is collectively financed and provided on our behalf. Under these conditions, the forces of demand and supply have been substituted by another mechanism and the processes described above do not take

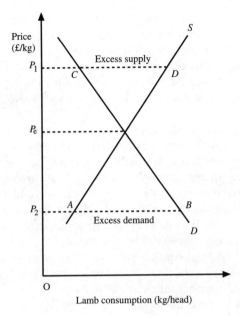

Figure 1.2 Equilibrium in the lamb market

place. When we speak of public policy reforms which use market-based approaches, we are referring to the setting of incentives which mimic the market in encouraging and defining more clearly the forces of demand and supply.

Shortages and surpluses

The market process can deal with shortages and surpluses by raising and reducing the price respectively. The role of prices is therefore to balance the conflicting forces of supply and demand. However, the concept of need is different to demand and it is here that the market processes may be limited. Take the case of poverty: this is something quite different to shortages. Poverty suggests that some basic level of need has not been met. The absence of shortages means that not just has some basic need been satisfied but as much of the good as we want has been provided. There is no reason why the market mechanism should distribute according to the principle of need.

Shifts in the demand and supply curves

The description of the process leading towards equilibrium price makes a number of assumptions: certain things remain equal. In the case of demand this refers to the price of related goods, the income of consumers and consumers' tastes and preferences. Referring to the example of lamb, if we change one of the assumptions and imagine that the price of beef, a substitute, has decreased,

7

we can analyse this impact on the demand for lamb in Figure 1.3. Beginning at output Q and price P, there is now a reduction in the demand for lamb, at each and every price. On Figure 1.3 this would result in a shift of the demand curve to the left from D to D_1, the equilibrium output would fall from Q to Q_1, and the equilibrium price would fall from P to P_1. Following the same logic, changes in consumers' income and tastes and preferences will also bring about shifts in the demand curve.

The supply curve is drawn on the assumptions that the technology available to producers and the costs of inputs remain constant along the supply curve. When one of these conditions changes, it will result in a shift of the supply curve. This represents a change in the amount that producers wish to supply at each and every price. In the case of lamb production, if a new improved fodder is introduced, which reduces the cost of producing lamb, new producers may come into the market and existing producers may be able to expand their output. Producers will be able to supply a greater quantity at each and every price, and the supply curve will shift to the right. Beginning from equilibrium output Q and price P, the supply curves moves downwards and to the right, from S to S_1. Equilibrium output has increased from Q to Q_1^*, and price has fallen from P to P_1.

The reason why we need to describe the process of shifting demand and supply is that, in theory, it demonstrates that markets are highly interrelated and that changes in circumstances necessarily produce changes in other things. Free markets allow prices to be determined by the forces of demand and supply. However, in many of the markets or sectors studied in this book, the forces of

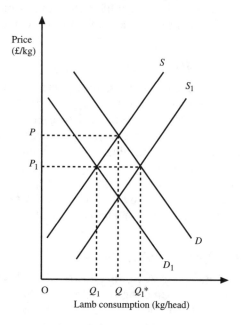

Figure 1.3 Shifts in demand and supply curves

demand and supply are non-existent or do not have a very strong impact on outcomes, or take a long time to respond and react. In other words, changes in circumstances are not always met by responses in these markets. This condition can arise because of the nature of the good or because of government intervention. In some cases, like the provision of higher education, the changing demands of consumers have not led to immediate changes in supply. Public policy reforms have been aimed at clearing the channels of interrelatedness: for example, allowing students a greater range of choice in higher education courses. In this case, market-led approaches can mean that changes have a better chance of exerting an impact on subsequent outcomes.

The market mechanism and efficiency

We have to ask the question: if a free market did operate in the manner described above, what could we expect in terms of resource allocation? The answer is that a perfectly competitive market is an appropriate mechanism to use to achieve economic efficiency. Economic efficiency is a term which means that for any given level of effort (cost), we obtain the largest possible benefit. This can be put another way: we obtain a given level of benefits with the least possible effort. Economic efficiency is about getting the most out of the available resources.

The next question to ask is: how do we ensure that the maximum is attained from the available resources? Two conditions are necessary for economic efficiency:

- An economic action should be undertaken if it results in more benefits than costs for the individuals in an economy.
- No economic action should be undertaken if it results in more costs to these individuals.

The economist Pareto introduced a way of evaluating the efficiency of resource allocation. It was based on a value judgement: that economic welfare is increased if one person is made better off and no one else is made worse off. This is called a Pareto efficiency or welfare improvement. Similarly, welfare is decreased if one person is made worse off and no one better off. Being made worse off or better off in terms of welfare involves a change in the level of utility: for example, in the consumption of goods and services. If a person increases the consumption of a good and their utility increases, it is assumed that there is an increase in the welfare of society. Pareto optimality is an ideal position: we say that it is not possible to reallocate resources so as to make one person better off without making another worse off. Economics breaks down the notion of economic efficiency into two broad areas:

- Efficiency in production.
- Efficiency in consumption.

9

Efficiency in production

Efficiency in production does not refer to a situation where everyone is working flat out and machines are overheating. In economics it is a very specific term. A starting point is to describe what inefficient production means. Have you ever been in a family-run restaurant where all the family members are helping in the running of the business? Let us imagine that situation now and assume that the grandparents are involved too. They may be working very hard, but they are not so fast on their feet and may get in other people's way. This is an example of inefficiency in production. It may be possible to reallocate the grandparents' effort to uses which best suit their ability. For example, they could be involved in menu preparation or training other people when the restaurant is closed. In economics, we say that there is inefficient production when the factors of production are not, given their relative strengths or values, being combined in the best possible way. In this example, costs are not being minimized.

Alternatively, let us assume that the grandparents are fast on their feet, are efficient and can handle new technology competently: for example, the food-processing equipment. But this time they do not get along with their spouses. There are problems with the day-to-day running of the restaurant because no one can agree on how and when the equipment should be used. In economics we say that, even if the best production techniques are being used, so long as it is possible to reorganize resources so as to increase the production of a good without producing less of another good, by making better use of existing resources, then production is inefficient.

Finally, let us assume that all family members work efficiently and get along together. Will this be enough to assure total efficiency? The answer is: not necessarily. Let us assume that this time the grandparents like to use old-fashioned recipes. They produce meals which are reasonably enjoyed by consumers, but no one raves about them. In economics, we say that production is inefficient if it produces things which people do not really want. Production can be made efficient by producing more of one good, such as a more modern recipe, and less of another. Hence, we say that efficiency in production means two things:

- Producers produce goods at a minimum cost.
- They produce goods in combinations that match people's willingness to pay for them.

In other words, production is not efficient if goods are being produced at above minimum cost. This can occur when there are few incentives to be cost conscious. Moreover, when goods are not produced in relation to the amount which people want or at the price they wish to pay, production can also said to be inefficient.

Efficiency in consumption

Efficiency in consumption does not refer to eating everything on your plate or using goods until they fall apart! This is a very specific term and it means that consumers purchase goods in accordance with their personal preferences and finances. For efficiency in consumption to be reached, no final redistribution of outputs among people will make them better off. In other words, if you and I purchase in the same markets and pay the same prices, and we each buy according to our tastes and preferences, it follows that it is unlikely that we will end up with the wrong combinations of things.

Putting the two sides of the equation together, we can summarize what total efficiency means:

- Efficiency in production is where, for a fixed supply of inputs, it is not possible to produce more of one good without producing less of another; nor is it possible to reduce the use of one input without increasing the use of another to produce a given output.
- Efficiency in consumption is where it is not possible to increase welfare by changing the distribution of goods among consumers.
- Total efficiency is where there is maximization of both output and the welfare derived from the consumption of goods.

What we are saying here is that the rate at which consumers weigh up consuming a good in terms of other goods, is the same rate at which producers weigh up producing a good in terms of its alternatives. A competitive market leads to efficiency in the absence of market failure. If a market is in disequilibrium and there is excess demand for a good, this means that a consumer values one good more in terms of another, and its price will be bid up. The rate at which consumers value these goods is the relative prices of the goods in question. Producers must then alter their rate of producing the goods, increasing production of one good in response to its rise in price. This will continue until supply equates with demand. Here, it is not possible to reallocate resources to make one person better off without making another worse off. In economics, we say price equals marginal cost under perfect competition. When the price of a good is greater than the marginal cost of producing that good, society gains value by producing more of that good. When the price of a good is less than the marginal cost of producing that good, society gains value by producing less of that good.

The market mechanism and public policy

So far, we have built a model of the perfectly competitive firm that produces an efficient mix of output and an efficient distribution of that output to consumers. Prices are the indicators which ration scarce goods. The Laws of Supply and Demand ration goods to consumers who are willing to pay the highest prices.

Prices guide consumers to choose on the basis of what they are willing to give up. Under a market system, there is a tendency for resources to be allocated to those who value them most highly: that is, the company which is willing to pay the most for the raw materials and the consumer who is willing to pay the highest price. The perfectly competitive model assumes that there is economic efficiency. We now need to relate these ideas to their meaning in relation to public policy. This will be done in relation to two aspects:

- Reflections on the perfect competition model.
- Uses and limitations to public policy.

Reflections on the perfect competition model

This model has been criticized on the grounds that the assumptions are very unrealistic. We just need to look around us to see the presence of large, dominant, price-giving firms, people not making rational economic decisions, price being only one of many considerations in determining choice, and people not having perfect information. We need to assess whether these variations from the assumptions are large or small. If there are small variations, then we can be reasonably content with the perfect competition model. If there are large variations between the assumptions and reality, then the model has limited applicability. This is an ongoing debate and there does not appear to be any consensus on the matter.

The model has also been criticized on the grounds that it is not internally logical. One issue is the meaning of competition. Does this mean people vigorously striving to better their lot, and in production, does it mean everyone producing the same or producing something which is different? Is competition a state or is it a process? Some people have claimed that the perfect competition model is useful as a way of explaining how the price mechanism works, but it is limited in explaining how competition works. Competition is something which is broader, incorporating time, risk and the interrelatedness of things. One of the paradoxes of the perfect competition model is that profits motivate producers, but that this process continues until profits are eliminated. It can be argued that there is no competition in a perfectly competitive market.

The Pareto criterion, which states that for a welfare improvement one person must be made better off without making someone else worse off, is very restrictive. Any public policy will inevitably make some people worse off, even if it is a small number of people, thereby infringing the welfare rule. The measurement of the effectiveness of policies has tended to expand this rule. In some cases the policy is judged upon the basis of who the gainers and losers are, and how the losses can be minimized: for example, how the least number of people can be hurt.

Uses and limitations to public policy

We need to ask: what are the attributes of the market and what use are they to policy making? One can claim that the attributes are rationing and motivation. The role of price is that it rations goods and services. There is a tendency for each resource to be rationed to the company that evaluates it most highly, that is willing to pay the most for the resource. In addition to rationing, the market also motivates people towards the productive processes. Entrepreneurs and business people are motivated to undertake producing a good or service because they believe that people will be so willing to pay for it that they will pay in excess of the costs of production. Pursuit of personal interests by producers will lead them to act in a way which benefits consumers. This means that millions of goods and services can be produced and consumed through the market mechanism.

The perfect competition model has been used in many policy-making approaches. For example, privatization, international trade and economic integration in the European Union all rely on the predictive qualities of this model. More specifically, new directions in public policy which seek to give consumers greater choice, to increase the number of producers of a public service or to introduce a price mechanism have one thing in common. They all seek to take market elements and use them in a way which will promote competition and increase efficiency.

However, we must be aware of the limitations of relying on this model and the Pareto optimum. Both are developed in isolation of social, moral and political considerations. If we wish to teach people how modern capitalism works, few teachers would advocate looking at the perfect competition model alone. It is too limited in its assumptions and scope to be able to capture the complexities of how markets and competition work.

Q1 Why is it necessary to examine the workings of a perfectly competitive market prior to a discussion of public policy reforms?

Q2 Why is it that, although the perfect competition model has serious shortcomings, it still influences much thinking about the workings of markets?

Q3 What is your vision of an economy which is running well?

Q4 How much do you think markets and the way they operate are products of the fundamental nature of humans and the way that they think?

Further reading

Introductory level

Begg, D., Fischer, S. and Dornbusch, R. (1994) *Economics*, 4th edn, Maidenhead: McGraw-Hill, ch. 3.

Hardwick, P, Khan, B. and Langmead, J. (1994) *An Introduction to Modern Economics*, 4th edn, Harlow: Longman, ch. 3.

Lipsey, R. and Chrystal, K. (1995) *An Introduction to Positive Economics*, 8th edn, Oxford: Oxford University Press, chs 4, 5 and 6.

Sloman, J. (1994) *Economics*, 2nd edn, Hemel Hempstead: Harvester Wheatsheaf, ch. 4.

Intermediate level

Bailey, S.J. (1995) *Public Sector Economics: Theory, Policy and Practice*, Basingstoke: Macmillan, ch. 1.

Brown, C. and Jackson, P. (1990) *Public Sector Economics*, 4th edn, Oxford: Basil Blackwell, ch. 1.

George, K.D. and Shorey, J. (1978) *The Allocation of Resources: Theory and Policy*, London: George Allen and Unwin, ch. 1.

Gwartney, J.D. (1977) *Microeconomics: Private and Public Choice*, London: Academic Press, ch. 3.

Isachsen, A., Hamilton, C. and Gylfason, T. (1992) *Understanding the Market Economy*, Oxford: Oxford University Press, chs 2, 3 and 4.

Pindyck, R.S. and Rubinfeld, D.L. (1992) *Microeconomics*, 2nd edn, New York: Macmillan, ch. 2.

Other sources

Roper, B. and Snowdon, B. (1987) *Markets, Intervention and Planning*, Harlow: Longman, ch. 1.

Self, P. (1993) *Government by the Market?* Basingstoke: Macmillan, ch. 7.

Seyf, A. (1996) 'Reflections on "perfect competition": what's in a name?', *Economics and Business Education*, vol. 4, part 3, no. 15.

Chapter 2

The economics of market failure

Key words used: public goods, externalities, monopoly, adverse selection, property rights

Chapter 1 introduced the perfectly competitive model. It was recognized that this state of perfect competition does not apply throughout the real world. In fact, there are many cases where markets fail and where the assumptions of perfect competition are not met. Welfare economics is a branch of economics which asks the question: what should governments do? The answer is based around the notion of an efficient allocation of resources generated by a perfectly competitive market. Welfare economics suggests that, when market failure occurs, it would in principle be possible for government to intervene to improve the allocation of resources to make everyone better off. It is important to note that welfare economics begins with the notion that governments will act so as to ensure that the market worked as if it were perfectly competitive. In addition to market failure, there is nothing in the perfect competition model which suggests that an efficient use of resources will bring about a socially desirable distribution of income. It is possible that any outcome achieved by perfect competition could be matched with an appropriate redistribution of income. This chapter describes both the economics of market failure and problems with the inequalities of the market process.

The presence of public goods, merit goods and externalities

Public goods

Some goods have the characteristic that once they are available to one person they are available to everyone: it is impossible to exclude them from another person. This is called non-excludability and it is one of the key features of a public good. One example is ships using a lighthouse. It is nearly impossible to exclude individual ships from benefiting from the service it provides. The other feature is non-rivalry in consumption. This means that one person's consumption of a good in no way reduces the amount available to others. An example is where someone brings an electric heater into a room full of people, and everyone enjoys the heat without taking away the consumption of it from others.

National defence is a public good. Once it is provided it is difficult to exclude one person from being protected from an invasion by another country. People consume the good collectively, and one person's consumption of defence in no way takes away the amount available to another person. People do not have the incentive to pay for the good because they know that everyone else is receiving it anyway. Public goods suffer from the free-rider problem. A free-rider is an individual who consumes a good without paying for it. This is a feature of public goods because if one person bought the good then it would still be available for everyone else to consume.

With public goods the presence of free-riders makes it impossible or difficult for markets to provide the good efficiently. We all benefit from a national vaccination programme: there is a reduction in the chances of catching the disease. Also, it is difficult to exclude someone from consuming this good: that is, from benefiting from a reduction in the chances of catching the disease. In a free market these goods will not be provided at the socially efficient level of output. Suppliers cannot easily devise methods of excluding individuals, nor can collective consumption be reduced. In the case of defence it is neither desirable nor feasible to do either.

In addition to pure public goods, like national defence, there is an important category of goods called semi-public goods. These are important because many of the services discussed in this book have semi-public good qualities. These are goods which have, to varying degrees, elements of non-excludability or non-rivalry in consumption. From a public policy point of view, we have to ask whether it is either feasible or desirable to exclude these goods. For example, in the case of roads, it is possible to exclude road users from using them, but this would require setting up a road toll and charging for the use of the road. This might be feasible, but would it be desirable? Imagine a toll on every road and the difficulty of cases where some roads run into each other. More specifically, the additional car user imposes only a small cost on that road, so setting up a toll in order to collect the small amount from each road user is undesirable.

Private market solutions to public goods

If the market can find ways of excluding consumers and preventing free riding, then there is hope for a more efficient level of output. This can sometimes happen. Technology is something which has changed the degree of excludability of some semi-public goods and services. For example, cable television means that producers can now charge for the use of television. Developments in electronic smart cards has meant that roads can become more excludable. Cars can now be fitted with an electronic card that allows them to pass without delay, deducts a monetary amount for the use of the road, and prevents a potential user from using the road without payment.

Merit goods

The idea of merit goods is important in relation to public policy. It centres on the belief that some people do not consume enough of a particular set of goods, even though consumption of these goods is good for them and for the community at large. Merit goods are those which society thinks everyone should consume whether or not the individual wants them. Examples of merit goods are primary school education and health care. In Chapter 1 we noted the assumptions of the perfect market. The Pareto optimum assumes that consumers are the best judges of their own welfare. But people do not always act in their best interests. The market does not tell people to consume primary school education. This is a role for governments. Some people dislike having to go to school, but they often agree afterwards that they were glad they were made to do so. The second reason for merit goods relates to externalities. If going to school increases the productivity of an individual, it also creates a production externality. Working alongside a productive worker increases the productivity of everyone. This consideration may not be taken into account when the individual decides how much education to consume. Merit goods are those goods or services which are underconsumed. Conversely, demerit or bad goods are those which people overconsume in terms of what is good for them, such as alcohol.

Private sector solutions to merit goods

In a free market, people may underconsume because they have poor access to information. One solution is to increase the quantity and improve the quality of information. However, this may be more difficult than it appears. Increasing information on the benefits of consuming a good or service may be an inadequate solution where some groups in society cannot access the information or do not know how to use it for their own benefit. In this instance, government intervention to encourage consumption in the form of direct incentives may be a better solution. The merit good argument, like the public good case, does not justify government provision, but it does justify a government policy which indicates how much should be consumed.

Externalities

If a perfectly competitive market exists, it will result in a Pareto optimal allocation of resources. This assumes that there is no divergence between social and private costs. One of the assumptions of the perfect market is that individuals act in their own self-interest, and that this self-interest leads companies or consumers to consider only their private marginal costs. Where private costs are greater or smaller than social costs, the market outcome will result in too much or too little of a particular good: that is, resources will have been misallocated. This is called an externality. It arises when the production or consumption decisions directly affect a third party, other than through market prices. A simple way to think of externalities is that they have a spill-over effect. There are numerous examples of externalities in the real world. There are spill-over effects from polluted air, from having a local town festival and from the Channel Tunnel. The key thing to remember is that, in all of these cases, there are benefits and costs which are going to one and to all.

Externalities can be classified into several categories. There are positive and negative externalities, and consumption and production externalities. There are environmental externalities like those which affect the quality of air and water. These may be global or local in nature. The former externalities affect everyone, in all nations, like global warming. An example of a negative externality in production is the disposal of waste material. This is something which becomes undesirable after it has reached the end of its economic life. A company decides to place its refuse in a nearby river. Let us imagine that this causes pollution to the local pub owner further downstream. The externality may cause unpleasant smells which put people off going to the pub, and subsequently lowers the profits of the pub owner and results in higher prices. This is an example of the adverse side effects of dumping waste anywhere: in this case, the external costs are those which the pub owner has to bear. These costs are not reflected in the market price of waste disposal. Unless the company is charged the full cost of its action, then the true cost to society will be understated.

There are also many examples of positive externalities in everyday life. For example, someone painting their house in a street increases the attractiveness of the street generally; the action spills over to their neighbours. The cost of the paint does not reflect the external benefit to the community. In public service areas, the production and consumption of many goods and services confer benefits to those who have not directly consumed the good. For example, someone who has become more productive through the consumption of higher education can influence less productive people in the workplace.

These ideas can be represented pictorially, using an example of a negative externality. The terms used are the marginal social cost (*MSC*) and the marginal private cost (*MPC*). The *MSC* refers to the additional costs to society incurred in supplying an additional unit of a good. The rule is that resource allocation is optimal when $P = MC$ or $p = MSC$. With the production of some goods, $MSC = MC$, but in the case below, the *MSC* does not equal the *MPC* of production.

Figure 2.1 shows the demand and supply curves facing a company in the production of steel. The marginal private cost curve gives a typical steel company's marginal cost of production. The supply curve shows the quantity of steel supplied at each price received by the steel producer, and it is also the marginal cost of producing an additional unit of steel. In the absence of externalities, the market equilibrium Q_m is efficient. This is where the marginal private cost curve intersects the demand curve. The demand curve represents the marginal social benefit of producing steel. Now, assume there are negative externalities involved in the production of steel. We will assume that the company cannot change its production processes, it can only reduce pollution by reducing output. In the production of steel, toxic fumes are emitted into the

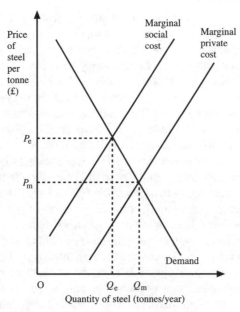

Figure 2.1 Negative externalities in the production of steel

environment. The company supply curve will not reflect marginal social cost, only marginal private cost. If expansion of the good increases pollution levels, the total costs of that expansion are not just labour, raw materials and equipment, but also the costs imposed on society of the extra pollution created. These costs are not accounted for by the producer. If they are added to the private costs, the social (private and external) cost curve would become the marginal social cost curve, with an equilibrium output of Q_e and price of P_e.

Efficiency rules developed earlier in this book require that the marginal social cost equals the marginal social benefit of increasing output. On this basis, production should occur at Q_e, so the efficient level of production is lower than the market equilibrium level. The presence of a negative externality means that the marginal social cost exceeds the marginal private cost, and the market equilibrium will produce excessive quantities of steel. It is important to point out that this particular externality arose because of the presence of a common property resource. Steel producers were able to emit pollution because the atmosphere belongs to one and all. In a free market there is unrestricted access to using the atmosphere.

Private sector solutions to externalities

When market failure occurs and the situation needs addressing, it is useful to think of private and public solutions. Markets can, under certain circumstances, sort problems out themselves. In the case of externalities and in the absence of government, there are at least two broad private sector solutions. The first is where the affected parties get together and form an economic unit of sufficient size that the consequences of any action occur within that unit. For example, students tend to be naturally energetic and noisy. This can have spill-over effects in terms of accommodation and other residents. A student landlord owning two flats in a private house of four flats could unitize the externality (noise) by buying up all the remaining flats. The externality is thus internalized and is no longer a problem to non-student residents. However, this solution will work only if the house is sufficiently large to contain all the students and their noise.

The second solution is where the two affected parties get together and bargain with each other. This idea came from Coase in 1960, who identified the problem of externality as the absence of markets and property rights. The Coase Theorem states that externalities arise from the broader problem of property rights. These are rights or laws assigned to individuals or groups which state how they can use and charge for their property. Consider the case of fishing in the North Sea. The sea is overfished and future stocks are being run down. The challenge is to discourage overproduction. The Coase Theorem states that, when externalities exist, parties of individuals can get together and agree a set of arrangements whereby the externality is internalized. Alternatively the group may get together to compensate or bribe an offending party or individual, such as the fisherman who fishes all day long for seven days a week. The determination of who compensates whom is very important in the final distribution of outcomes. Clearly the group of fishermen are better off under a regime in which this fishing activity is banned unless the group is compensated, than under a regime where fishing is allowed unless the fisherman is paid not to fish.

A final solution, which is not economic in nature, is about modifying externalities through social sanctions. Through the socialization process, people can be taught actions which are to be encouraged, like good manners or picking up litter. This is about being considerate to others. For example, schoolchildren could be taught the principle of, 'do unto others as you would have them do unto you'. Certainly some external effects such as litter could be reduced or avoided through this process, but clearly it is limited in terms of the number of situations it could be applied to.

Other important issues

Besides describing specific reasons why markets fail to produce an efficient allocation of resources, economists use a number of other concepts in order to explain in greater depth how, for example, externalities arise.

Property rights

The absence of these rights gives rise to externalities and public goods. If property rights are present and clearly defined, there is usually no externality. Property rights state what action an owner may take over their property. For example, if I have property rights over a stretch of river, this could mean that anyone can use the river, but that only I can make a claim on others for using the river. If my next-door neighbour disposes his refuse there, I have the right to take action because I can enforce my property rights. In this instance I can be assured of the outcome, but if property rights are absent or vague then problems can arise. So, in the case of the river, this time assume that there are an ill-defined set of property rights. I could sue my neighbour for damages for the polluted river, but the outcome would not be certain; I may or may not win compensation. The point about property rights is that they are needed for a private market to operate; they prevent individuals from damaging, stealing or abusing the property of others.

Common property resources

The relationship between property rights and public policy issues is that for some goods there are no rules governing certain assets, or it is not feasible to have rules. This means that the resources are not used wisely. This is true of the sea, rivers, open countryside and the atmosphere. Access is unrestricted and the resource can be used intensively. In a way, such resources are free to individuals, but not to society. As it is too difficult for anyone to establish property rights to the air, for example, this leads to an overuse of this resource.

Transaction costs

Public goods, merit goods and externalities are all related to an important concept in economics known as transaction costs. These are not the same thing as administrative costs; transaction costs are those costs involved in making a market exchange. Imagine that you are buying a pop CD. On the whole you are roughly familiar with the contents and names of the tracks and are willing to pay for the CD at the price offered for sale in the display. All you have to do is walk into the shop, select the CD and offer payment for it. Economists call this a frictionless exchange: there are no or very few transaction costs involved. Compare this with a case where you are buying a house. You are not familiar with the structure of the house; nor are you certain of the price that you will pay. These facts give rise to imperfect information and can increase the amount of transaction costs. Consider the different types of transaction costs involved in buying a house:

- Search costs: the costs involved in finding out more about the house and how many other people are interested in its consumption.
- Bargaining and negotiating costs: the costs involved in determining the boundaries of what the exchange will be (e.g. the form and timing of payment, and what exactly will be traded for that payment).
- Contract costs: the costs which clarify the conditions of trade (they might

involve a solicitor, for example, where the purchase may be contingent on a number of steps being undertaken).

How does this idea relate to issues about public policy? Many public goods and services have high transaction costs (high relative to the value of the transaction). This occurs because of the presence of free riding and the absence of well-defined property rights which, as we have seen, are common in public goods and externalities. An example is trying to prevent people from dumping their rubbish in the countryside. A market in rubbish collection which prevented people from doing this would mean closing the possibilities for free riding. This would mean assigning property rights to the countryside, banning people with cars from visiting it, or some other expensive action. High transaction costs lead to market failure because the costs of monitoring, agreeing and enforcing contracts are large relative to the value of the transaction.

Q1 Many goods produced in the public sector have elements of a public good: in other words, they are not pure public goods. Give examples of those goods or services which can be described as having non-exclusiveness, but rivalry in consumption. One example is a public road which has the tea-time traffic on it. Also, think up examples of goods or services which have exclusiveness, but are not rival in consumption. One example is Sky Television.

Q2 Private solutions exist for externalities. In what ways could the following scenario be improved upon by private solutions? You are walking on a public access path through agricultural land and enjoying it (a positive externality because of the spill-over effect of the agricultural production), when along comes a farmer and tells you to get off his land as he is fed up with people's footprints damaging the ground.

Q3 List the transaction costs involved in deciding which higher education course to study and where to study it, in terms of: (a) the search costs; (b) the bargaining costs; and (c) the contract costs.

The presence of market imperfections

Market imperfections are a different type of market failure to those discussed above. They relate more to problems emerging from a market structure or the presence of imperfect information which causes problems in exchange and in provision. One problem of all these imperfections is power. This is about suppliers or consumers having greater control over the other. A starting point for discussing these issues is to divide the market imperfections into three groups:

* Information-related imperfections.
* Capital market imperfections.
* Market structure imperfections.

Information-related imperfections

One of the key assumptions of the perfect competition model, outlined in Chapter 1, is that of perfect information. This is rare in reality. When firms and individuals are not well informed, this affects their decisions and choices. They may take action which does not suit their interests. Many reasons explain the presence of imperfect information. On the supply side, private markets may not produce the right amount or quality of information, since there may be no incentive to do so. On the demand side, people may not be able to access information simply because they do not know how to find it or how to use it when they do. Examples of imperfect information occur in health care where the market rarely produces long-term health forecasts. Unregulated drug companies could produce 'wonder drugs' without due regard to safety because the general public does not have the information to judge the drug. This is why we have government regulation.

Private sector solutions to imperfect information

The markets can find solutions if there are incentives for it to provide the information. For example, information can be provided through institutions, the Internet and consumer magazines. Some information problems arise because of uncertainty about the future. The market can address this type of uncertainty through insurance. We can assure that our quality of living continues at the same level when we retire, by taking out a private pension. However, under certain circumstances, when it is impossible to insure against some risks or when there are problems with insurance markets, discussed in detail below, then it is likely that the market will bring about an inefficient supply of these goods.

Asymmetry of information

Asymmetry of information is about unevenness of knowledge between two parties. Figure 2.2 illustrates pictorially what asymmetrical information means when comparing the purchase of a pop CD and the 'purchase' of a medical prescription.

The vertical axis shows the range of information known, from total knowledge to total ignorance. The horizontal axis shows the buyer and the seller positions. In Figure 2.2(b) we say that the amount and type of information, such as the type of music, the price of the CD and the quality expected is roughly similar between the retailer and the consumer. Compare this with a good such as a drug prescription, shown in Figure 2.2(a). We see that patients' knowledge about their condition and the type of cure required is relatively low. The doctor, on the other hand, knows relatively more. A full rectangle is not drawn because, while doctors may know more, they do not know every single thing there is to know about a person's health. Nevertheless, we say that between the two people there is asymmetrical (not even) information.

23

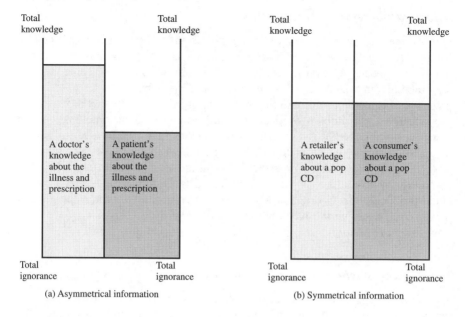

Figure 2.2 Asymmetry of information

This has important implications for an efficient market provision because things like choice of product, quantity, timing, price and quality may be totally different when asymmetric information is present. The significance of this in relation to public policy is that, while imperfect information may exist in the exchange of private goods, it is undesirable to have people in positions of power when it comes to necessity goods. This leads on to another key idea: the principal-agent problem.

The principal–agent problem

Information-related problems extend to relationships in work and at home. A perfect market assumes perfect knowledge and the continuous monitoring and extraction of information, but this rarely happens in reality. The implications are that one person might be able to act in their own interests and follow their own goals (the agent). Another person's welfare or profit may be dependent on that person (the principal). These are called principal–agent relationships and they exist in many aspects of economic life. There is the potential for people to have power in influencing outcomes. Agency relationships can be found in public enterprises. The problem arises when managers (the agents) pursue their own goals, and this impacts on the profits and outputs of the owners (the principals). As it is expensive to monitor the behaviour of public managers, there are no guarantees that they will produce an efficient level of output. The problem occurs, generally speaking, when one party can affect the value of the transaction to the other party and there is no mechanism whereby the second party can enforce or control the outcome. The problem with this situation in relation to public policy is that the agent is making decisions about resources which have the potential to be based on their own personal agenda and not on the interests of the owner. Agency relationships are also present in housing, where managers of housing may have the potential not to act in the interests of the owners of the housing stock.

Markets with asymmetric information and agency relationships are not necessarily markets which are operating efficiently. With the former, situations where sellers are better informed than buyers, and the reverse, can lead to market failure. There are private market responses to the presence of asymmetrical information, such as warranties. The difficulty of purchasing certain types of insurance like health and pensions offers a strong economic justification for government intervention. It is particularly relevant in insurance markets. Examples are pensions, social security, health and motoring. In all these cases one side of the exchange (i.e. purchaser or seller) is much better informed than the other. Asymmetrical information gives rise to two further economic features which are often referred to when discussing market failure and insurance markets: adverse selection and moral hazard.

Adverse selection

This is a situation which arises between a producer, or a supplier, of a good or service and a consumer. Adverse selection is where asymmetric information means that high-risk individuals or goods drive out low-risk individuals or goods from the market. Why might people over the age of 65 have greater difficulty in buying life or health insurance than a young person? Could not the price of insurance rise to reflect the higher risks associated with older age? In a free market, health care could be provided by people purchasing health insurance. People who buy health insurance know more about their health situation than private health insurance companies. Let us assume that unhealthy people are more likely to want health insurance. Health insurance prices are then bid up, the proportion of unhealthy people insured increases relative to healthy people, and the latter, knowing their own healthy disposition, do not choose to be insured. The remaining insured are predominantly unhealthy, and at this point health insurance is unprofitable and inefficient.

Insurance markets have attempted to overcome these imperfections. Insurance companies have recently become more sophisticated. They now request more information than ever before in order to identify different types of consumer. For example, prior to selecting an appropriate private health insurance, people are often asked to take a medical examination. When the problem of adverse selection is severe, it is likely that the market will fail to provide an efficient quality and quantity of the good.

Moral hazard

Insurance works by setting a price or premium which represents the probability of the event occurring and the size of the expenditure which would have to be covered. Moral hazard refers to a situation where one party is fully insured and their post-insured behaviour cannot be accurately monitored by the insurance company, which has limited information. The behaviour of the insured party may change after the insurance has been purchased. Consider the example of someone who takes out a house contents insurance. Once insured they subsequently decide against getting the front door lock mended, which it needs. This is the problem of moral hazard. The probability of the outcome is affected by the subsequent actions of the insured person. The presence of moral hazard can lead to imperfections in the market price and in provision.

Market solutions exist for the problems of adverse selection and moral hazard. This is the function of warranties, which are a form of security. For example, during the mad cows disease scare in the UK, supermarkets gave guarantees that their beef came from other countries, like New Zealand. In the absence of perfect information, such warranties solve the information problem. However, they are not perfect solutions. In health and pension insurance there is a case for national insurance or related forms of government health insurance for the elderly.

Capital market imperfections

Capital markets have a number of functions, one of which is to supply finance. The suppliers of finance are banks and other lending institutions. The problem arises with credit and imperfect information. In very simple and general terms, these financial institutions prefer to lend money to people who have secure jobs with average or regular earnings and some collateral (backing). This preference arises because of the absence of full information. Banks can lend money to low-income borrowers with little collateral, but this would be very expensive. This is because of the high risks perceived in the absence of perfect information. What is the implication of this? The consumption of some goods, such as merit goods, identified earlier in this chapter, would rely on the private capital markets to finance an efficient amount of investment in education and in health. However, this is not reliable. It is likely that finance might be provided, but at a cost. This would also lead to inequalities, where some people would be unable to access finance on the basis of their income levels or profession. In a free market, it is likely that inefficiencies and inequalities will be present to the extent that knowledge, power and access to capital markets are associated with socio-economic status.

Market structure imperfections

The perfect competition model assumes that there are many sellers, that they are price-takers and that they earn normal profits. However, there are some goods and services where these conditions do not occur and these give rise to market structure imperfections. This section focuses on the monopoly market structure. There are many sources of monopoly. A monopolist is the single seller of a good or service. Such a market is said to be imperfect because a monopolist can earn high profits by restricting output and raising prices.

Sources of monopoly

It is important to describe the sources of monopoly because they help us to understand the nature of many public policy changes which are taking place. A monopolist is a single supplier in a market. Local monopolies are very common and examples include the university bookshop, the local electricity company and the ice-cream stand in the cinema. A unique product can give rise to a monopoly structure. This means that there are no close substitutes to the monopolist's good. It may have come about through an innovation, and may prevail until imitators come along.

Barriers to entry mean that there are constraints to prevent new firms entering the market. These barriers have different sources and it is worth differentiating them as they are important to understanding public policy reforms. First, ownership of a vital resource gives rise to monopoly and can act as a barrier to entry. An example is the single owner of an oil field. Second, legal barriers may be a result of institutional and historical action by governments, which prohibit entry via franchises, patents, copyright and licences. One example is the statutory postal monopoly in the UK, which prevents other competitors providing a specific postal service.

The presence of economies of scale can lead to a situation where it is not efficient to have many competitors, and a monopoly structure may emerge. Technically, economies of scale are where the long-run average cost curve declines as the company increases output. As a company becomes larger, its unit cost of output falls and is lower than that of a smaller competitor. The latter eventually leaves the industry because it has no cost advantage and a single supplier emerges. In this case a monopoly structure arises not because of legal barriers or the ownership of a vital resource, but because of the relationship between costs and output. In economics, we say that when one supplier emerges in an industry because of this relationship, it is a natural monopoly. This is where the average cost of production declines throughout the entire market. Public utilities, such as water, local telephones, gas and electricity, are said to be examples of natural monopoly.

The relevance of this market imperfection is that the presence of monopoly is likely to lead to economic inefficiencies, which we shall explore below. This book is interested in monopoly from the point of view of the public utilities and industries of national importance, like the railways and the postal services. We wish to describe developments in policy towards these industries. In order to do this we need to establish the constraints present in the market structure, so as to understand what is required in terms of policy approaches. This can be done by using models in the first instance, and by comparing the monopolist's position with that of the perfectly competitive market structure.

Figure 2.3 shows the short-run position of the two market structures. The efficiency rule developed from Chapter 1 is that perfectly competitive firms will set price equal to marginal cost, and in Figure 2 3(b) this is at price P_e and output Q_e. When the marginal cost of producing the last unit is equal to the marginal benefit, perfect competition achieves efficiency. Compare this with Figure 2.3(a) where the monopolist's average revenue or demand curve is the price per unit received. The demand curve is downward sloping because the monopolist is the only producer in the market. So if the monopolist wishes to increase sales by one unit, the price must fall. This time the price falls for all units sold, so *all* units earn less revenue. The average revenue (*AR*) is the total revenue divided by price. Marginal revenue (*MR*) is the change in total revenue of producing the last unit divided by the change in price. The latter will lie below the average revenue curve.

Applying the same rule again, price must be set equal to marginal cost. In the case of the monopolist, this is where marginal revenue (*MR*) equals marginal cost *(MC)* at output Q_1, and we read off from the demand curve the price P_1 that corresponds to this quantity. This is the profit-maximizing output level. What this means is that the production of the last unit adds as much to cost as it adds to revenue. If the monopolist were to increase output, *MC* would exceed *MR* and

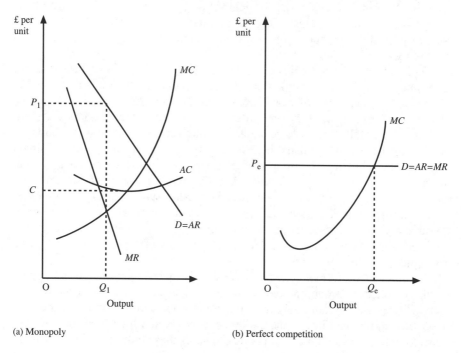

(a) Monopoly

(b) Perfect competition

Figure 2.3 Equilibrium of monopoly and perfect competition

it would be in the monopolist's interests to reduce output. From the analysis, we can see at output Q_1 there is a gap between the marginal cost of production and the price. This gap is referred to as the monopolist's profit. Why might this be inefficient from a social point of view? Output Q_1 is produced, because it is in the interests of the monopolist, but there may be consumers wishing to purchase more than output Q_1. If they are unable to purchase more than Q_1, this is called the social loss from monopoly or the deadweight loss of monopoly. Moreover, the price set exceeds marginal cost, and this excess of price over marginal cost can be seen as a measure of monopoly power.

The relevance of this to public policy is that, while there are thousands of monopoly structures prevailing in an economy, it is the nature of the good which determines whether there is a case for government intervention: that is, whether the good or service in question is of a high necessity value to everyday life and business; produces national positive or negative externalities; and leads to a redistribution of income. Take the case of energy: few economic activities can take place without it, and it would be socially undesirable to have a situation of restricted output.

Q4 *Give examples of where asymmetrical information might occur when you (a) buy a mountain bicycle; (b) ask a lecturer for a reference; (c) make new friends; and (d) go out on a date!*

Q5 *The principal–agent problem arises from incomplete information and costly monitoring. Explain the relevance of each or both of these in relation to the following situations, pointing out who is the principal in each case: (a) a life insurance salesman who informs you that you must take out one of the policies of the company now because he thinks that you will be considered too great a risk in the future; (b) the objectives of a manager employed in a state-owned industry; (c) housing letting agencies who are supposed to act on behalf of the owners of a particular house.*

Q6 *The suppliers of capital do not lend to just anyone. This has implications for public policy. Explain why you, with student status, might have difficulty in borrowing under the following circumstances: (a) wishing to buy a flat; (b) wanting to do a master's degree in the USA. If you had been working for ten years and had some savings, would this have changed the outcomes?*

Q7 *There are many industries in the private sector which have monopoly structures, such as the Premier Football League and the steel-making industry. Why then is there such a concern about the presence of monopoly in the transport, communications and energy industries?*

The presence of inequalities

The first two sections have presented a rationale for why free markets may not lead to an efficient allocation of resources. The Pareto criterion in Chapter 1 is concerned with ensuring that resources are efficiently allocated among competing uses. It is possible to have several Pareto optimal outcomes, each with a different distribution of income, but the market does not claim to produce a *fair* distribution of income. If society places emphasis on greater equality, the government has grounds to intervene. A free market allocates resources so that the marginal cost of production equates to the marginal benefit derived from the consumption of that good. Consumers' marginal benefit comes from their willingness to pay, which in turn stems from the amount of money they have. Irrespective of their willingness to pay, if the funds are not available, their utilities will not be maximized. Free markets can leave a distribution of income where some people are permanently on low incomes, with bad housing and little educational opportunities. These everyday facts of life are ignored when a test is begun for optimality of resource allocation.

There are two problems with equity. The first is that it is not as easy to define as efficiency; there are many possible interpretations. Second, inequalities in life are not just restricted to income. Inequalities can manifest themselves in living conditions and opportunities to participate. For example, consider these three commonly used assertions of equity:

- Everyone should have equal treatment for equal needs.
- Everyone should be given equal opportunities.
- Everyone should have a minimum standard of living.

The first relates to the idea that, if a consumer wishes to have a particular health service or to take a higher education course, they will receive the same service or treatment, irrespective of their income, race or gender. The second idea is that everyone should be given the opportunity to choose to do something. So, for example, if they meet the educational criteria, all 18-year-olds should be able to choose whether to go to a higher education institution. If they do, they will be given a grant. If they choose not to go, the grant will go to someone else. The important point is that the statement means that everyone has the same opportunity. The third assertion is that there is some basic level of living which everyone should have access to. This can mean income level, housing and primary education.

We only need to look around us to see that, in our mixed economy, some people are endowed with better abilities, better health, higher income and higher socioeconomic status. The market will work well for these people, but it will struggle to meet any of the assertions listed above. Markets are not principally concerned with ensuring that the gains from the competitive process are distributed to one and all. We say that the market has failed to bring about an equitable distribution of resources.

Another problem relates to the relationship between equity and efficiency. The attainment of one can often reduce the attainment of the other. For example, if your taxes are reduced in order to encourage you to work more, but you know that all your efforts and outcomes will be redistributed to all people whether they are workers or not, this might make you work less hard. In this case, equity has been achieved, but at the cost of reduced efficiency. On the other hand, being efficient may mean that someone is made redundant, and they now have less opportunity to ensure that their standard of living is equal to that of others. Efficiency has been achieved, but at the cost of less equality in a society.

One final issue is that of whether economists should be addressing issues of equity. There are three reasons why economics has a role to play in this area. The first is that efficiency objectives interfere with equity outcomes, as we have seen from the above examples. They cannot be easily separated. The second is that economists have a toolbag of concepts which can be usefully transferred to the study of equity problems. Third, public policy reforms should be aimed at finding solutions which can creatively increase efficiency and equity at the same time or, at least, increase efficiency and not reduce outcomes in terms of equity.

Discussion

This chapter has discussed why markets in reality do not operate in the way the perfect competition model suggests. Either markets can correct these problems or governments can intervene. The reason why it is important to discuss market failures is that this discussion provides a foundation for understanding the direction and rationale for current public policy reforms. Many of these new directions have gone back to the drawing board and asked how governments can intervene again to improve the efficiency of markets and public provision. These new approaches use market-based ideas. We now understand that to use a market-based idea is to introduce something which the market uses: exchange, a price system, information, incentives, allowing consumers to choose, allowing the real costs of provision to be made clear to the producer. Many of the public policy reforms discussed in this book seek to draw out some of the strengths of the market and use them in a public sector environment, to help address the problems of allocation in the mixed economy.

Further reading

Introductory level

Begg, D., Fischer, S. and Dornbusch, R. (1994) *Economics*, 4th edn, Maidenhead: McGraw-Hill, ch. 16.

Hardwick, P., Khan, B. and Langmead, J. (1994) *An Introduction to Modern Economics*, 4th edn, Harlow: Longman, chs 12 and 13.

Lipsey, R. and Chrystal, K. (1995) *An Introduction to Positive Economics*, 8th edn, Oxford: Oxford University Press, chs 23 and 24.

Sloman, J. (1994) *Economics*, 2nd edn, Hemel Hempstead: Harvester Wheatsheaf, chs 11 and 12.

Intermediate level

Brown, C. and Jackson, P. (1992) *Public Sector Economics*, 4th edn, Basingstoke: Macmillan, ch. 1.

Cullis, J. and Jones, P. (1992) *Public Finance and Public Choice: Analytical Perspectives*, Maidenhead: McGraw-Hill, chs 2 and 3.

DeSerpa, A. (1988) *Microeconomic Theory: Issues and Applications*, 2nd edn, Boston, Mass.: Allyn and Bacon, chs 11, 17 and 19.

Gwartney, J. (1977) *Microeconomics: Private and Public Choice*, New York: Academic Press, ch. 17.

Pindyck, R. and Rubinfeld, D. (1992) *Microeconomics*, 2nd edn, Basingstoke: Macmillan, chs 17 and 18.

Other sources

Bailey, S. (1995) *Public Sector Economics: Theory, Policy and Practice*, Basingstoke: Macmillan, ch. 2.

Coase, R. (1960) 'The problems of social costs', *Journal of Law and Economics*, October.

George, K. and Shorey, J. (1978) *The Allocation of Resources: Theory and Policy*, Hemel Hempstead: George Allen and Unwin, ch. 8.

Roper, B. and Snowdon, B. (1987) *Markets, Intervention and Planning*, Harlow: Longman, ch. 1.

Chapter 3

The economics of government

Key words used: policy objectives, policy approaches, intervention, taxes and subsidies

The economics of government has undergone change in recent years. For over a century, welfare economics has guided our thinking on the question of what governments should do. The answer was that governments had a specific but limited role, in intervening to overcome market failures. In practice, governments play a much wider economic role in the market economy, but recently there has been a revival in the *laissez-faire* approach: that is, the approach which says that governments should leave the allocation of resources to market forces. These shifts in economic thinking are very important in terms of public policy. Many of the new directions in public policy are underpinned by the idea that the government's role should be one of 'clearing the way' for market forces. This chapter explains the traditional economic functions of government and uses this as a starting point to understanding the rationale for the new approaches which are subsequently described in this book.

Government objectives and approaches

Government objectives

This section takes a closer look at the objectives of governments. There are two reasons for looking at objectives. Changes in government objectives can help to explain changes in public policy. Different objectives require different approaches and this is a key learning outcome of this book. The objectives of government are different to those of the private sector. Although governments are trying to overcome the failures of the market, they are also trying to balance other objectives at the same time, like maintaining employment and macroeconomic stability. Sometimes being able to understand why the task of setting objectives is difficult in the public sector can help us to understand why it can be difficult to evaluate the efforts to achieve those objectives.

Setting objectives in the public sector is infinitely more difficult than in the private sector. The best way to illustrate this is to think of objectives in the private sector. A firm might have an annual profit target, to increase profits by 5 per cent, among its range of objectives. Why is this so different from public sector objectives? First, it is very tangible, it is a monetary figure. Profit is typically why a firm exists and there is more likely to be a consensus on this objective. Contrast this with a government objective of increasing the number of people in higher education by 5 per cent per annum. Here the outcome is not as tangible – issues arise such as how much public expenditure will be required, will quality suffer, should anyone be educated, and what can be expected in the long run from such an increase?

One of the most famous examples of difficulties with setting objectives can be found in the recent history of the UK nationalized industries. The government wished to meet a range of economic, social and political objectives, some of which were in conflict with each other. The objectives set were generally vague, inadequate for different industry circumstances and, in some cases, rather ambitious. The aims were more like aspirations than objectives, and industries drew little guidance from them on how to allocate their resources.

The objectives of governments, in relation to the concerns of this book, can be grouped into three categories:

- Economic efficiency objectives.
- Administrative efficiency objectives.
- Equity objectives.

Economic efficiency objectives

Economic efficiency is about wanting to get the maximum out of the available resources. Put in another way, it means that for any given level of costs, we wish to obtain the largest possible benefit. This is about achieving an allocation of resources which reflects the value in consumption that society places on it. This valuation is the same as the value that producers place on using the resources, in terms of its opportunity cost to society. Being efficient is an idea anchored in the notion of scarcity and choice. As we saw in Chapter 1, opportunity cost is an important idea in choice because every decision made involves an opportunity cost. We can compare every decision in production and consumption in terms of the alternative goods and services which could have been produced and consumed. This is the forgone opportunity. The value of this criterion is that it provides a starting point for the analysis of objectives. Economic efficiency objectives fall into three categories:

- Allocation efficiency objectives.
- Production efficiency objectives.
- Internal efficiency objectives.

Allocation efficiency objectives

These types of objective refer to ensuring that resources are distributed in a way which matches consumers' demand for them, in terms of both the quantity and the price. An example of inefficiency in allocation is where resources are being over- or underproduced in relation to the demands of consumers. Why divide efficiency into different groups? One reason is that governments have altered in their pursuit of one over the other, so it is worth looking at what each is made up of. In the UK, the government nationalized over forty industries after the Second World War. The policy focus was on allocation efficiency. Initially, the government laid down pricing and investment rules. Specifically, the industries were encouraged to set prices equal to the marginal costs of supply. The government undertook reviews to ascertain whether these rules were being adhered to. Eventually, the government changed its focus and, for a number of reasons, addressed production efficiency aspects.

Production efficiency objectives

These types of objective focus on production and cost effectiveness. For an economy to be efficient, it must produce goods at a minimum cost for a given level of output. This is simply about getting the best from the inputs to production. With the UK nationalized industries, the government changed from focusing on allocation to emphasizing production efficiency objectives in the 1970s. One example of this change in policy was the setting of targets for industries to reduce the costs per unit of production over a specified period. Subsequently, government saw privatization as a means of obtaining production efficiency through competitive forces.

Internal efficiency objectives

This type of efficiency refers to things like improving organizational slack and the inefficiencies which arise from an organization being too bureaucratic. This can arise, for example, when people have the opportunity to meet their own objectives, which are not necessarily those of the organization. This type of inefficiency also arises when companies or organizations are large and there are difficulties in monitoring how resources are used. The nature of relationships within a company, and between it and government, can impact on internal efficiency.

Administrative efficiency objectives

This refers to the costs of administering a policy approach. There are two broad aspects. First, there is administrative efficiency, which relates to accountability and improving the quality of decision making in resource use. Second, there are the administrative costs involved in executing a particular approach: for example, the costs of material produced to inform the public, the costs of loopholes in the system and the costs of non-take-up of benefits. Ideally, administrative efficiency of any policy means that it should be simple, easy to understand and as cheap as possible to administer. This is easy to define, but the situation becomes more difficult when we combine this with economic efficiency.

An example serves to illustrate the complexities. Child benefit in the UK is administratively efficient, in the sense that it is given to those who are parents. This benefit is not means-tested, so its administration is relatively simple and relatively cheap. However, it could be argued that it is not economically efficient. People are not receiving benefits in relation to need: some people have less need of £40 per month than others. In this example, there is a trade-off between an efficiency loss and an efficiency gain in lower administrative costs.

The relevance of economic or social efficiency to public policy reforms is that, when a particular policy is executed, we need to be able to think in terms of the net economic benefits and costs produced, but we must also include the costs of moving from one approach to another. This is relevant in the case of the privatization of certain industries, where a huge amount of resources has been expended in the privatization process. The gains at the end of the day must be weighed up against these administrative costs.

Equity objectives

The distribution of income and wealth are important government aims. They are quite different in nature to economic efficiency objectives. The latter are about how utility is distributed, how factors of production are combined, and whether the Pareto optimum is met. Equity objectives are about how income, basic services and the much wider concept of wealth can be distributed in a way which is fair. Economics has much to offer the shaping of such objectives. For example, economists are able to measure the degree of income inequality in a country. They do this by dividing the population into tenths, and working out how much income the top income group earns as a proportion of total income earned. If, for example, it were found that this group earned 50 per cent of all income earned, then we would say that this economy had serious inequalities. If a tax policy redistributed the income, so that the percentage fell to 20 per cent, we could say that this tax policy has led to more equitable outcomes.

A starting point is to illustrate that equity, unlike efficiency, has many meanings and that each and every meaning is difficult to define. Consider the following interpretations of the equity objective:

- The elimination of poverty.
- The reduction of inequalities in the distribution of income and wealth.
- The promotion of greater equality in the spread of specific goods and services, including housing, health and education.
- To ensure that people do not receive a dramatic decline in their income and living standards in the event of an unexpected mishap.

Along with these objectives, economists can offer concepts, methods of analysis and ways of thinking about the nature of the problem. So, for example, one of the most common methods of defining equity used by economists is to use the concepts of horizontal and vertical equity. Horizontal equity is the identical treatment of people with identical needs. Vertical equity is the different treatment of people with different needs. Horizontal equity has a value in that, in principle, it rules out racial, sexual and other forms of discrimination among people: the concept is about judging people who have similar economic features. Vertical equity is about redistributing income, usually from the better off to the less well off. This concept causes the greater controversy because people disagree about the extent to which resources should be redistributed.

The first objective on the list above addresses the extremes in society. Poverty is a relative concept. It relates to the relative position suffered by a proportion of society in relation to what is regarded as a normal standard of living. This means that governments have to make a judgement about what is normal. The following list serves to illustrate exactly the type of issues concerned in defining this objective:

- The choice of poverty indicator that should be used: for example, a broad single indicator of economic resources, individual items of consumption, poverty over time, or a minimum level of income.
- The poverty level: for example, using the subsistence level, adjusted for changes in the level of prices, or using absolute or relative values.
- The unit of analysis that should be used: for example, accommodation, expenditure or income.
- The group of people to be used or compared: for example, families, individuals or couples.

The second objective is about reducing the overall amount of inequality. This objective focuses on redistributing income from higher-income to lower-income groups. The difficulties here are deciding on how much to redistribute and which methods best suit the objectives. The third objective concentrates on the idea that there are other things in life, besides income, which are of a basic nature and have a high necessity value. Most governments have social objectives for housing, health care and education which justify intervention in those markets. These are in addition to any objectives they may have for improving the efficiency of those markets. The last objective relates to the merit good argument, in that some people do not consume enough of certain goods. Whether this is because they do not perceive the benefits of current consumption or for some other reason, it is true to say that some people could be left with huge medical bills or no pension on retirement. Governments develop equity objectives to ensure that these events will be insured against.

Another objective that governments might wish to follow is that of ensuring that provisions are made for people to be able to participate in society. These are different to setting minimum standards of living. Examples of participative goods and services are employment, education and mobility. So, for example, the provision of a good standard of transport can assist people to participate in modern life. As we can see, many of these objectives are semi-economic in nature, and there are strong social objectives at play here too.

Government approaches

Discussion so far has centred on the aims of policy. The next step is to consider approaches, which can also be referred to as methods, tools or instruments. These all refer to things which governments might adopt in order to overcome the market failings which they have identified and to meet the policy objectives they have established.

Governments can intervene in three broad ways: finance and public provision; regulation; and taxes and subsidies. Finance involves taxes and subsidies. These can be used to fund the provision of a good or service, or to alter the prices people have to pay. Sometimes it is a combination of both. For example, provision of higher education is often funded through the general taxation system, which is used to subsidize the cost of attending a course. In the UK, higher education fees are paid by the government, and a grant system subsidizes the costs of maintenance. Alternatively, the whole price can be subsidized, as in the case of free medical prescriptions for the elderly. Taxes can be used to alter the price of specific goods, such as a tax on petrol.

Governments can intervene in the production of goods and services with a combination of providing finance for provision and regulation. For example, in housing markets, local authorities directly plan for the provision of social housing; they also regulate the housing quantities and standards. They may finance housing construction through block grants or subsidies. It is important to separate government finance and production. Governments can intervene by financing a good, like higher education, but often it is independent organizations which actually provide the service, such as universities. Alternatively, governments can take over the provision and financing completely, as in the case of health care in the UK.

Regulation has two aspects: there is economic regulation and standards regulation. The first refers to setting guidelines on the quality and quantity of the goods and services provided. So, for example, in the UK, the nationalized industries are owned by the government and managed by the industries, but they are subject to economic regulations on pricing and investment decisions. Standards regulation does not directly intervene in prices. Examples include setting road construction requirements, the requirement to attend school, and making car insurance compulsory.

Taxes and subsidies are also used to meet the objectives of redistributing income and wealth. They involve income transfers: for example, specific expenditures on social security and family income supplements are raised through the tax system. Governments can change the incomes of individuals in the form of a cash transfer. In this instance everybody contributes to the expenditure, but only a specific proportion of the population directly benefits.

Q1 Sort the following statements into the different categories of objectives: production, allocation, administrative and equity: (a) users of the postal service in the Outer Hebrides are to pay the same amount as users in London; (b) public enterprises are to reduce their operating costs by 2 per cent per annum; (c) price structures must reflect both the willingness to pay for the service and the benefits received from consuming the service; (d) higher education institutions are made to account for how they spend public funds.

Q2 Give examples of where a policy intervention brings about an increase in efficiency, but at the same time increases inequalities.

Q3 Finance and production are entirely different forms of intervention in theory and in practice. Illustrate this idea with reference to different sectors of an economy.

Government approaches to improving the problems posed by public goods, merit goods and externalities

Public goods

Chapter 2 explained that the problem with public goods or semi-public goods is that an inefficient level of provision may occur. Market solutions are unlikely to work when they lead to feasible but undesirable outcomes. Governments can intervene in 'markets' for public and semi-public goods by direct public provision. This book examines an important example of a semi-public good: roads. Governments directly plan for future road demand using traffic forecasts. Governments, often local authorities, design roads and allocate their budgets accordingly. In many countries, governments raise the finance through the general taxation system. However, in countries like France, the Netherlands and Belgium, finance is generated by user charges. These take the form of road and motorway tolls.

In the case of roads, regulation can be employed as a means of ensuring that safety standards are laid down and met in terms of how roads are built and constructed. In many cases, government departments do not undertake the building work themselves, but contract private companies. Legislation can be used to define what is legal. Taxes can be used to change the price of producing or consuming a public good. For example, road pricing can be used to increase the costs of driving to the road user.

Merit goods

Chapter 2 also explained that the case for merit goods rests on the idea that governments should intervene to indicate the efficient level of production and consumption of specific goods like health and education. Imperfect information gives rise to merit goods. Consumption and production in a private market may result in underallocation.

Governments could intervene through provision, specifically by providing more information: for example, informing the general public about drug use, the use of seat belts, taking more education, or the relationship between housing and health. The idea is that, as people become more informed and aware of the overall benefits, they should produce and consume more. The other form of provision is direct public provision, although this is difficult to justify on the basis of the merit good argument alone. With the two principal examples of merit goods, health and education, there are in fact other reasons why governments may intervene.

In the case of health, governments intervene substantially either by publicly providing health care or by regulating private provision. These forms of intervention are undertaken to address a number of market failures. In the case of primary education, there is mixed provision in most western European countries between private and state schools. In higher education, there is less mixed provision, but a different organizational form, that of the separate publicly funded higher education institution. Health care is funded either directly by the government through the general taxation system or by a private/public health insurance scheme. Education is most typically funded by the first method: taxation. The costs of educating an adult are also shared by students and their parents, in many countries. As merit goods are underconsumed, the government can use subsidies to encourage greater consumption. In the housing market, many governments view owner occupation as a merit good. As such they have pursued policies which aim at extending this: for example, the sale of council housing in the UK.

Externalities

Chapter 2 described the idea of externalities as spill-overs. They exist because there is a divergence between the private costs/benefits and the social costs/benefits. They can cause a misallocation of resources. Private solutions exist but, as we saw, they are limited by the assumption of a small number of people being involved. Once the nature of the externality involves more generators and more affected parties, governments can intervene in a number of ways. As this book devotes much space to negative externalities, these will be used as examples.

Provision

Governments can take over the ownership of companies which are major polluters. For example, the French government owns the electricity industry, which is largely generated from nuclear sources. Nuclear power does relatively less damage to the environment than gas or oil-generated electricity. This, it claims, is a valuable reason for the continuation of public ownership.

Taxes and subsidies

Using a tax or subsidy to overcome an externality was first suggested by Pigou. Take the example given in Figure 3.1, which shows a graphical analysis of a market which fails to include the costs of externalities. Steel production produces pollution, as the burning of high-sulphur coal causes pollution of the air. The cost of this pollution is called the external cost. Imagine that steel producers ignore this pollution. The demand curve for steel is horizontal because we are assuming a perfectly competitive market. We can say that for every tonne of steel produced there are two sets of costs: the direct production costs, which we term the marginal private costs, and the marginal social costs, which include the external costs of pollution. Ideally, we wish the steel producers to take into consideration the additional cost, which is the vertical distance between the two cost curves.

Economic theory tells us that a socially efficient output level occurs when the marginal social cost (MSC) is equal to the marginal social benefit (MSB). The MSB is represented by the demand curve. In the absence of the cost of pollution being included in the price of steel, companies produce more steel and pollution than is socially desirable. This is at price P_m and output Q_m. Resources are overallocated at the market equilibrium. What we desire is that price is set at P_e and output at Q_e, where $MSC = MSB$.

Governments can intervene, according to Pigou, by forcing companies to pay the full costs of their activities: that is, by taxing the steel producers by an

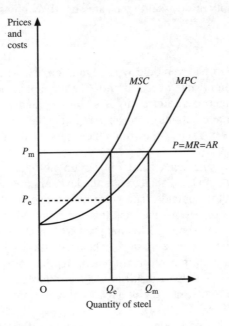

Figure 3.1 Solutions to external costs

amount which equals the external costs. On the diagram this is the distance between P_e and P_m. Conversely, a subsidy can be paid to the person or parties which have suffered from the pollution, to compensate for the damage done. The payment of the subsidy does not, however, reduce the level of pollution in this case.

This approach appears to be simple to describe, but in practice it has a number of shortcomings. The solution requires not that pollution be eradicated altogether, but that the right amount of output and hence pollution is produced. The function of the tax is therefore to try and make the full cost of the externality reflected in decision making. In practice, it is difficult to measure this vertical distance because it requires that a monetary value be placed on the damage that, say, sulphur causes to the local residents. If people claim that it makes them cough, how do we translate this respiratory problem into a value?

Another problem arises because the cost curves are not drawn parallel to each other. This means that, at different levels of output, the vertical distance will change. We need a tax which varies in proportion to the external costs. Second, Pigou assumed that all other markets work efficiently and that there are no other market failures. Clearly this is not the case: many of the markets discussed in public policy suffer from a number of market failures. Third, it is assumed that there is perfect knowledge about the cost of the polluting firm, the amount of damage and the costs to society. It is unlikely that all this information will be available. Finally, it is assumed that the government or regulatory authority imposing the tax will have access to company information and will act in an efficient manner. Both these assumptions are very demanding.

Regulation

Externalities can also be overcome with regulation. This can take the form of legislation which might state a legal limit to the amount of pollution that can be emitted. This is sometimes referred to as setting a standard. Governments can regulate the undesirable outputs or they can regulate the inputs to the production process. If companies exceed the limit, they may face financial penalties or criminal proceedings.

Figure 3.2 shows the legal limit on certain pollutants associated with a negative externality. The horizontal axis is the level of emissions and the vertical axis shows the value in pounds. The marginal social cost (MSC) of pollution curve rises up. This represents the idea that the more pollution is emitted, the more damage there is to society. The marginal cost of abatements (MCA) curve falls in relation to the level of emissions. The curve shows the additional cost to firms of installing pollution control equipment. It is downward sloping because to reduce emission levels by a small amount is relatively inexpensive, but to reduce levels substantially, say to 2 or 3 levels of emissions, incurs much greater costs.

The efficient level of emissions is where the marginal social cost of emissions is equal to the marginal cost of abatement: this is at a level of 10 units. If a

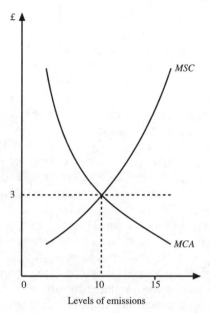

Figure 3.2 Standards and fees

standard were used, this is where it would be set. If a company emits at a higher level – for example, at a level of 12 units – a penalty may be incurred. In theory, the setting of a standard ensures that a company produces at the efficient level.

A tax is a charge levied on each unit of a company's emissions. Let us assume that the tax is set at the charge of £3 per unit of emissions. There is no incentive for the company to produce beyond levels of 10 units because the marginal cost of abatement is less than the tax: it pays the company to reduce emission levels. For levels below 10 units, the *MCA* exceeds the tax and there is an incentive for the company to pay the tax rather than reduce emission levels further. A tax of £3 per unit will lead to an efficient outcome because, at the level of 10 units, the marginal social cost of emissions is equated to the benefits associated with lower abatement costs.

When would a government use a regulation rather than a tax? Much depends on how the incentives work and on the amount of information available. Under a tax system, the company pays both the costs of abating the pollution and the tax. Companies have different abilities to reduce their pollution levels because they have different types of equipment and production processes. If a government or regulatory body decides to reduce total emission levels to a specific amount, the imposition of a tax allows each company to abate by different amounts to reach the total level. So companies which can reduce at less cost per unit should in theory reduce emission levels by more. In intuitive terms, it is cost effective to allow companies which incur more expenses to reduce levels by less.

This situation must be compared with the setting of a regulation, which requires all companies to reduce their emission levels by the same amount. This approach loses out relatively in that it does not take into consideration differing abilities of abatement. Taxes also provide a strong incentive for companies to install new equipment, allowing them to reduce their emission levels even further.

If companies emit beyond the standard, some penalty system must be in place and represent a larger loss to the company than the cost of abating its pollution. There must be a perceived probability of being caught, which requires monitoring and therefore access to information. Let us now assume that there is imperfect information and that monitoring is expensive. It is the government's responsibility to monitor. Regulatory schemes only require companies to prove that they have not exceeded the regulatory limit. If we compare this with a tax system, which requires information on the exact level of pollution, we can say that taxes are more costly to monitor than regulation.

Governments could alternatively subsidize the cost of pollution abatement equipment. The subsidy would be the difference between the private and social costs of production. What this does is reduce the costs of pollution to society, but at the same time reduce the marginal private costs to the producer. The problem with this approach is that, when producers decide how much of the good to produce, they do not take into consideration the extra costs of the public subsidy. They could increase production to beyond the efficient level and use the subsidy to abate the pollution, but the fact remains that they would not be producing at the efficient level.

Another aspect of regulation involves the use of voluntary agreements and cooperative international agreements. The former can be loosely defined as risk reduction agreements. They are slightly different to regulation because they have a moral basis. There is more of an exchange of terms involved with agreements. They are contracts between industry and the regulatory authorities. Generally they supplement and strengthen existing regulation. They include a general statement of the objectives on the environment, a timetable, methods of achieving these objectives and a responsibility to publish the results. In France since the 1970s, sectoral contracts have been made between the Ministry of the Environment and a number of trade associations. The aim is to encourage industry to carry out certain programmes to reduce pollution in exchange (compensation) for financial assistance from the government. The idea behind these agreements is that they are self-enforcing. Governments intervene by setting up the contract and then the industry is left free to decide how best to achieve these standards. Many negative environmental externalities require nations to work together. This involves international co-operation and is altogether more difficult to implement. One of the problems is that certain air pollutants are blown into other countries, leaving the question of who should pay for the damage. In theory, there are greater gains to be had from coordinated international action than from uncoordinated national action.

Finally, many economists make distinctions between market- and non-market-based approaches when dealing with negative environmental external-ities. Market-based approaches fall into two broad groups: taxes and the use of tradable permits. The first, as we saw, is logical but suffers from implementation problems. Despite these shortcomings there is much debate going on at present about an EU-wide carbon tax. The ideal tax is one which is the same size as the external cost. Where this is difficult to achieve in practice, another approach is to use a tax to shift the use of pollution-causing inputs. This is what the carbon tax would do: it would tax the carbon content of fossil-fuel energy industries.

Tradable permits are an exciting idea and may be applied if uncertainty exists and if it is undesirable to impose high costs on companies. Permits are pieces of paper that are distributed to companies in an industry and which give them the right to generate emissions. If they manage to reduce their pollution levels to less than the amount on their permit, they acquire credits. These can be bought and sold among companies depending on their differing ability to reduce pollution. The government decides on the total level of emissions, just like a standards system. Costs will be minimized as companies which are efficient at abating pollution have an incentive to do so, because they can sell their credits to another company. Companies which accrue debits have an incentive to buy permits from another company. The advantage of this approach is that it combines the strengths of a standards system with the cost advantages of a tax system.

Government approaches to improving market imperfections

Market imperfections can be grouped into information, capital market and market structure imperfections.

Approaches to improving information imperfections

We saw in Chapter 2 that perfect information in markets is not something which occurs in reality. Two aspects of information imperfections can be addressed by governments. The first is imperfections arising from information being too complex and technical for consumers to make a rational choice. This is clearly the case in health care: consumers have to rely on the suppliers of information, doctors. The second aspect is imperfections arising from unequal power. This situation comes about because consumers need both full information and the power to enforce their choice; there must be equal power among consumers. However, this is not always the case. For example, some consumers know the uses and benefits that education and health will bring them. Unequal power can arise among consumers because of different abilities to articulate and different levels of confidence. If there is imperfect information and unequal power, consumers may make inefficient choices.

How can governments intervene to improve this aspect of decision making? Governments could provide information on a large scale about health, pension and education issues. But this might still not overcome the unequal power problem. When there are severe information problems to the extent that the market fails, then public production is a better solution. Take the case of health

45

care. Patients suffer from asymmetry of information relative to doctors. They do not know how ill they are; nor do they know about their future health. Private insurance could offer a solution – people could cover for any future health problems by taking out the appropriate insurance. However, as we have seen, private insurance markets suffer because of technical problems such as moral hazard and adverse selection.

Public production could improve on the efficiency of outcomes. Public finance and production can overcome the inefficiencies of insurance markets and meet equity objectives. In the case of health care, instead of an insurance policy, a publicly funded health insurance programme means that everyone pays an amount in the form of a tax, which then goes to finance the public provision of health. The moral hazard problem, which arises because insurance makes people alter their behaviour, is reduced under a publicly funded and provided system. There are no adverse selection problems: the government is not selecting healthy over less healthy people; everyone is in the pool. The premium paid will ensure that there will be enough money in the pot to pay for the less healthy.

Approaches to improving capital market imperfections

Capital market imperfections arise because of restrictions made by lending institutions, which naturally focus more on the risks associated with lending money to different types of consumer, and less on the economy-wide benefits of educating more people. Governments can intervene by providing the finance for investment required in education and in housing. Alternatively, governments can provide an implicit subsidy. For example, the purchase of council homes was made accessible to more people because the government reduced the market price of the homes. This enabled many people to obtain finance which was within their means. Also, governments can give guarantees. Student loan systems can be administered by the banks or private lending organizations, but they may have a government assurance that it will follow up debtors. In the case of social housing, the UK government has worked in partnership with investors to provide finance for the construction of new homes. In this way, risk is shared between a greater number of finance providers. In specific bridge-building projects, governments can embark on joint funding arrangements, and they can allow a private operator to run the bridge tolls, thereby allowing the generation of revenue to be made from a public asset.

Approaches to improving market structure imperfections

Chapter 2 demonstrated that there is a loss of welfare resulting from monopoly, and that a monopoly structure prevails in many of the 'necessity' industries or public utilities. A monopoly structure can lead to higher prices, reduced output and monopoly power. Governments can intervene in a number of ways, including the following:

- Nationalizing the monopoly.
- Directly regulating the monopolist's prices or profits.
- Subjecting the market to franchising.
- Removing artificial barriers to entry and making the market contestable.
- Creating internal markets.

Nationalizing the monopoly

This means that the assets are under the ownership of the state. The UK government nationalized key industries in order to meet economic, social and political objectives. It set a guiding principle of control: the 'arm's length' approach. The industries would manage their commercial affairs independently of the government, while it took the role of overseeing the public interest. An innovation at the time, sadly it was too optimistic, and the 'arm's length' approach gradually became the interfere-with-everything approach.

Governments can use nationalization to overcome the social losses, control the problem of monopoly power and meet equity objectives. This can be done by setting out the industry's duties and objectives. So, for example, all the UK nationalized industries had a duty to protect the public interest and most importantly to provide a universal service. This is an interesting idea and it relates to the principle that everyone should have access to certain basic goods and services. Also, there was to be a uniform price, irrespective of the costs of supplying to distant locations. This applied to the postal service, electricity, gas, water and telephones. This meant that some services which are clearly loss making were cross-subsidized by profit-making services, all under one organization.

The disadvantage of this form of intervention is that, although it meets equity objectives, it can lead to inefficiencies. An inefficiency arises because of the presence of costs which are not unbundled. Bundled costs mean that, in the production of a good or service, it is not clear what the profits and losses are for each service. A situation could arise where a service is no longer needed or where the managers of a nationalized industry do not act in the most cost-effective way. Both these situations would be made clearer under a private sector arrangement. Cross-subsidization can be said to be distortive. Governments could address this situation with annual reviews or a change in organizational structure. The latter, which is studied in the case studies, works by changing the incentives under one organization without privatization. For example, services can be grouped together and made into separate businesses with specific responsibilities. Managers could then be given operational targets, like the reduction of operating costs over a specific period. What this does is increase accountability and provide a greater degree of commercialization.

The problem of monopoly power causing higher prices was dealt with by the UK government in an order to set prices roughly equivalent to the marginal costs of supply. Let us reconsider the model presented in Chapter 2, this time comparing the monopoly price with that set under nationalization. Figure 3.3 shows that P_m is the monopolist's price and Q_m its output. Under nationalization the government instructs the industries to set prices equal to marginal costs. This is at output Q_c and price P_c. We can see that under these instructions output is greater, and the price is lower, than under monopoly. The problem, as we shall see in the case studies, is that many industries did not comply with setting prices at marginal cost levels.

Another problem with this approach arises when there is a natural monopoly. Economic theory tells us that this means that the average costs of production are declining. If average costs are declining, marginal costs are below average costs. An approach which specifies that prices should be set at the marginal cost of production means that a company will incur a loss. Governments would have to provide a subsidy to cover this loss. In essence, the pricing approach is right in principle: resources will be allocated efficiently when price is set equal to marginal costs. But this situation must be weighed up against alternatives, like average cost pricing and monopoly pricing, and this is discussed below.

Directly regulating the monopolist's prices or profits

This approach might be required if the monopolist operates in the private sector. Price regulation is about ensuring that monopoly power is kept to a minimum, in terms of prices, and this means setting a limit on price increases for an individual or a group of services. Price regulation aims for a form of average cost pricing. This is because if the industry is in the private sector, it will need to make some profit in order to attract investment. The regulated price must be pitched somewhere

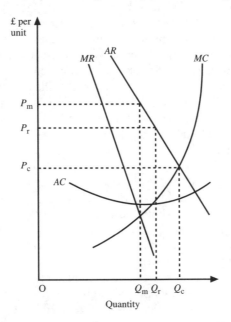

Figure 3.3 Government approaches to monopoly

between the monopoly and the competitive market price. On Figure 3.3, let us place this at price P_r and output Q_r. In this instance, there will be some deadweight loss because output is not at the efficient level of Q_c, but there is an improvement by a reduction in the deadweight loss of the monopolists' output, Q_m.

Profit regulation is another form of intervention practised in the USA. This is based on the rate of return that the industry earns on its capital. The task for the regulatory authority is to set a fair rate of return, which provides incentives for profits, innovation and expansion, but at the same time is based on a maximum price that depends on the expected rate of return. This approach has suffered from implementation problems, especially in determining the expected rate of return and the actual cost of capital. So far this type of regulation has not been widely adopted in Europe.

Regulation can also address the other problem which has the potential to arise under a monopoly structure. This refers to quality of service and meeting the universal service obligation. Governments can ensure that both these concerns are addressed by conferring on the regulatory authority the right to ensure that certain standards are met. There could be a legal obligation to provide services to one and all through the granting of a licence. If the operator does not comply with the specifications, the licence can be removed and trading will become illegal. A less stringent option is for the authority to have the industry practices reviewed and also to make requests for greater information.

Subjecting the market to franchising

This refers to a situation where there is a right granted to supply a market whose product or service may or may not generate revenue. The idea behind it is that there is competition for the market, but not competition within the market. This condition can arise when revenues may be produced, but when there is little point or feasibility in price competition. Take the case of catering services on a train. There is no point in having many different companies going up and down the carriages trying to sell sandwiches. There would be undesirable duplication. It is more efficient to have one operator, selected on the basis of the lowest prices or the best quality of service. There would be no price competition. Contracting out is another form of franchising, but in this case no revenues are generated: an example is the collection and disposal of refuse. In both these cases the monopoly is retained, but there is competition for the market. It is a way of trying to be more cost effective without breaking up the monopoly structure and in the absence of unfeasible competition.

Removing artificial barriers to entry and making the market contestable

Another approach open to governments in overcoming the problems of monopoly structures in the public services is to remove the barriers to entry which protect the monopoly, and to try and make the market more contestable. In the first instance, as we saw in Chapter 2, monopoly structures arise from

49

many sources. One of these is a legal barrier which only allows a single company to supply the service. Many postal services are protected by statute (an Act). If the government decides that the reasons for the protection are no longer valid, it can change the Act. This is a form of deregulation or liberalization. Contestability is an idea which has two strands. On the one hand, it is about changing the degree of competition in a market by reducing the barriers to entry; and on the other hand, the theory states that the behaviour of a dominant company can be changed through the threat of potential competition, but not actual competition.

Both these approaches have been used in the UK. In the first case, the postal services have had their statutory monopoly suspended for a temporary period, which means that any postal operator can deliver letters in the category which was once protected. This situation will be examined in the case studies. In the second instance, the idea about making the market more contestable relies on establishing a number of conditions in favour of the potential new entrant. For instance, there should be no sunk costs (i.e. costs which cannot be recovered), so that the entrant is not put at any disadvantage. This method was employed in the UK telecommunications industry.

Creating internal markets

A final approach open to governments relates to making improvements in the areas where there is a monopoly structure in government provision. An internal market is like a system of exchanges being undertaken within a market. The internal market approach means that independent providers rather than the government will compete with each other to win contracts to supply services. Internal markets are used when consumer purchasing power is expressed through budgets rather than cash; and these budgets can be state-funded. On the demand side, consumers' preferences are expressed through agents or intermediaries, such as a health authority or a higher education funding council. There may also be some competition between organisations which are purchasing on behalf of their consumers. The idea is that efficiency gains can be made on the supply side, and providers will be more responsive to consumers' demand and more accountable to those who fund their operations.

Government approaches to improve equity

As this book is focused mainly on the new directions in public policy associated with market-led approaches, this discussion will concentrate on the approaches available to governments to ensure that fairness is either maintained or improved as a result of these new directions. Many of the efficiency drives described in this book should improve the production and distribution of resources, but improvements to the level of fairness are not guaranteed. There must be mechanisms in place to ensure that the outcomes and the benefits are directed both at those who have paid for them and those who need them most. We will consider this in respect of the different types of intervention.

Legislation can be used to direct economic resources to help the needy or those on low incomes. For example, in housing markets, governments can require local authorities to draw up plans and schemes for the underprivileged in their area. Governments can also legislate on the allocation of houses to homeless people, or attempt to discourage the formation of ghettos by encouraging and establishing a policy of balanced allocation. Such legislation is often needed to supplement the existing funding arrangements.

Governments can intervene and overcome inequalities in the distribution of basic goods and services either by establishing a public monopoly and conferring on it the right to supply exclusively, or by regulating the behaviour of a private monopoly. With the first idea, equity concerns can be met through cross-subsidies to ensure that people can access the goods, irrespective of their income and geographical location. Public ownership with direct government subsidies may also ensure that regional and industrial differences are evened out.

Regulation can be used to reduce the potential for consumer exploitation in the consumption of goods and services in industries like energy and transport. This can be done through price, profit or quality of service regulation, set up and written in the licences of the suppliers. Regulation can set standards and request information on performance. Companies may be required to keep a number of customer service-related codes of practice. Failure to meet a guaranteed standard – for example, the response time for dealing with a customer complaint – could be dealt with by a regulator requiring compensation to be paid to all customers affected. Also, governments can put in place mechanisms which ensure that the benefits derived from greater competition are directed to the consumers, as well as the owners and shareholders of the company.

In many of the new approaches examined, governments have stressed the desire to increase consumer choice. This aspiration needs careful handling because consumer choice can be strengthened only if there are clearly defined channels for expressing a preference. In the housing market this may mean increasing the rights of tenants or allowing them a greater say in the running of the housing schemes or the setting of rent levels. Increasing consumer choice is also about educating people in how to access and use information to ensure that they receive, for example, the quality of service they have paid for.

Increasing access to information and improving its quantity and quality are ways which specifically assist certain sections of society. In higher education systems, there has been a tendency for students from middle-class backgrounds to attend. While this is a product of many factors, it is clear that if people can be helped to overcome perception problems of what higher education is like, then they may be more likely to enrol. At the operations level, this may mean that the providers, higher education institutions, may have to change the type of provision to meet the specific needs of different types of consumer.

Taxes and subsidies play a large role in reducing inequalities. These can be used to finance public provision or to alter the prices of goods and services. An example of the first case is a move from a largely privately funded health care programme to one which provides a compulsory and basic service to everyone. This means that those people who had not taken out private health insurance might at least be covered for basic medical services. Many governments have shifted towards using personal subsidies rather than production subsidies in the social housing market. This is a policy of targeting those in need, rather than providing a minimum level of housing.

There has been a change in the objectives and approaches used to overcome inequalities. After the Second World War, governments felt that a greater redistribution of income and wealth could be obtained through public ownership of the means of production. Thus, we witnessed a spate of nationalization. The idea was that having a government in control of these fundamental resources would ensure that people could access energy, homes, transport and communications nationally and at subsidized prices. This approach has now been replaced with the idea that private ownership of the means of production will bring its own benefits, particularly greater competition. This will, in theory, reduce costs, increase choice and lead to greater flexibility. The role of government in promoting equality in this instance has been to introduce independent regulation to promote the interests of the consumer and the nation. At the public service level, governments are increasingly using targeting as a means of improving the income levels of those with the greatest needs.

Q4 Why is it important to distinguish between government objectives and government approaches? Give an example of both an objective and an approach in the case of health care provision.

Q5 Give examples of an efficiency objective, an administrative objective and an equity objective for the provision of higher education.

Q6 What is the difference between a government financing the provision of a public service and using a tax in the provision of a service? Give an example of where a government directly provides a good and an example of where it directly finances the provision of a good.

Further reading

Introductory level

Begg, D., Fischer, S. and Dornbusch, R. (1994) *Economics*, 4th edn, Maidenhead: McGraw-Hill, chs 4 and 18.

Hardwick, P., Khan, B. and Langmead, J. (1994) *An Introduction to Modern Economics*, 4th edn, Harlow: Longman, ch. 15.

Sloman, J. (1994) *Economics*, 2nd edn, Hemel Hempstead: Harvester Wheatsheaf, ch. 12.

Intermediate level

Bailey, S. (1995) *Public Sector Economics: Theory, Policy and Practice*, Basingstoke: Macmillan, chs 2, 8 and 13.

Barr, N. (1993) *The Economics of the Welfare State*, 2nd edn, London: Weidenfeld and Nicolson, ch. 4.

Griffiths, A. and Wall, S. (eds) (1995) *Applied Economics: An Introductory Course*, 6th edn, Hawlow: Longman, chs 8, 10, 11 and 12.

Griffiths, A. and Wall, S. (1996) *Intermediate Microeconomics: Theory and Applications*, Harlow: Longman, ch. 12.

Gwartney, J. (1977) *Microeconomics: Private and Public Choice*, New York: Academic Press, ch. 18.

Other sources

Atkinson, A. (1995) *Incomes and the Welfare State*, Cambridge: Cambridge University Press, ch. 1.

Jackson, P. and Price, C. (eds) (1994) *Privatisation and Regulation*, Hawlow: Longman, ch. 1.

Minford, P. and Ashton, P. (1996) 'Rolling back the state: a proposal for reforming public spending', *Economics and Business Education*, vol. 4, no. 3.

Pigou, A.C. (1924) *The Economics of Welfare*, London: Macmillan.

Sawyer, M. (1996) 'The role of the state in a market economy', *Economics and Business Education*, vol. 4, part 3, no. 15.

Part 2

Social welfare themes

Chapter 4

Health care

Key words used: providers, purchasers, adverse selection, internal markets, contracts, universal access

How many times have you been to the doctor's and had to wait over an hour for a consultation? How often do you read or learn about the local ladies' group which is trying to raise funds for a new scanner machine? Have you ever read in the newspapers about the patient who had to travel miles to have an operation? These observations are signs of our times. Health care is a very much talked about subject. People's opinions and passions run high on this subject, and political elections can be won and lost on plans for health reforms. On the one hand, we all want to be assured of having access to good health care, and on the other, the costs of running health care systems are rising. Something has to give. Governments throughout the industrialized world are facing new challenges which have stimulated a variety of approaches to combat rising costs and improve the quality of and access to health care. This has prompted and sharpened attention on the respective roles of the public and private sectors in health care systems. Economics has a useful contribution to make to these challenges: it can provide a framework which helps us understand the unique features of health markets and an analytical set of tools to study and evaluate alternative policy approaches.

Background to the problem

This section considers the general tensions which have prompted governments to introduce reforms in their health care systems. Most industrialized countries are trying to fit expanding health care systems into tightly managed market economies. Which forces have put pressures on policy-makers to introduce reforms? There are at least three forces for change: the need to contain costs; changes in the demand for health; and the need to preserve equity.

The need to contain costs is about controlling the growth of health costs so that they do not gallop beyond either the rate of inflation or the annual rate of growth in an economy. Examples of health costs include doctors' salaries, the cost of medical equipment and the cost of running a hospital. The first question is: why are health costs any different to those of other industries? The answer is that they have a tendency to rise, and this occurs for a number of reasons. The first reason, which is enlarged on later, relates to the idea that the nature of health care products and services is such that, because most people cannot easily evaluate the type of treatment needed or its effectiveness, there is a tendency for health costs to rise without people really noticing or being able to do much about it. In addition, health care providers, who are seeking the best care for their patients, may not necessarily look for the most cost-effective treatment. For these reasons there appear to be tendencies for upward rather than downward pressure on costs.

Finally, medical technology impacts on health costs. There are thousands of health treatments, each requiring a different amount of resources. Technology often develops in response to health problems, and in health care it provides new treatments, but not all technology increases productivity. Some technological equipment requires just as many staff to operate it as before. Productivity in health care has the potential to fall relative to other industries, and the result is an increase in the relative price of health care. Technology means that some diseases that were not treatable decades ago can now be treated, and this takes up increasing resources.

How well do these ideas hold up against the statistics? There are at least two ways to look at health care costs. One is to look at how health costs have changed relative to other costs. The other is to look at changes in public expenditure. The key indicator is public expenditure on health care as a percentage of output, usually gross domestic product (GDP). Table 4.1 shows data collected by the OECD. Over the period 1981–90, in four out of the six countries, the share of GDP spent on health care increased, although this statistic says nothing about changes in GDP. If we look at the change in relative health prices, the health price index increased for four countries and there were increases in health prices over and above the changes in other prices. The statistics, although incomplete because they say nothing about changes in quality, suggest that upward pressure on expenditure and prices is being experienced by many countries.

Changes in health spending can be viewed as being influenced by both the demand and the supply side. So far only supply-side influences have been discussed. On the demand side, demographic changes are likely to impact on health care systems. One fact, in particular, is that most western European nations face an ageing population. Taking the UK as an example, Table 4.2 shows that in 1961 some 12 per cent of the population was aged 65 or over, but by 1994 this had increased to 16 per cent.

This trend is expected to continue, so that by the year 2031 there will be 23 per cent of the population aged 65 and over. Increasing longevity and a fall in the number of births are contributory factors. The implications of this are that we might expect the demand for health care to increase and there to be a change in the type of health care required. However, there is some evidence to suggest that, while this may become an important factor in the future, it does not make a

Table 4.1 Expenditure on health and relative prices

	Total expenditure on health (% of GDP)			Health relative price index (1985 = 100)		% growth in relative prices
	1981	1990	1981–90	1981	1990	1981–90
France	7.9	8.8	0.9	106.7	95.3	–10.7
Germany	8.7	8.3	–0.4	94.8	98.6	4.0
Italy	6.7	8.1	1.4	102.3	105.0	2.6
Netherlands	8.2	8.2	0.0	102.2	105.6	3.3
Sweden	9.5	8.6	–0.9	102.6	98.2	–4.3
UK	6.1	6.2	0.1	95.9	108.7	13.3

Source: After 'OECD health data', OECD, 1993.

significant contribution to health expenditures at present.

Finally, equity in health care is becoming an area of increasing concern. Changes in labour markets resulting from structural changes have led to higher levels of unemployment. This has two impacts on health care. One is that unemployment can bring its own bad health: people experience more stress and this expresses itself in a greater demand for health care. Second, having a greater proportion of a nation unemployed means increasing pressure to maintain the equity objective of equal access. Some industrialized countries have found an increase in the number of people not insured for health care.

Health care systems face many challenges, the most important of which appears to be the concern about costs. This has given rise to a further challenge: what are the best approaches to dealing with this problem? Many governments have recently placed faith in the virtues of market-led approaches and the

Table 4.2 Population by age, UK

	under 16	16–39	40–64	65–79	80 and over	All ages (millions)
1961	25	31	32	10	2	52.8
1971	25	31	30	11	2	55.9
1981	22	35	28	12	3	56.4
1991	20	35	29	12	4	57.8
1994	21	35	29	12	4	58.4
2001[a]	21	33	31	11	4	59.8
2011	19	30	34	12	5	61.3
2021	18	30	33	14	5	62.1
2031	18	28	30	16	7	62.2

[a]1992-based projections.
Source: Social Trends (1996).

introduction of competition. But how do you combine competition with equity objectives? This will be examined in the case studies. Significant reforms are taking place in most industrialized countries, in the UK, Germany, Belgium, Sweden, Spain, Canada, Israel, Ireland, France and the Netherlands. In publicly operated health care systems, competition among health providers has been proposed for Sweden and Finland and implemented for the UK. In countries with private health insurance, like the Netherlands, the approach adopted has been towards increasing competition among health insurers.

Current system of allocation

To begin with we need to ask: what would a free market in health care look like if there was no government intervention?

The market

To determine how health care would be allocated in a free market, we need to describe the economic conditions that a market in health care would face, some of which give rise to important types of market failures. In relation to health care, these failures are as follows:

- The presence of externalities.
- The presence of information imperfections.
- The presence of inequalities.

The presence of externalities

The first type of market failure, externalities, arise from the wider benefits associated with consuming health care services. These can be referred to as positive spill-over effects. Under a free market these wider benefits, such as a vaccination programme which immunizes everyone, would not necessarily be captured. A private supplier of vaccination services might provide injections only on the basis of willingness to pay. This might exclude a proportion of the population. The external benefits of everyone being immunized are not taken into consideration. A related argument is that a person's welfare is dependent on the health of another person. This is called a caring externality. In the absence of a market which places value on this caring aspect, if caring externalities do exist, there is a case for government intervention.

The presence of information imperfections

These are among the most serious of market failures in health care. Patients do not have the same knowledge as health providers about the type of remedy they require, the costs of the treatment, or their future health needs. They face uncertainties over their future and incomplete information on their state of health. This tends to make them dependent on others. In economics we say that imperfect information gives rise to a principal–agent relationship. A health provider, such as a doctor, is the agent, and the patient is the principal. The relationship is different to others in a normal situation of exchange. The consumer has little control over the choice, quantity and timing of health care services. The provider makes a decision in the interests of the patient. There is no way the patient can determine whether this was the right decision. There is also a principal–agent relationship between hospitals and doctors. Doctors cannot easily find out about where the best services are, as they do not receive the care directly. This means that their decisions are based on the information of others.

Also, what options are available to patients who feel they have received a poor medical decision? This would involve finding out about alternatives, their effectiveness and availability. In economics we call these the transaction costs involved in an exchange. These are likely to be high in health care, and when this occurs we can say that the market will not be very efficient.

How can the market respond to these problems? The lack of information about costs and about future medical needs means that patients require health insurance. But there are problems with health insurance markets. The principal ones are adverse selection and moral hazard, discussed in Chapter 2. Health care is plagued with adverse selection and it arises because of asymmetrical information between the health insurers and patients. The former have little means of identifying people with low or high health risks. Patients know their state of health better than the insurance company. This means the information between them is asymmetrical. The implication of this is that, when private markets provide health insurance, the individuals with poor health will tend to overinsure, which will increase the price or premium for everyone. Individuals with relatively good health, and therefore lower risks, may opt out. At this point the market may become unprofitable. There is likely to be an inefficient allocation of resources. One solution, via the market, would be for insurance not to be sold on the basis of health, for example, but to be sold to a company as a package for all its employees.

Moral hazard refers to uncertainties surrounding health costs, arising from imperfect information. A private health insurance company offering medical insurance might induce a person to overconsume in the first instance. Then, once insured, the person might take less care of themselves without the insurance company knowing. This occurs because insurance companies are not closely watching over the everyday activities and behaviour of their consumers. Both these outcomes could lead to increased costs. Private insurance markets may therefore lead to inefficiencies in terms of costs and provision.

The presence of inequalities

Markets do not ensure that there will be an efficient allocation of resources. It is likely that, under a system of private health insurance, some people will be either left uninsured or facing high prices. Markets are unlikely to ensure an equitable outcome in terms of the distribution of and access to health care. The merit good argument rests on the idea that governments feel that the consumption of the good should be increased, so that there are benefits to one and all. This suggests that some minimum level of health care should be provided.

Government objectives

Government intervention is justified on the basis of the market failures described above. Intervention assumes that it will improve the outcomes of the market. In this context we need to consider the objectives that governments might pursue, which were introduced in Chapter 3:

- Economic efficiency objectives.
- Administrative efficiency objectives.
- Equity objectives.

Economic efficiency objectives

What does efficiency mean in health care? We can begin to answer this question by thinking in terms of efficiency in the production and allocation of health care. An example of a production efficiency objective is one which attempts to deliver a medical service at the lowest possible cost and gives the maximum benefit. It is extremely difficult to define what maximum benefit or output means in health care. For example, it could be the number of days it takes to heal after taking a prescription, or how well one feels, or some other indicator. There is a growing body of literature and research on health output measurement. One attempt has come up with the idea of the quality-adjusted life-year (QALY). This has two dimensions. It takes into account life expectancy and a quality adjustment for the healthiness of those expected life-years. Comparison can then be made on how QALYs change with a medical procedure and without it. This can be a way of monitoring economic efficiency. One of the problems with this measure of output, however, is that only a limited amount of information can ever be imparted in a set of indicators.

Administrative efficiency objectives

These are about improving the systems which utilize the resources. An example of an administrative efficiency objective might be to keep health costs at the previous year's level, or to improve the cost and management accounting systems.

Equity objectives

These aims are pursued by policy-makers in all types of health care system. If we take an egalitarian approach (believing that all people should be treated equally), then a commonly used definition in this context is that of equality. This has many interpretations. In relation to provision, it could mean equal treatment for equal need, or equality of access, or equality of health. The first definition can be split further. Two terms were introduced in Chapter 3: horizontal and vertical equity. Equal treatment for equal need meets the former criterion, but it does not say anything about how people with unequal needs should be treated. Equality of access is about the time and money individuals have to spend in using health care facilities. This will depend on how they perceive the benefits they receive. Equality of health can mean that treatment and health are open to the population as a whole, as opposed to a sub-group. All these considerations are difficult to put into action, since they involve some degree of measurement of need, of treatment and of access.

Equity in financing might mean that payment for health care is related to ability to pay. This serves the vertical equity definition. Those with greater ability to pay should pay more. Again there are questions about whether this should be in proportional or absolute terms. If we desire an egalitarian system, the payments should be progressive. Setting health care objectives is difficult because, as we saw earlier, there are problems with measuring health output, which makes it difficult to assess the costs of health inputs. In practice, equity goals vary among countries. In the USA objectives tend to be defined in terms of minimum standards rather than equal treatment for equal needs. In Europe, and the UK in particular, the emphasis is more on everyone being treated equally.

Government intervention

Governments intervene in health care markets to overcome market failures and to achieve a set of objectives. We now turn to the types of approach that governments might adopt:

- Private financing and provision.
- Public financing and private provision.
- Public financing and provision.

Private financing and provision

Pure private financing and provision systems are rare, although the USA comes close. It has private voluntary insurance and private provision, but there is significant public provision through programmes which target different demographic groups. For example, there is Medicaid for the aged, the disabled and low-income groups. The problem with this form of provision is that, because of the problems with insurance markets and equity, there is little to prevent large groups of people being uninsured.

Public financing and private provision

Mixed public and private involvement avoids most of the problems of a wholly private system. In the provision of health care, much depends on how the fees are arranged for the provider: for example, a doctor's fee. This is called third party payment. Problems can arise because there are incentives for the provider both to overcharge and to overprovide. This could be overcome by government regulation of the amount of output, or placing a budget on the amount which can be charged. European countries such as Germany, France and the Netherlands have a significant degree of private provision which is subject to heavy regulation. In France, the government regulates the schedules for fees to providers, and regulates expansion of medical equipment through strict controls.

Some of these countries have mixed financing arrangements. There are two ways finance can be organized: private finance plus government finance for special cases; and wholly government-financed systems, where medical bills are paid from tax revenues. In the first instance, the financing of income-earning individuals can be left to health insurance markets. Here they might offer a minimum standard of coverage. The problem with this arrangement is: what happens with risks like chronic health problems and the poor? Governments could subsidize the insurance companies in order for them to cover these cases; alternatively, they could make cash transfers to cover the patient's health bills. But what happens with borderline health cases and with people whose income is just above the state assistance level?

Public financing and provision

Public production and finance is common in the Scandinavian countries and the UK, where health care facilities are publicly owned in the former and there is a small private sector in the latter. These arrangements are justified on the grounds that they improve on both of the systems described above. If finance is publicly provided, this typically means that the system is compulsory. Premiums are not based on ability to pay or on risk; a compulsory government-financed system means that everyone is covered. This meets equity concerns. Third party problems which give incentives for overprovision and overcharging can be overcome. On the question of overprovision, public production can ensure that increases in health care output are constrained by the use of budgets. The problems that patients have in monitoring the quality of the service can also justify public production.

The problems with public finance and provision on the demand side are that a form of rationing is required. Demand may be rationed by some patients not being treated or joining waiting lists; others may take out private insurance, while urgent cases can be allocated on a priority scheme. These can all cause an inefficient allocation of resources. On the supply side, there is monopoly provision, and management are subject to political constraints. Managers' objectives will focus on putting the case for more resources. Ministers cannot monitor health costs because they rely on management to provide proper information, and the latter have incentives not to provide this information.

Options for reform

The challenges facing health care systems in the industrialized countries were discussed in the first section of this chapter. Whether they have private insurance, public insurance or government programmes, all countries must find ways to improve the quality and administrative efficiency of their systems, control costs and maintain equity. Reform strategies fall into three groups and it is through these categories that policy options will be discussed:

- Approaches to contain costs.
- Approaches to increase efficiency.
- Approaches to increase equity.

Approaches to contain costs

How can health costs be better controlled? Costs can be controlled through the use of budgets or by trying to keep down health care providers' payments. A national health care budget can set limits on total expenditure. Alternatively, budgets can be set for different sectors of the system. For example, heart surgery costs might not be allowed to rise above a specified amount per annum. Budgets can also be set for specific institutions; this is the historical method used in the UK. On the question of providers, their fees and payments could be set or capped. This could be done by a cost-based or a fee-for-service approach. Hospitals could be paid prospectively: that is, after they have provided what they said they would provide. Another method is selective contracting. Here insurers or other financial institutions would be free to select and agree formal contracts with health providers who can offer the best quality at competitive prices. This is a reform which is gathering favour in the Netherlands. A further option is capitation. This is where providers receive a fixed sum of money for each person in their service area. Capitation is the principal method used in the UK to pay general practitioners. The methods used will be evaluated in the case studies.

Approaches to increase efficiency

Increasing efficiency through the adoption of market concepts is an approach which is attracting the attention of many governments. This approach has a number of aspects. It could include introducing some form of competition, through an internal market, setting incentives for efficiency, or privatization. Competition in health care is about creating choice: choice between providers, and choice for patients. There are two types of competition. There are the exchanges which exist between two health institutions, a health funder (insurer) and a health provider. If there is little choice, no prices and little difference in the quality of product offered, this is called guild competition. Market competition is something different. It involves health insurers selecting from a range of providers on the basis of differences in prices and service quality. Most public provision systems have guild choice. A move from this to a market choice might represent a potential improvement in efficiency. In order to achieve this, it might be necessary to separate activities out: for example, dividing the purchasing activity from the providing activity and then getting the two organizations to exchange on the basis of prices or quality of service. This is a first step towards creating an internal market.

Incentives have a role to play in market-based approaches to health care reforms. Incentives motivate people. Typically, there are rewards and penalties involved. Examples include performance-related pay and GP practices being allowed to earn a surplus from their budgets. If they manage their budgets correctly, the reward might be a surplus, which they can then use to develop the practice. When incentives are in place, GPs can in theory encourage cost-effective behaviour and try to get the best services for their limited budget. In the UK, there are GP fundholding practices which have responsibility for their funds and patients, and which can bargain with other providers for the best arrangements. Also, the UK government has given trust hospitals (see below) greater freedom to manage their production. This means that there are incentives to be cost efficient.

Privatization is now a common practice in the sense that parts of health care systems are being transferred to not-for-profit or for-profit organizations. Hospitals can be made self-governing, as in the case of the UK. They receive funding from contracts with purchasers, GPs and private companies. The idea is that they will purchase high-quality, low-cost health care from providers. It means that the organizations can have a greater degree of freedom from central funding and manage their own production.

Approaches to increase equity

Efforts to increase equity are a real concern for countries with private health insurance systems which rely on people taking out health insurance. In America, a growing proportion of the population is totally uninsured against the possibility of illness or accidents. Governments can intervene in the private insurance market by directly funding health care for specific groups, like the mentally ill. Alternatively, they can make health insurance compulsory. Here there would be universal access to health insurance as well as health care. This type of intervention is not as easy as it sounds. Governments have to identify the uninsured and fund the insurance. The latter could be undertaken through a general fund or through specific taxes.

Institutional arrangements

The European Commission is at present less involved in health care than in areas like energy and transport. However, it has published a report on social protection in 1995, covering topics such as pensions, social insurance and health care provision. The Maastricht Treaty also commits the EU to a high level of social protection.

Q1 What factors have put pressure on governments to rethink their role in the financing and provision of health care systems?

Q2 List the reasons why governments intervene in the provision and delivery of health care.

Q3 The introduction of an internal market in health care operates by introducing incentives for competition to take place between the purchasers and the providers of health care. Explain the role of each of the following in an internal market: separation of purchaser from provider; the necessity of incentives to supply information; the use of contracts; the existence of surpluses; and greater choice in provision.

Q4 List the different types of interpretation which can be used to define equity objectives in health care. Increasing equity in the provision of health care is different from increasing equity in the financing of health care services. Explain the differences.

The following case studies have been chosen to illustrate market-based approaches used in the provision of health care. The two approaches demonstrate the strengths and weaknesses of the use of the market and the changing role of government.

Case study The Netherlands: The Dekker plans

Objectives

The principal aims of the reforms are to promote workable competition among health insurers, to contain costs and to preserve universal access.

Objectives for the EU

None relevant to this topic.

New approaches

The Dutch have sought to reform their national health insurance system on a number of occasions, but this case study will concentrate on the most recent attempt, the proposals from the Dekker Committee which reported in 1987. The proposals are studied from the following aspects:

- Approaches to increase efficiency.
- Approaches to contain costs.
- Approaches to increase equity.

The background

In the Dutch health care system, the financing and delivery of health care are separate from each other. The financing of health care is done through the sickness funds and private insurers. The former organizations provide insurance for individuals and families whose income falls below a certain level. The private insurers offer health insurance on a voluntary basis. Figure 4.1(a) shows the position before the proposals. A percentage of gross income is taken from individuals and placed in a General Fund. Governments also contribute about 12 per cent of their revenues in the form of subsidies. The Sickness Funds then contract with providers. Providers are independent GPs and independent hospitals. No price is negotiated between the two. The providers then treat the patients, who do not pay for the services directly. The other half of the operation is the private insurers, where one-third of the population have private insurance. They do not contract with providers. There was also a national insurance programme to cover uninsurable medical expenses such as nursing home care and long-term care.

Approaches to increase efficiency

The Dekker proposals recognized that the position of the health insurers was very stagnant: given the large amount of private involvement, there was little competition. Specifically, there were no incentives for either the Sickness Funds or the private health insurers to find providers which provided the health care services efficiently. The Sickness Funds were fully reimbursed for medical expenses, so they did not mind how the services were delivered to their members. This is a form of guild competition.

The proposals were aimed at increasing competition among health insurers. This was executed through three methods: changing the way payments were made; making all the different types of health insurer compete in the same market; and selective contracting. In the first case, health insurance companies were to make prospective payments (as opposed to full retrospective reimbursements) to providers. This meant that the bills would be paid only after the treatment had taken place.

In the second method, Sickness Funds, which typically insured for the low-income groups, and private insurance companies, were to be allowed to offer insurance to anyone in any location. This effectively meant that both faced more competition because they were addressing the same markets.

The third method, selective contracting, meant that the health insurers would be encouraged (through various regulations) to make contracts with providers on the basis of the price and quality of service they could offer. At the same time, consumers would be free to choose between different insurers on the basis of the cost of the health insurance package offered. Clearly, there would be incentives for

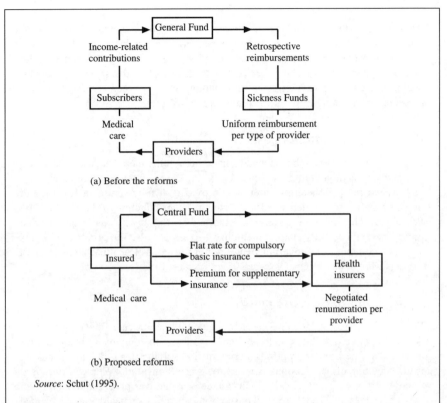

(a) Before the reforms

(b) Proposed reforms

Source: Schut (1995).

Figure 4.1 The Dutch health care financing system

insurers to shop around and get the best deals, and they would be rewarded by attracting more consumers.

These methods appear to make sense in theory, but the problem was that with increased competition, there might be a tendency for quality of service to decline, or for high-risk and therefore costly patients to be refused coverage. The government had to operate a system of managed competition. The principal proposal was that the Central Fund (see Figure 4.1(b)) would pay about 75 per cent of the insurers' costs, which would be risk adjusted. This means that payment would be on the basis of the age, gender and health status of the patients treated. If an insurance company did decide to cover a high-risk patient, these costs would be reflected in the payments from the fund. The remaining 25 per cent would be a flat premium. This means that they had to charge a flat rate for identical policies, but that the rate could vary among insurers, depending on their ability to contain costs. This aspect effectively formed the price aspect of the health insurance package.

The idea was that consumers would be free to choose from the different insurers for an insurance policy which best suited them. If insurers received bad feedback from patients, there would be incentives for them to renegotiate better terms. Insurers were to act as intermediaries between providers and patients. The problem with this was that it relied on consumers identifying a poor-value-for-money health insurance package and making the decision to change to another insurer. However, health consumers have imperfect information, and also there are costs to the consumer in changing from one health insurer to another.

Approaches to contain costs

Cost containment was to be achieved partly through the methods described above and partly though government legislation to break the cartel arrangements which had existed between health insurers and providers. The government had tried to break up these arrangements in 1982 through the introduction of the Health Care Prices Act. This gave the government the power to intervene and monitor what providers could actually charge, including the fees of GPs. The problem with this was that, although the government was acting to control health charges, health insurers were not exerting any pressure on providers to lower their costs.

Approaches to increase equity

Previously the Netherlands had a very segmented health care financing system. About 30 per cent of the population were not subject to compulsory insurance for acute risks. The Dekker proposals were aimed at solving this problem by making insurance compulsory. A compulsory national health insurance plan was proposed to cover all basic benefits. A basic insurance package was proposed, covering 85 per cent (later increased to 95 per cent) of total spending on health care and social services. A supplementary package was to be made available on a voluntary basis.

The Committee also proposed that there should be open enrolment. This meant that insurers were to offer their services to anyone. Exclusions were to be dissolved, so, for example, where legal requirements excluded patients or care levels, these were to be outlawed. Equity was to be increased by everyone paying into the Central Fund, but the large part of this contribution was to be income related. One problem with this system was the difficulty of deciding what constituted a basic coverage.

Old arrangements

There was a lack of incentives for efficiency. Although there were private providers and insurers, there was little effective competition between them. There was choice, but it was of the guild type.

New arrangements

The Dekker proposals aimed for universal coverage through a single, comprehensive system, but with competition among health insurers. Under the new arrangements, the Sickness Funds are forced to offer coverage for anyone in any region, and can compete both on their services and on their premium. Private insurers, on the other hand, are allowed to offer health insurance to anyone, and this effectively means that the two types of insurer are competing in one market.

Change of relationships

As a result of the Dekker reforms, new relationships have emerged between the insurer and the insured. The insured person pays the insurer directly; if the insured does not find the package satisfactory, they may choose another insurer. The insurer and the provider now voluntarily enter into contracts, negotiating on volume, price and quality of health care. Selective contracting by the insurer means, in theory, that only qualitatively good providers will be offered a contract. The Sickness Funds will no longer be able to draw up a contract with a physician in the community who expresses a wish to do so; now the insurers will be acting as intermediaries.

The government's role will change. Previously it was involved in regulating price and volumes; now it will be monitoring quality levels, and regulating for anti-competitive practices.

Q5 *Describe the reforms which have taken place in each of the three areas: cost containment, increasing efficiency and equity.*

Q6 *If you were a patient trying to choose among different health insurers, what type of problem might you encounter in deciding who was the best insurer for you?*

Case study The UK: The NHS reforms

Objectives

The aim of the UK government has been to increase efficiency through competition in the provision of health care.

Objectives for the EU

None relevant to this topic.

New approaches

These objectives were to be met through a number of key measures which were introduced in 1991. These involved the following:

• Approaches to contain costs.
• Approaches to increase efficiency.

The background

The National Health Service (NHS) is a publicly funded body which provides public health care. It accounts for approximately 94 per cent of the total expenditure on health in the UK. There is, in addition, a small private health sector. General taxation accounted for some 83.4 per cent of the financing of the NHS budget in 1994/95, and a further 13.4 per cent of the budget was financed from NHS contributions. Public provision has been based on an administrative structure. The previous arrangements were that District Health Authorities (DHAs) received an annual budget from the Regional Health Authorities. They then had to provide a range of medical services for the district population. The rationale for the reforms, introduced in 1991, was a belief that the health providers, such as hospitals, had little incentive to be efficient. They did not have to compete for either funds or consumers, and they were part of the DHAs' responsibility. Consumers had little choice of service provider, and because there was no price system, there was little systematic information about the quality of service being provided. There were many proposals which sought to address these problems, but we will concentrate here on the changes in provision.

Approaches to contain costs

The UK government has embarked on a number of ways of exercising control over the costs of health care provision. For example, it has been proposed that doctors should receive indicative prescription drug budgets and if their costs exceed these specific budgets, then their drug-prescribing patterns should be reviewed. On the hospital side, trust hospitals have been created as non-profit-making, self-managed organizations. They are accountable to the NHS Management Executive, free from health authority control, and can establish their own management systems, raise capital and employ staff on an independent basis. These new arrangements are intended to provide for greater freedom in production and to be more cost efficient, as any surpluses earned can be used to improve future services. However, there are two problems. The first is that there is said to be overcapacity in the current system, which makes earning a surplus more difficult. Second, many hospital accounting systems will be required to provide detailed information on different services, as this will allow treatments to be priced separately, and this information will take skill and time to develop. Also, there are strong incentives for hospitals to cut costs by reducing service quality levels. Measuring quality is of little financial value to hospitals, so there must be incentives from outside to provide this information. Few hospitals are likely to voluntarily provide commercially sensitive information on costs.

Approaches to increase efficiency

One of the most interesting aspects of the 1991 reforms is that the responsibility for purchasing health care was separated from the responsibility for providing health care. Thus two separate bodies were formed: the purchasers and the providers. The purchasers are the DHAs and the general practitioners (GPs). They must decide on the health needs of their local population and purchase the appropriate health care. They receive a budget from government and can buy the health care from any provider they wish. Providers, on the other hand, are the suppliers of health care and they include the hospitals, categorized as state, trust and private. Before the reforms, the providers were under the authority of the DHAs. The idea is that purchasers will have incentives to seek out the most efficient providers, whether in terms of cost or quality of service. Information will be required only if purchasers ask for it. So far, apart from in London, there has been little change in patient referral patterns from GPs to hospitals.

The internal market in the NHS is based on the idea that providers will compete for contracts with purchasers. In theory, if a patient does not like the quality of medical service given at a hospital, the GP may not necessarily renew the contract or do so only on different terms. GPs come in two forms: those who have opted to become GP fundholders, and who therefore have a budget and a purchasing role, and those who do not have a purchasing role.

The intention is that the benefits of the competitive process will outweigh the costs. One of the expected benefits is greater awareness of the costs of provision. This will occur only if effective competition among providers takes place. However, this may be blurred by a number of considerations. The first is that it depends on a supply of accurate information. One set of purchasers, the DHAs, are in a weak position to accumulate this type of information. They do not see their patients directly and so they would not hear of the effectiveness of service without some form of questionnaire. GP fundholders, on the other hand, have better relative access to information because they may see their patients again.

The Audit Commission found that £65 million in savings had been made by fundholders in 1994. Against this, it found that fundholding practices had incurred large management costs, and the savings figure did not take into account the late invoicing by health providers. Also, the scope for these savings to increase steadily is dependent on the system having a higher take-up of GP fundholders and self-governing hospitals. So far the number of trust hospitals has grown from 57 in 1991 to 449 in 1995, but this growth slowed down between 1993 and 1995. The number of GP fundholder practices is 2000, with 8889 doctors, out of a total number of 26 387 doctors in 1994. The scope for the number of GP fundholding practices to increase is limited partly by the number of patients required for this status (over 9000) and partly by the fact that in some areas there are few providers to choose from. Finally, there have been concerns over the potential opportunities for cream skimming with GP fundholders. This refers to where high-risk patients are not taken on by a practice.

Old arrangements

The NHS had a monopoly in provision. It both financed and provided the health care services.

New arrangements

Health authorities are now contracting with independent trusts, their own managed hospitals and private hospitals. In parallel, GPs are being given budgets so that they can purchase hospital care, from providers, on behalf of their patients.

Change of relationships

Districts and GPs have to develop information systems which measure quality and build up negotiating structures with providers. The nature of relationships will tend to focus on the information needs of purchasers. Purchasers and providers will have to work closely with clinicians to implement change and use contracts as levers to bring it about.

Q7 Describe the UK efficiency reforms in terms of how they will, in theory, contain health care costs, increase choice, increase access to information and increase the flexibility of the system. In what ways do you think quality of service and equity might be influenced by these reforms?

Q8 Although both the UK and the Dutch governments are aiming for a form of managed competition, what are the differences between the two types of health care reform?

Discussion

This section looks at two things. It evaluates each approach in relation to how it might improve efficiency and equity, and it contrasts the different approaches undertaken. Beginning with the UK, internal markets are supposed to enhance consumer choice, improve accountability and increase cost efficiency. Internal markets will increase efficiency only if a number of conditions are met. There must be lots of competition on both the provider and the purchaser side. There must be access to information, otherwise how do purchasers and patients decide what an efficient service is? Third, providers must be really trying to increase the quality of their services because they see that there is some reward in it for them. Fourth, there must be few loopholes where purchasers can pick and choose low-risk patients.

How do the reforms stand up in terms of efficiency? We can only theorize at present because reforms take time to develop. On the positive side, health care savings have been made and the take-up of fundholding and hospital trust status was rapid in the early 1990s. There is scope therefore for bad hospitals and unsatisfactory GPs to raise their standards and be rewarded for doing this. The internal market provides a competitive environment where GPs can discover the facts and use them to make improvements. These facts would never have become known without the competitive process, or at least would not have been used.

On the negative side, trust hospitals are still subject to considerable central regulation, and the negotiation of preferential contracts for their patients by GP fundholder practices has led to cries that patients are not being treated in the same way. In terms of the system as a whole, the UK health care market is not obviously competitive. In some cases there are a handful of purchasers and a single provider. The purchasers are dependent on the providers for information. If they do not request the information, it is not provided. There are likely to be substantial information gaps. It is expensive to collect information from providers on medical services, and this is compounded when there are no direct financial incentives for doing so.

This point could be extended to an argument about incentives for providers. There are incentives for providers to attempt to avoid the high-risk patients. This is referred to as cream skimming and occurs when providers are able to differentiate between people and to reject high-risk ones. GPs are presently well positioned to determine the health status of individuals and therefore could save part of their budget by not accepting high-risk patients. If a two-tier system evolved on the basis that healthier people received better service, this would have serious equity ramifications.

In the Dutch reforms, the government introduced incentives for competition between health providers and health insurers, although the government plays a role in setting regulations on price in order to contain costs. Ironically, this was an intervention which did not reinforce the role of the market, but rather that of the government. It was much opposed, and it seems unlikely that efforts to contain medical fees will be sustainable. The ideal solution would be to have some form of competition between providers and insurers which results in a reduction of fees. Either the government could negotiate fees directly with providers, or it could force insurers to accept prospective payments (it was unsuccessful here initially). Attempts to increase efficiency in these circumstances have been hampered by the unwillingness of insurers to cooperate.

The second reform, which aimed to increase competition among insurers, with the government managing this competition, has had mixed success. On the one hand, the collective bargaining situation between insurer and provider has been weakened through government intervention. For example, some price cartels for medical devices have been broken, thus reducing prices. The government also introduced hospital expenditure caps and fee controls. On the other hand, there is some doubt about the sustainability of these measures, as it seems that government involvement is increasing rather than decreasing and this was not the intended outcome. On the issue of equity, the Dutch health care reforms appear to have been successful. In order to preserve universal access, a redistributive financing mechanism was devised. A basic package was introduced and made compulsory for everyone.

Finally, we have witnessed two examples of market-orientated reforms. Both arose from objectives of increasing efficiency in the delivery of health care where there were believed to be serious inefficiencies. Some comparative observations can be made. Both systems are adopting a managed competition approach. The Dutch reforms aim to introduce competition among insurers and through selective contracting, while the UK is only introducing selective contracting and separating provision and purchasing. Similar competitive elements have been introduced, including increasing cost consciousness and breaking anti-competitive practices. There appear to be potential efficiency gains with this type of arrangement, but they must be weighed up against the costs. Both systems have experienced problems in implementing the reforms and clearly time and further refinements are required. High costs are involved in collecting information on the part of the purchasers, the insurance companies or administrators, and consumers.

Further reading

Introductory level

Griffiths, A. and Wall, S. (eds) (1995) *Applied Economics: An Introductory Course*, Harlow: Longman, ch. 12.
Le Grand, J., Propper, C. and Robinson, R. (1993) *The Economics of Social Problems*, 3rd edn, Basingstoke: Macmillan, ch. 2.
Roper, B. and Snowdon, B. (1987) *Markets, Intervention and Planning*, Harlow: Longman, ch. 8.

Intermediate level

Barr, N. (1993) *The Economics of the Welfare State*, 2nd edn, London: Weidenfeld and Nicolson, ch. 12.
Griffiths, A and Wall, S. (1996) *Intermediate Microeconomics: Theory and Applications*, Harlow: Longman, ch. 12.

Other sources

Anand, P. (1995) 'Objectives, information and incentives in the NHS internal market', *Health Services Management Research*, vol. 8, no. 1.
Besley, T. and Gouveia, M. (1994) 'Alternative systems of health care provision', *Economic Journal*, October.
Blomqvist, A. and Brown, D.M. (eds) (1994) *Limits to Care: Reforming Canada's Health System in an Age of Restraint*, Toronto: C.D. Howe Institute.
Brazier, J.E. and Normand, C. (1991) 'An economic review of the NHS White Paper', *Journal of Political Economy*, vol. 38, no. 1.
Caines, R. (1995) 'UK healthcare, 1995 market review', London: Keynote.
Chalkley, M. (1996) 'The NHS – does efficient mean better?', *Economic Review*, February.
'Britain's sickly health reforms', *The Economist*, February, 1994.
Green, D. (1992) 'The NHS reforms: from ration-book collectivism to market socialism', *Economic Affairs*, April.
'Working for patients: the Health Service – caring for the 1990s', HMSO, Cmnd. 555, 1989.

Kirkman-Liff, B. (1994) 'Health care reform in the Netherlands, Germany and the United Kingdom', in Blomqvist and Brown (1994).

Le Grand, J. (1992) 'Quasi markets in welfare', *Economic Review*, November.

Locock, L. (1995) 'Pull the other one', *Health Service Journal*, February.

MacFarlan, M. and Oxley, H. (1995) 'Reforming health care', *OECD Observer*, no. 192, February/March.

McGuire A., Fenn, P. and Mayhew, K. (1994) *Providing Health Care: The Economics of Alternative Systems of Finance and Delivery*, Oxford: Oxford University Press.

Minford, P. (1989) 'A policy for the National Health Service, part II', *Economic Affairs*, December/January.

'The reform of health care: a comparative analysis of seven OECD countries', OECD, 1992.

'OECD health data', OECD, 1993.

'OECD health systems – facts and trends, 1960–1991', OECD, 1993.

Propper, C. (1993) 'Incentives in the new UK health care market', *Economic Review*, February.

Raftery, J., Gibson, G., Hamilton, I. and Perkin, I. (1994) 'Perspectives on purchasing band-aid', *Health Service Journal*, February.

Schut, F. (1995) 'Healthcare reform in the Netherlands: balancing corporatism, étatism, and market mechanisms', *Journal of Health, Policy and Law*, vol. 20, no. 3.

Chapter 5

Social housing

Key words used: finance, provider, purchaser, internal market, incentives, deregulation of housing finance

We have all seen the homeless on the streets and in the parks of major cities throughout Europe; they are a very visual reminder that economic prosperity has missed a proportion of society. Housing is an important aspect of life, since having a home can bring security and a feeling of well-being, while life without a roof over your head is a miserable existence. Governments have long been associated with housing markets, and their policies have had mixed successes. The economic developments of the 1980s changed the way social housing is organized in many countries; it became more decentralized and market orientated. As a consequence of these and other factors, the changes in the system have affected the position of the poor, and housing affordability has become a real and worrying issue. Economics has much to offer this subject. It can provide a rationale for why there should be government intervention and provide a framework of analysis to evaluate different approaches. Economics can contribute to discussions on reforms and assess the possible new role for governments and for markets.

Background to the problem

This chapter is about social housing – housing which is provided or funded by the public sector. Housing markets are made up of different housing tenures or sectors. Broadly, there are owner-occupied private rented, social (or non-profit) rented, cooperative and other tenures. Table 5.1 shows how these sectors vary in size between countries.

The social rented sector is by no means insignificant, and varies in size from 7 to 44 per cent of the total housing tenure. In England, unlike the other countries, the social rented sector was predominantly made up of council housing, but changes in policy towards this sector, including the right to buy and reductions in expenditure, have brought about a fall in its size. This has occurred despite a growth in the housing association sector. The owner-occupied sector has grown for all countries, although it is less marked in Germany, the Netherlands and Sweden. In some of

Table 5.1 Housing tenures at the end of the 1980s (%)

	Owner-occupied	Private rented	Non-profit rented	Cooperative sector	Other or unknown
Netherlands	44	12	44	–	0
Germany	42	42	16	–	–
France	54	20	17	–	9
Belgium[a]	59	31	7	–	3
England	68	8	24	–	–
Denmark	55	18	17	4	6
Sweden	43	21	21	15	–

[a]1981.
Source: Boelhouwer and van der Heijden (1992).

these countries, governments have followed policies to promote home ownership; in England generally this has led to the sector significantly increasing above the size of the others. The private rented sector is in decline in most countries, but this is more marked in some countries than others: England has a significantly smaller sector than the other countries.

Housing markets and government policies have both been subject to changes. It is not possible to summarize all these changes in the space available, but an attempt will be made to divide the sources of change into two broad groups: those which have occurred within the housing market (the endogenous changes) and those which have been exogenous to or outside the market. Within the social housing market three aspects will be addressed: changes in government policy, the need to contain costs and the affordability problem.

Government policy has undoubtedly been influenced by the general deregulation drive in the public sector, and this has expressed itself in housing policies which have placed greater reliance on market forces. Specifically, governments have shifted from production to consumer subsidies, raised rents and, in the case of the UK, reduced the role for local authorities in the provision of social housing. As a result of an erosion of tenants' rights in some countries, and reductions in rent controls and in the level of government assistance in other countries, there has been an increase in housing costs. Other factors have played a role too: many governments faced problems with rising maintenance costs associated with social housing and there were various management difficulties with looking after large estates. For a variety of reasons, the provision of social housing and access to it had been reduced, culminating in problems of affordability, placing upward demand pressure on the private rented sector and increasing homelessness. The promotion of owner-occupied housing, and in some countries the reduction in public expenditure, have accelerated and accentuated these problems in the social housing sector.

Government policies cannot be seen in isolation of their objectives, and exogenous factors like demographic and socioeconomic changes and economic development also affect the functioning of housing markets. Demographic factors, such as changes in population size and composition, have altered housing demands, but as yet it is difficult to say exactly how this affects housing markets. Some countries have experienced population growth, from unification in the case of Germany and from migration generally. Socioeconomic changes, like changes in family size and composition, have occurred because of increases in divorce rates and the number of single-parent families, and this will continue to change the demand for housing both in terms of its type and in terms of the amount of rent people can afford. It is likely that changes in housing demand are also caused by the growing proportion of elderly people, who have specific housing needs. Finally, economic development, inflation and unemployment all affect the housing market and housing conditions, which in turn affect the position of the less well-off.

In summary, governments face a number of problems in the social housing market. There has been an increase in the costs of housing and there have been changes in the demand for housing. Governments have responded to these problems by altering the way in which social housing has been provided and financed, in the hope that consumers' demands would be better met through a more market-orientated approach, and many have shifted public expenditure from production to personal housing allowances. These policies, as we shall see, have impacted on the housing market and created subsequent constraints and opportunities.

Current system of allocation

This section discusses the special properties of housing and begins by asking why market provision alone might be unfeasible or undesirable.

The market

Using the assumptions of the perfect competition model discussed in Chapter 1 and the failures of markets described in Chapter 2, we are in a position to discuss the problems a pure market would have in allocating resources in housing. This can be viewed from the following perspectives:

- The presence of externalities.
- The presence of market imperfections.
- The presence of inequalities.

The presence of externalities

Housing cannot be said to be a private good because there are spill-over effects to third parties. Externalities can be said to arise from the effect of one property on the surrounding environment. Likewise, the surrounding neighbourhood can have an impact on the value of a property. These may be positive or negative effects: for example, a well-cared-for house in a street may affect the value of other properties and give rise to a positive externality. If all the residents decide not to make improvements to their homes because it is not a worthwhile investment to them, this may give rise to a negative externality, and without intervention, a neighbourhood may turn into a slum.

Housing externalities are also associated with housing conditions and their impact on a person's life, which then impacts on other people's lives. For example, health, crime, fire safety and educational achievement can all affect the quality of life. Good housing conditions can have widespread effects: they can eliminate the spread of disease to others, improve educational achievement and productivity. A private house-builder may not take into consideration the wider impact of better housing conditions. It is likely that, in the presence of externalities, a free market will lead to an inefficient allocation of resources.

The presence of market imperfections

Housing markets are subject to imperfections from a number of sources. These are perhaps less serious than in health care and arise from imperfect knowledge and imperfections in the capital market. Imperfect information arises in two ways. First, consumers' information on every aspect of house purchase or rental is limited. They enter the housing market relatively infrequently and are dependent on others for information. Agents such as building societies, banks, surveyors, estate and letting agents improve the channels of information, but as they are involved in price setting, they will tend to affect decisions on both behaviour and prices. Second, moving to a new home involves relatively high transaction costs. For example, searching out available properties will take time and effort, and the likely impact will be to discourage consumers from changing accommodation frequently. There is likely, therefore, to be slow adjustment on the demand side.

On the supply side, houses are long-term assets and there is only a small proportion of the total housing stock available at any one time. Given that it takes a relatively long time to build a house, if demand increases, there can only be a slow response from the supply side. House-building activity is very speculative and tends to rise and fall with the economic cycle. On the whole, house-building activity is relatively slow to respond to market changes and upward pressure on demand is therefore more likely to impact on house prices than on the supply of housing. On the rented side, private landlords may respond by increasing supply, but even if demand is met, there is the potential for housing needs not to be met, since people may be supplied with relatively expensive or unsuitable accommodation.

Capital market imperfections arise from the supply of loan finance being restricted to particular circumstances: for example, to those with regular and above average incomes and with collateral. In the rented sector, because houses are both a consumption and an investment good, there may be problems arising from the contract between a landlord and a tenant. This factor is likely to impair the workings of a market in housing. A related problem is that the balance of power is likely to lie with landlords. This is because houses after a while tend to become homes. People become comfortable and begin to build up their lives in the locality. These aspects increase the value to the individual of living in the property, but do not increase the value of the property; nor can this value be transferred. The monopoly power of the landlord means that rents can be raised to the point where they equal or exceed the marginal value to the tenant. It is possible that households may end up paying rents at above the market rate because of this type of market power.

The presence of inequalities

The presence of inequalities gives rise to a theoretical argument for intervention. There are two issues: capital market failures and access to housing. With the first issue, certain socioeconomic groups may be charged a higher rate of interest, reflecting higher perceived risks. Those on low or irregular income may not even be offered a loan in the first instance. With the second issue, access to housing can be viewed from the horizontal equity perspective discussed in Chapter 2. In the housing market, horizontal equity will exist if people can make rational decisions and have equal power to those supplying property. Some people claim that housing is a merit good; that everyone should consume housing of at least a given standard. If society has decided on a minimum standard, or a basic need, it is not clear that a market mechanism will achieve this. If people cannot afford basic housing, then this becomes an equity argument for intervention. There is a case for government intervention if we accept the merit good argument.

In summary, what we have described is largely a set of imperfections relating to housing markets. The problems are not as severe as in health, and housing is probably closer to a private good than a public good. Government intervention has been justified largely on the externality case, rather than on the imperfection arguments. Nevertheless, leaving the provision of housing solely to the market is likely to lead to an inefficient and inequitable allocation of resources.

Government objectives

If governments intervene in housing markets, there are a number of different types of objectives that they might pursue:

- Economic efficiency objectives.
- Administrative efficiency objectives.
- Equity objectives.

Economic efficiency objectives

An example of an economic efficiency objective in the housing market is one which is concerned with the efficient size and quality of the housing stock. Clearly, if a government decided to spend all its resources on houses, we would live in splendour, and if only a tiny proportion was devoted to housing, there would be many people living rough or in cramped conditions. An efficient allocation of resources lies somewhere in the middle. In economics, we say that the value of the marginal unit of consumption equals the marginal social costs of resources used. Many governments built large amounts of social housing after the war, but this was largely driven by the objective of providing a minimum standard of housing, rather than producing an efficient amount of housing. More recently, governments have become concerned with efficiency objectives and this has been expressed through increases in rent levels and the shift from production to consumption subsidies.

Administrative efficiency objectives

Governments are involved in housing markets, but some policies incur more administrative costs than others. For example, many governments have shifted from using production subsidies to consumption subsidies. Both policies have economic strengths and weaknesses. One problem which has emerged is that, in order to qualify for housing benefit, households may have to be on very low income. For a group of households it is possible that, as income levels rise, housing benefit falls and they face a poverty trap. This loophole could be overcome with further modification and refinement. However, this might require more information on individual cases and might be very expensive. The costs of administering particular policies must therefore be added to the economic outcomes.

Equity objectives

Governments can develop policies to overcome the horizontal equity problems: for example, ensuring that consumers are in a position to make rational decisions, and that they have equal power to enforce those decisions. Also, public intervention can take place to ensure that the treatment of different types of housing tenure is fair. This might mean, for example, that there is no financial difference for a consumer when deciding between renting and buying property. Establishing objectives to meet vertical equity relates to deciding on the best way to redistribute income.

Government intervention

Governments intervene in housing markets through a number of approaches or methods, including the following:

- Provision.
- Taxes and subsidies.
- Regulation.

Provision

Governments could intervene either wholly with direct public provision or by having a mixed public/private provision arrangement. Social housing has been largely publicly provided. Governments have directly planned for and designed social housing, although they typically contract out the construction to private companies. In the UK, council or local authority housing has been publicly provided to overcome the problems of housing supply, and the subsidized rents have addressed the equity problem. Recently, governments have embarked on joint ventures with the private sector to build homes for sale rather than for public renting. This form of intervention has had its strengths and weaknesses. There is little doubt that the provision of social housing played an important role in meeting housing shortages after the war in most western European countries. On the other hand, many governments subsequently faced problems emanating from poor design and layout, which led in some cases to high repair and maintenance costs.

Taxes and subsidies

These can be used in two broad ways. First, taxes are a way of funding the public provision of social housing. This meets the merit good and the externality arguments. Second, taxes and subsidies can be used to alter the costs of housing. Price subsidies can be used to help enhance the appearance of houses and prevent the development of slums. This overcomes the externality argument. Subsidies can also be used to lower rents. Housing benefit subsidizes housing costs for the less well-off. These forms of intervention can help overcome the equity concerns with housing. Consumption subsidies are where consumers of housing are directly given a supplement to cover their rent. They are free to choose which type of accommodation they wish and to use the subsidy as they like. On the whole, there are fewer conditions attached to a consumption subsidy. Consumption subsidies are preferable to production subsidies as they give the consumer some power on the demand side. Production or supply subsidies are less popular than consumption subsidies now with many governments. There are, however, problems with this form of intervention. If the aim of subsidized rents is to meet the merit good argument, there are incentives for overconsumption. People who could afford higher rents may understate their income and remain in property that was not intended for them. If this situation applies to a significant proportion of social housing tenants, then we can say that this has increased the tax burden without assisting those who are in more need of help. If the purpose of the subsidy is to assist those on low income, it is preferable to use housing benefits. However, increasing individuals' purchasing power does not necessarily lead to increased housing consumption; rather, the price of housing may rise.

A final role for subsidies is to give people an incentive to purchase their own homes. In the UK, council tenants were given the right to buy at substantial discounts, ranging from 30 to 70 per cent. This policy was criticized on the grounds that it was the more well-off tenants who bought the better-quality property, leaving less social housing and poorer quality property to those in need. It may be argued that this has subsequently led to ghettos and increased inequality.

Regulation

This is used to overcome the externalities problem of housing conditions. Regulation ensures that minimum standards are met with regard to the quality of housing, safety aspects and planning of land use. Regulation can also be used to ensure that landlords do not exploit their monopoly power over tenants. In the UK, rent control legislation regulates the level of rent.

Government intervention varies widely in practice throughout Europe. On the whole, most countries have a market system of allocation with varying degrees of government support. In the UK, social housing financial support is through consumers and the housing allowance. There are land use planning controls, no one has the right to build and there are no taxes on gains from land development. In France there are income supplements to consumers and reduced-interest loans for both owner-occupiers and owners of housing to rent. The UK has a more indirect form of intervention than France, which has a more defined system of land use regulation and financial control over house prices. Other countries like Sweden have a considerable degree of control over dwelling types, production levels, and land and house prices.

Options for reform

The first section described the pressures for change on governments and housing markets. Having described the objectives and the current system of allocation, the next step is to ask what options are open to governments. These can be discussed in relation to the following approaches:

* Approaches to increase efficiency in social housing finance.
* Approaches to increase efficiency in social housing provision.

Approaches to increase efficiency in social housing finance

In the first section we saw that governments face a number of challenges. On the one hand, they wish to reduce the level of public expenditure or to increase the efficiency with which public funds are used to support the provision of social housing; on the other hand, they must meet changes in the level and composition of demand. Many governments have relied on meeting these challenges by using

85

market forces. There are a number of options: privatization, the creation of an internal market and the encouragement of private sector funds. Privatization, or the policy of allowing social housing tenants to buy their own homes, in theory saves the government money by getting people to pay their own housing costs. The other benefit of this policy is that it gives people a sense of well-being, since they can have both a home and an investment. The problem with this policy, mentioned earlier, is that it can lead to social polarization between owners and renters.

The creation of an internal market involves the creation of providers who supply the housing, purchasers who buy on behalf of the consumer, and a financier, usually the government. The function of an internal market is to create competition for public funds on the supply side, while on the demand side, the consumer's purchasing power has to be expressed through some mechanism. The overall aim is to increase choice to the consumer, promote greater efficiency in supply and inject incentives for cost effectiveness and greater accountability in the use of public funds.

For these aims to be met, a number of conditions need to be in place. For example, on the demand side, consumers would need to have vouchers, which in the case of housing would take the form of housing benefits. This means that if consumers are dissatisfied with their housing, they can be transferred. Consumers would also need to be able to express their preferences within the housing arrangements. So having formal channels through which to express their dissatisfaction, such as tenants' rights, is an important aspect of the function of demand. On the supply side, there must be many providers and purchasers: for example, there would be little impact on prices and quality if there were only a few purchasers. If only one or two purchasers existed, they would have a large monitoring role in ensuring that housing provision was at the required quality and price. There must be many providers bidding for public funds, otherwise dissatisfied purchasers cannot seek out alternatives. Also there must be adequate access to information, so that the purchasers can decide whether the provisions made are meeting those specified in, for example, a contract between the purchaser and the provider. Profit or some other factor must be present to motivate suppliers, otherwise there may be few incentives for providers to supply their services or seek to minimize their costs. Finally, there must be few opportunities for providers to select some consumers and reject others. If this occurs, the provision of social housing will fail.

An internal market works by increasing competition among providers for public funds. This could be for the construction of new homes for renting or buying purposes. Contracts could be set up containing specific requirements on the quality of housing, rent levels and the amount of public funds which will be used.

The final approach to increase efficiency is to encourage private sector finance. This means that, if social housing can be built with public and supplemented with private funds, it effectively lowers the public cost of provision. The challenge of this approach is to encourage private investors to fund housing schemes, and this involves governments meeting any requirements and concerns private investors may have.

Approaches to increase efficiency in social housing provision

Many governments have been the sole providers of social housing and, as we have seen, there have been a number of problems with this form of provision. One option is to increase the number and type of providers: for example, using more independent, not-for-profit organizations. This can be done by transferring ownership and responsibility to existing providers, by ensuring that these organizations undertake new housing schemes, or by allowing any housing provider to bid for public funds. The advantages of this approach are that it tends to move social housing out of the political arena, it can lead to provision being run on a more commercial basis, and it can lead to greater diversity in terms of size, quality and flexibility of provision. The problem with this approach is that commercial and social objectives have to operate together. There needs to be regulation on the quality and level of rents and to ensure that cream skimming is not possible.

Institutional arrangements

The European Commission has not been directly involved in setting directives in this area, which remains a national responsibility. However, there is growing interest in what is happening to housing systems in the EU member states, and this is becoming manifest in a handful of international studies. Eventually housing systems will have relevance to issues surrounding European economic integration.

Q1 List those factors which have necessitated reforms in policy towards social housing. Put them into two categories: those which are a result of the market and those which are a result of factors outside the market.

Q2 Housing has been described as more a private than a public good. Discuss.

Q3 Governments can intervene in housing markets in a number of ways. Describe some market-based approaches to overcoming the following problems: monopoly provision in social housing; declining housing conditions; the need to increase social housing output with a constant level of public funding; and the need to give housing consumers greater choice.

Q4 Evaluate the likely efficiency and equity gains of the successful development of an internal market in social housing provision.

The objectives of the case studies chosen are to illustrate approaches taken to increase efficiency and equity in the provision and allocation of social housing, and to contrast the different approaches adopted.

Case study The UK: The role of housing associations

Objectives

To reduce public expenditure on social housing, while maintaining the investment programme.

Objectives for the EU

None relevant to this topic.

New approaches

A number of changes in social housing policy have been developed in recent years. These will be discussed in relation to the following:

*   Approaches to increase efficiency in the provision of social housing.
*   Approaches to increase efficiency in the financing of social housing.

The background

The change in the roles of local authorities and housing associations has resulted in an innovative and dramatic change in how social housing is provided. Previously, the UK had a situation whereby local authorities (LAs) were the dominant landlords for social housing. They financed, provided and allocated housing. LAs were responsible for meeting housing needs in their area, approving the planning and building of houses, and managing and letting houses. Housing associations (HAs), which are private, non-profit-making organizations, had a small role in provision. In the early 1980s they accounted for only 3 per cent of total housing stock, whereas in England they now account for 24 per cent. Central government gives subsidies and capital grants to LAs. It also gives subsidies and capital grants to the Housing Corporation (HC), which allocates its money to housing associations. The HC was established in 1964 to promote and coordinate the activities of HAs. This role has been strengthened in recent years.

Approaches to increase efficiency in the provision of social housing

The government has introduced many initiatives to increase efficiency, many of which have been market led in nature. This case study concentrates on developments with housing associations. Four market approaches will be discussed here: expanding the number of providers by transferring housing stock to other landlords; altering the basis of funding; raising rent levels; and introducing competition for funds among providers. The first approach was introduced in the mid-1980s. The government wished to change the role of LAs as monopoly providers, so the idea was to encourage other landlords to manage LA property.

LAs were allowed to sell off whole housing estates, but although this was a start, it was not successful. LA housing stock was eventually directed to be sold off to housing associations. The outcome of this was that the number of providers increased, and stock of houses held by HAs increased. However the National Federation of Housing Associations (NFHA) reported in 1992 that housing output was becoming more standardized and of lower quality.

Altering the basis of funding and raising rent levels were both introduced by the 1988 Housing Act. These both represent steps towards the creation of an internal market. The idea behind altering the basis of funding was to ensure that increases in the provision of new housing still took place, but not at the expense of public funds. Previously, the government had provided a 100 per cent grant, the Housing Association Grant (HAG), for new housing developments. The Act required that any HAs using HAG would have to find a proportion of their total costs from elsewhere. Grants were reduced to 75 per cent of the total costs of construction, which meant that HAs had to find about 25 per cent of the funds from the private sector. (The grant currently stands at 57 per cent.)

This approach has had a number of strengths and weaknesses. On the positive side, since 1990 the proportion of costs of building new housing association properties borne by the government has declined from 79 per cent to 58 per cent. Another 2 per cent cut in grant was announced in 1996. Spending on housing grants has declined from £12.5 billion in 1979–80 to £4.9 billion in 1994–95. These benefits must be weighed up against the costs. We would expect private finance to increase total housing stock. This it did achieve, but we can see from Table 5.2 that, despite the increase in new housing starts from HAs, this was not at a rate which counteracted the decline in LAs' new housing starts, with the net effect of a decline in the number of new social housing starts over the period 1980–91.

Approaches to increase efficiency in the financing of social housing

The second initiative of the 1988 Act was that it allowed HAs to set their own rents on all new lettings, with a general guideline for HAs to set sensible rents within the means of tenants. This enabled providers, the LAs and the HAs, to determine their own rents rather than these being determined by an independent rent officer, which had been the case for decades. The efficiency gains of this approach, in theory, were that the raising of rents in new housing developments would attract more private investment, which in turn meant that more social housing could be produced per public pound. To date a total of £10 billion of private finance has been used to build new homes.

These benefits have to be weighed up against the costs. Much of the saving to government has been offset by increases in housing benefit payments. As higher rents increase the retail price index, this feeds into other government benefits which are linked to the index. Between 1991 and 1996, housing benefit, used to pay for higher rents, more than doubled in real terms to over £10 billion. The NFHA reported in 1990 that rents had increased in real terms since 1989 and that, between the second quarter of 1988 and the first quarter of 1989, HA rents rose

Table 5.2 New housing starts, Britain and France, 1980–91
(thousands, per annum)

	France					Britain			
	PLA	PAP	PC	Free	Total	LA	HA	Private	Total
1980	60	120	100	117	397	44	15	102	162
1981	56	126	82	136	400	29	12	120	161
1982	64	127	81	72	344	38	19	145	202
1983	58	115	90	70	333	39	15	179	233
1984	55	113	92	35	295	30	13	166	209
1985	65	93	105	33	296	24	13	173	210
1986	50	86	99	51	296	22	14	187	223
1987	54	78	114	64	310	22	13	204	239
1988	54	60	108	105	327	18	15	228	261
1989	50	48	105	136	339	16	16	177	209
1990	47	38	102	123	310	9	19	141	169
1991	60	33	90	120	303	5	22	140	168

Notes: PLA = subsidized rental
PAP = subsidized owner occupation
PC = *prêts conventionées*
LA = local authorities
HA = housing associations
Source: Kleinman (1995).

by 43.6 per cent, compared with a retail price index rise of only 12.7 per cent and an increase in tenant income of 11.2 per cent. Local authority housing rents also increased, but by the lower figure of 13.5 per cent in 1990. Some new housing association properties are charging rents of £85 per week, which means that for a family with two children earning £250 a week, a substantial proportion of their income goes on housing costs.

Finally, there are social impacts of too much dependence on housing benefit: people may be discouraged from seeking work and they may try to cheat the system. Many social housing properties have been left with a high proportion of households on benefit and these people may feel socially outcast.

The final approach encouraged competition between providers for public grants. The creation of a UK internal housing market has already begun in that there is one purchaser, the Housing Corporation (HC), and many providers. Competition exists in that providers have to bid for HC grants (in addition to attracting private sector funds). These grants are allocated not to every HA, but only to those building new housing, and three-quarters of the total of 750 housing developers might apply for a grant in any one year. On what basis are funds allocated? Unlike the internal market in health care, the HC does not use contracts, it uses regulation. Regulation covers three areas: aiming to ensure that the new housing developments are managed efficiently; that service provisions are made for tenants; and that social objectives, like housing the homeless, are met. How does the purchaser ensure that these aims are met? It uses performance indicators, requests financial information and has direct inspections. If an HA does not meet these standards, non-financial sanctions are applied, such as firing committee members. Once the funds have been received there are no financial rewards or penalties.

Two recent developments have been introduced to both sharpen the competition among providers and allow for greater price competition. These are contained in the government's consultation paper, 'More Choice in the Social Sector'. The first is about the licensing of non-housing association landlords. Private companies will be allowed to compete on a fair basis with HAs for capital funds to provide new housing. The idea is that the competition for capital grants will be based on costs, including the impact on rents and housing benefit. Second the HC has had its role strengthened. It is to regulate rents and limit surpluses or profits made by social landlords.

A final note is that the shift from production to consumption subsidies has facilitated the creation of an internal market. It gives consumers vital spending power and an opportunity to exert their demand. If production subsidies had remained the main financial assistance, it would have meant that consumers could only afford those houses which had subsidized rents. Now consumers have the means to choose the housing to meet their specific needs, providing it is available. Housing benefit was introduced in 1983 under the Social Security and Housing Benefit Act 1982, which revised and replaced earlier arrangements. It is paid by local authorities and it subsidizes people in local authority and private rented property. In 1995, over 3 million households received housing benefit to assist with all or a part of their rent. Housing benefit was just part of a general tendency towards subsidizing people rather than houses. It represents a move away from a general subsidy to local authorities towards subsidy on an individual basis.

Old arrangements

Local authorities provided the bulk of social housing. Central government provided them with the bulk of social housing finance. The government directly paid housing associations their development costs. The Housing Corporation monitored the activities of the HAs generally.

New arrangements

Provision of new housing is now mixed rather than being supplied by a monopolist. Finance for new housing by HAs is also mixed, with the private sector funding a small but growing proportion of total funds. Non-housing association landlords are to be 'licensed' by the HC. Companies are to be allowed to compete with HAs for capital funds. Competition for funds is to be allocated on the basis of the impact of rent and rent pooling on housing benefit expenditure. To ensure that equity objectives are being met, the HC is to regulate rents and limit surpluses made by social landlords, and to encourage voluntary participation by tenants.

Change of relationships

The HC's new statutory powers imply a greater regulatory role in monitoring the various licensed landlords. So, for example, the HC can transfer social housing assets to another landlord following revocation; it can also impose financial penalties where rents are raised above the specified level. The government, having made housing associations the instruments of public policy, now has to regulate them more and this may lead to a fall in their autonomy and a loss of flexibility.

Q5 What steps has the UK government taken to improve efficiency in the financing and provision of social housing?

Q6 The creation of an internal market in social housing is contingent on a number of conditions being met. Can you see any ways in which the present arrangements will lead to efficiency gains at the expense of equity ones?

Case study France: Habitations à loyer modéré (HLMs)

Objectives

Deregulation in the French social housing market sector.

Objectives for the EU

None relevant to this topic.

New approaches

French housing policy reforms, and particularly those which envisaged an important role for the free market, began as early as the mid-1970s. Since then a host of piecemeal approaches have been introduced and some of these will be discussed in relation to the following:

* Approaches to increase efficiency.
* Approaches to increase the quantity of social housing stock.
* Approaches to increase access to housing.

The background

The social housing providers are the *habitations à loyer modéré* (HLMs), which means 'dwellings at moderate rents'. These are loosely equivalent to housing associations in the UK, although their activity is on a much larger scale and is principally focused on new building rather than on renovation. They provide housing for sale or rent. There are currently 1200 HLMs, managing a total of 3 million dwellings, with an average number of 4000 dwellings per organization. They have been responsible for the building of more than a million social owner-occupied dwellings.

The principal groups of HLMs are the 276 *offices publics* (OPs), which are sponsored by the local authorities and are considered non-profit organizations, and the 354 *sociétés anonymes de HLM* (SAHLMs), which are limited liability companies, sponsored by private companies, public enterprises or local authorities. These are mainly concerned with the construction of subsidized owner-occupied housing for those on low incomes. In addition, there are smaller public sector groups which play a modest role in providing housing. Both public and private HLMs are entitled to public finance. SAHLMs may obtain finance from the '1 per cent'. This is where employers with more than ten employees have to contribute 0.43 per cent of their wage bill to housing finance.

Approaches to increase efficiency in housing finance and provision

France, like the UK, has embarked on market-led approaches to increase the efficiency in provision and financing of housing. Specifically, it has adopted the raising of rents, a move from production to consumption subsidies and the more targeted use of subsidies.

The Housing Act 1977 envisaged only a secondary role for the government and left the provision of housing up to the market as much as possible. Among other things, it proposed that housing expenditure should be reduced and that rents should be raised to increase housing costs. As a result of the Housing Act, housing costs were increased by raising rents. People on low incomes were given assistance in the form of demand rather than supply subsidies, and this subsidy was called the *aide personnalisée au logement* (APL). The idea was that public money should be directed towards individual households. At the same time, expenditure on the bricks and mortar subsidies was reduced.

The main 'bricks and mortar' subsidy for social housing in France is the *prêt locatif aidé* (PLA). These loans are made through a special state agency, the Caisse des Dépots et Consignments (CDC). It gets its money from the system of public saving banks. The loans can be used either for new housing construction or for improvements. The loans can be used by non-HLM developers so long as they build social housing. HLMs receive 95 per cent of their housing costs from the CDC. Companies which provide housing for their employees receive 65 per cent and other organizations 55 per cent. As with the housing associations in the UK, there are clear social housing regulations concerning the quality, costs, rent, rent increases, the allocation of housing and income ceilings. There is a recommended limit on the rent-to-income ratio, taking housing allowance into account, of 25 per cent.

The impact of these approaches was not quite what was expected. Expenditure on the APLs and the PLAs increased, by 25 per cent in the case of the former. At around the same time, there was an increase in the rate of interest on loans made from the government to the HLMs. Set at about 5.8 per cent in the mid-1980s, this was considerably higher than the 1970s level of about 2 per cent, but it was closer to the market rate of interest. In effect, HLMs' rent had to increase. The problem with this was that many people could no longer afford the higher rents. This fact, combined with a rise in the number of empty HLM dwellings, posed financial problems for HLMs. A new approach was adopted in 1985, which allowed HLMs to sell their property.

The deregulation described above, the increase in rents and the raising of the interest rate on the loans made to the HLMs have led to some unexpected results. The responsibilities of the HLM movement had to alter as changes took place in other tenures. As more middle-class people became owner-occupiers, as in the UK, the private rented sector had an increasing proportion of low-income households. This led to more low-income groups applying for HLM accommodation, leaving even fewer units available for the poorest groups. HLMs are not permitted to make a loss, and this can cause problems for tenants on very low income. People are temporarily or seasonally employed and the unemployed have difficulty in renting from HLMs. Another problem is that many HLM tenants are relatively well off, whereas HLM housing was intended for people on low incomes – ironically, the very groups which were being excluded. These problems have formed the basis of some of the reforms which have taken place in the last decade.

Approaches to increase the quantity of social housing stock

A number of factors prompted the French government to provide incentives for increasing housing stock in the 1980s. General slum clearance, urbanization and the unintended result of the Rent Act 1982, in giving tenants more power had caused the rented market to contract. The policy response to these outcomes was to stimulate housing construction, to deregulate housing construction finance, to tighten the rights of tenants and to increase public expenditure on the number of new dwellings being built. In 1993 some 11 000 PLA loans for social rented construction in the HLM sector were created. Table 5.2 shows that the subsidized rental housing starts have been maintained at a consistent level over the period 1980–91.

Approaches to increase access to housing

In 1989, in recognition of the plight of the homeless and the affordability trap, the French government introduced a number of measures to improve access to housing. The 'Law for Implementing a Right to Housing' 1989 introduced a range of specific measures. These included: requesting a scheme to be set up in every region for the underprivileged; giving tax rebates to those who rent out property at below a fixed rent level; introducing a new low-interest loan, the *PLA d'insertion*, to encourage social housing companies to take old property and do it up for those on low incomes; planning to have a state officer allocate housing in order to avoid ghettos; setting a minimum income whereby the government pays the difference between a ceiling income it has determined and a person's actual income; and extending the means-tested housing allowance to more individuals.

It is not possible to evaluate each of these approaches, but this was an important piece of legislation and some of the measures are very significant. However, it is easier to pass laws than actually to achieve the intended results, and it can be argued that these measures are more aspirations than goals. The right to housing must become the realization of that right.

Old arrangements

Production subsidies were the principal source of finance for the HLMs. Housing finance was very centralized and the regulations on housing construction were complicated.

New arrangements

The French appear to have used market-led approaches to improve efficiency in the provision of social housing. There has been a shift from production to consumption subsidies and increases in rents. In addition, the government has increased financial assistance to housing construction companies and introduced legislative measures to remedy the access and affordability problem among poorer households.

Change of relationships

The French government sees itself as very much a supporter of market relations. There has been a withdrawal from the government having a direct role in housing provision, but a stronger role has emerged in setting specific measures to be adopted at local government level.

Q7 The French have tried to introduce market-led approaches while at the same time ensuring access to housing. What approaches have been taken to achieve these objectives? From a consumer's point of view, what are the disadvantages of this piecemeal approach?

Q8 In French social housing, there are a great number of housing providers and great diversity in their type of provision and objectives. What are the advantages of this in terms of efficiency and equity?

Discussion

This section considers the efficiency and equity aspects of the various approaches adopted, and contrasts differences in these approaches. In the case of the UK, approaches to increase efficiency in finance and provision include: shifting the responsibility of social housing construction to housing associations; creating an environment in which these providers and non-HAs can compete for public funds from a central organization, the Housing Corporation; encouraging private sector funders; and raising rents. With regard to provision, the benefits have been an increase in the number of new HA housing starts and low cost to the public. The costs of this approach are that the rate of increase in housing starts has not kept up with the rate of decline of LA new housing starts. There is also some indication that the quality of housing has deteriorated. In relation to financing, there has been some success in attracting private finance, and the internal market provisions have meant that HAs are competing for public funds

95

and that there are incentives in place for providers to manage their costs more effectively. The cost of this approach is that, although there is supposed to be greater accountability of public funds between the HC and the HAs, this will occur only if there are a large number of purchasers. It is difficult to see at present how one purchaser, the HC, can adequately monitor the quality and other requirements laid down for the providers. This regulatory mechanism may require more refinement. Rents have increased in some periods beyond the rate of inflation, thereby making some people worse off. Also, savings from grants have been offset by increases in rents which have fed into increases in housing benefit. One possible solution to this problem is for HAs to pool their rents across the whole of their housing stock.

In France, there have been a number of deregulations. The approach has been piecemeal in nature and has tried to address the efficiency and the equity issues together. The efficiency approaches have included increasing rents, increasing the rate of interest on loans, shifting from production to consumption subsidies and deregulating housing construction finance. The French have suffered similar problems to the UK, in that there is an increasing affordability problem, a contraction of cheaper rented housing and the marginalization of people. In recognition of this, legislation has produced specific measures to increase both access to housing and assistance in the construction of new housing. In this respect, the French have managed to maintain the level of new social housing starts. This may have been facilitated by the greater number and diversity of housing providers. Unlike in the UK, the provision of social housing in France is the responsibility of many providers with different sources of finance and different objectives. It may well be that the UK could benefit from the French approach, by increasing the diversity of housing providers.

Further reading

Introductory level

Begg, D., Fischer, S. and Dornbusch, R. (1994) *Economics*, 4th edn, Maidenhead: McGraw-Hill, ch. 4.

Griffiths, A. and Wall, S. (eds) (1995) *Applied Economics: An Introductory Course*, Harlow: Longman, ch. 12.

Le Grand, J., Propper, C., and Robinson, R. (1992) *The Economics of Social Problems*, 3rd edn, Basingstoke: Macmillan, ch. 4.

Intermediate level

Barr, N. (1993) *The Economics of the Welfare State*, 2nd edn, London: Weidenfeld and Nicolson, ch. 14.

Griffiths, A. and Wall, S. (1996) *Intermediate Microeconomics: Theory and Applications*, Harlow: Longman, ch. 12.

Robinson, R. (1979) *Housing Economics and Public Policy*, Basingstoke: Macmillan.

Roper, B. and Snowdon, B. (eds) (1987) *Markets, Intervention and Planning*, Harlow: Longman, ch. 7.

Stafford, D.C. (1978) *The Economics of Housing Policy*, London: Croom Helm.

Other sources

Barlow, J. and King, A. (1992) 'The state, the market, and competitive strategy: the housebuilding industry in the United Kingdom, France and Sweden', *Environment and Planning*, vol. 24.

Bartlett, W., Propper, C., Wilson, D. and Le Grand, J. (1994) *Quasi-Markets in the Welfare State*, Bristol: School of Advanced Urban Studies, ch. 1.

Boelhouwer, P. and van der Heijden, H. (1992) *Housing Systems in Europe, Part 1: A Comparative Study of Housing Policy*, Delft, Netherlands: Delft University Press.

Diamond, D.B. and Lea, M.J. (1992), 'The decline of special circuits in developed housing finance', *Housing Policy Debate*, vol. 3, no. 3.

'Social housing: a conundrum', *The Economist*, August, 1996.

Emms, P. (1990) *Social Housing: A European Dilemma?*, Bristol: School of Advanced Urban Studies.

Hallet, G. (ed.) (1993) *The New Housing Shortage: Housing Affordability in Europe and the USA*, London: Routledge, chs 3 and 6.

'More choice in the social rented sector: government consultation paper', *Housing Association Weekly*, July, 1995.

Kleinman, M. (1995) 'Meeting housing needs through the market: an assessment of housing policies and the supply/demand balance in France and Great Britain', *Housing Studies*, vol. 10, no. 1.

Muellbauer, J. (1992) 'Housing markets and the British economy', *Economic Review*, November.

Myers, D. (1993) 'Housing markets and government policy', *Economic Review*, November.

'Urban housing finance', OECD, 1988.

Pryke, M. and Whitehead, C. (1992), 'The provision of private finance for social housing: an outline of recent developments in funding existing housing associations in England', *Housing Studies*, vol.8, no. 4.

'Partial voluntary transfers: a special report', *Social Housing*, November, 1995.

Chapter 6

Higher education

Key words used: imperfect information, finance, provider, performance indicators, quality regulation, vouchers

This chapter is about higher education. This is a sector which is undergoing a set of rapid changes, and in many countries there has been a shift from an élite to a mass higher education system. The surprising thing is that higher education systems are experiencing similar pressures throughout many western European countries. The development of mass higher education is not something which has happened in isolation of other changes; it is a transformation which is a product of the larger changes in society, in technology and in industrial structures. In the UK, there has been a doubling of the number of universities, a quadrupling of the number of students and a whole new way of structuring courses. The experience of the next generation of students is likely to be very different from that of ten years ago: they will be seeking skills as well as knowledge, selecting modules in a café-style arrangement, and independently evaluating higher education institutions. It is likely that the environment of learning will be unrecognizable. For one thing, the campus could be empty! If the information technology revolution persists in the way it is developing now, it could mean that people will be able to interact with lecturers and institutions from afar and not need to be present on campus.

Governments have always been involved with higher education systems. The question is: what is their role in this transformation and what is the role for the market? Economics can help answer these questions by describing the special economic properties of education, providing an economic analysis of education, and evaluating government and market-based approaches to persisting issues.

Background to the problem

This section explains those factors which have brought about the need for change in the way higher education systems are organized. The chapter focuses principally on the teaching and learning aspects of higher education reforms. A starting point is to say how important education is and this can be done by considering the amount of resources dedicated to it. The OECD found that 12 per cent of all public expenditure goes on education, of which 7.3 per cent goes on primary and secondary education and 2.8 per cent on higher education. Expenditure on education per student varies between countries. For example, in the UK it was £6500 in 1992, compared with £4100 in Germany and £3600 in France. Differences also exist in enrolment rates in different age groups.

Consider Table 6.1, which shows the percentages of people enrolling in different countries, in three young adult age groups. In six out of the ten countries, the greatest proportion of young adults are enrolled in the 18–21 age group. However, in four of the countries this percentage rises in the 22–25 age group. It is interesting for the case studies in this chapter that the UK enrolment percentages are the second lowest in the 22–25 age group and only a quarter of the figure for Germany in the 26–29 age group. Sweden is the third lowest in the 18–21 age group. Although these figures are influenced by the type and length of course, they do suggest that formal education in some countries, particularly the UK, tends to end at an earlier age.

A number of factors have brought about a need for change within higher education systems. These are socioeconomic changes, inadequate responses to these changes by the providers of higher education, and investment issues. Socioeconomic changes are reshaping both the economy and society of the developed nations and this is impacting on higher education systems. The first impact relates to changes in demand and these come from a number of sources. First, there is a growing demand for higher education from secondary school-leavers, eager to stay off the long unemployment lines. In some countries this has been encouraged by governments. Second, there has been an increase in the demand for higher education from 'mature students'. This may have come about through changes in industrial structures. Many industrialized nations face a

Table 6.1 Enrolment[a] in public and private higher education: by age, EU comparison, 1992 (%)

	18–21	22–25	26–29
Belgium	31	10	2
Denmark	9	20	10
Finland	15	22	11
France	29	14	4
Germany[b]	10	17	11
Greece	24	5	1
Netherlands	20	16	5
Spain	23	15	5
Sweden	11	13	7
UK	18	7	3

[a]Percentage of each age group enrolled.
[b]Former Federal Republic.
Source: Social Trends (1996).

decline in their manufacturing bases. This has brought a rapid decline in the number of unskilled jobs and a new demand for skilled workers. These people require new training and retraining courses. The outcome of these factors is that the level of demand increases and there is greater diversity of demand. The higher education sector has a role to play in meeting and providing for these new demands.

Has this increase in demand, and the increase in its diversity, been adequately met by the providers or suppliers of higher education? The providers are the universities and other higher education institutions. These providers as a group will henceforth be referred to as the HEIs. There have been at least three problems with provision. The providers generally, across Europe, are either state or public institutions. Providers are dependent on government for funds, and many of them have had a significant degree of autonomy. The problem with this arrangement is that, loosely defined, a situation where there is a guarantee of funds, plus little accountability for the use of those funds, can lead to inefficiencies and inflexibilities. In recognition of this, efforts have been made to increase the level of accountability between governments and HEIs.

A second problem was that there was little diversity of course provision. Given the growth of diversity in the backgrounds of many students, there has been a need to alter both the number and type of courses, but also to change the way students learn. The third problem was that there was very little competition among providers for funds. HEIs competed for students on the basis of their reputation and status, but there was no competition in the sense that HEIs had incentives to reduce their costs of provision, improve the courses offered or increase their intake of students. In this respect, the conditions in which HEIs have operated have tended to lead to inefficiencies and an inflexible response to the changing demands made on higher education systems.

Governments on the one hand recognized the wider benefits of expanding the higher education system, but on the other hand took the view that there should be better value for money for public funds, and that expansion should not entirely be made at public expense. These constraints have led to a wide-ranging change in the provision of student finance and the method through which HEIs are funded. Governments from many industrialized nations are now seeking value for money, which involves: identifying high-cost and low-cost universities; encouraging higher education institutions to raise money from the private sector; introducing a variety of market-led reforms such as per-capita funding; dividing up purchasers and providers; using league tables to differentiate performance; and increasing the accountability of HEIs.

One important aspect of expansion relates to maintaining the quality of teaching and provision generally. The issue is that, if expansion takes place without dramatic increases in real public expenditure, the quality of education may decline. In order to ensure that this does not occur, governments have had to play a greater role in setting up regulation for quality standards and assurances.

In summary, higher education systems have had to change in response to a number of factors. On the supply side, incentives were needed to make HEI provision more responsive and flexible to meet increases in the demand for different types of higher education service. At the same time, governments have sought to increase efficiency and provide incentives for systems to expand.

Current system of allocation

What are the special economic properties of higher education, and how much do they justify government intervention?

The market

Chapter 2 outlined various market failures. In relation to higher education these are as follows.

- The presence of externalities.
- The presence of market imperfections.
- The presence of inequalities.

The presence of externalities

Higher education can be said to have a number of intangible benefits. A higher level of education is said to accelerate the rate of technical progress in a country. This can enhance productivity levels and make people more adaptable and more flexible to changes in technology. Also, someone who has become more productive influences the productivity of others. There is also an inter-generational externality, in that education benefits future generations, as well as the current generation. The problem is that economists have not yet learned how to evaluate and quantify these external benefits. Until this is done it will not be possible to add these values in to the higher education process. An associated point is that higher education is a long-term experience good. This means that its benefits become apparent only after a long period of time. Private providers are unlikely to identify and value these external benefits. The presence of external benefits, where the social returns exceed the private returns, means that there is unlikely to be an efficient level of provision.

The presence of market imperfections

In Chapter 2, we identified types of market imperfections. In a free higher education market, it is likely that information and capital market weaknesses would exist. Information imperfections in education relate to the asymmetry of information experienced by prospective students. In a free market, students would have to decide which course they require in order to fulfil their intellectual and career needs. They have no way of knowing how the consumption of one course will influence their careers in twenty years' time. The benefits are uncertain. An added problem is that everyone has an opinion on what constitutes

101

a good education. There may be many different opinions. Students do not have perfect information about courses, on what they want and what they hope to achieve in the future. There may be differences in confidence and ability to articulate. It is likely, therefore, that under free markets, imperfect information would lead to underconsumption.

An added problem is the principal–agent relationship which exists in higher education. Students are dependent on an agent, typically a funding council, to purchase courses on their behalf. This assumes that central planners are better at making choices about which courses to fund in relation to the needs of the economy. It also means that the final consumer is likely to have less direct impact on the type of higher education courses provided. This could lead to a misallocation of resources.

A further point relating to information imperfections is the argument that education is a merit good. Underconsumption will result because consumers do not act in their best interests. Could the government intervene in free markets and overcome these information imperfections? Governments could supply the relevant information through an advisory service or advertising, or could direct HEIs to produce consumer guides. It is not clear whether these measures would guarantee that consumption would rise to its optimal level.

A free market in higher education is likely to suffer from capital market failures. This arises because education, as a good, is expected to bring benefits in the future, the principal private one being a relatively larger salary. Empirical studies for the most part have confirmed this assertion. However, even if students were motivated to consume higher education, they would still have to find the means to finance themselves. Lending institutions are unlikely to offer loans; there are too many risks associated with lending to a young or low-income borrower, often with little collateral. A free market would not be guaranteed to finance the investment required to educate a student. For these reasons it is unlikely that an efficient allocation of resources would prevail in higher education.

The presence of inequalities

Free markets are unlikely to ensure that everyone has equal access to higher education because of the capital market imperfections described above. Provision would be based on prices, and without some form of support this might exclude people on low incomes. This is about vertical equity. Unequal incomes would lead to unequal access to education. Markets are unlikely to take these factors into consideration. On the horizontal equity side, there is a problem with not being able to access information (on course and finance provision). Even if this information became available to individuals, it is not clear that it would be used efficiently. This may be especially so with individuals from lower socioeconomic backgrounds.

There are some grounds for government intervention to improve efficiency and equity outcomes under a free market. The externality arguments provide the strongest economic justification for government intervention. Education is primarily a private good and many of the market imperfections described above are important, but they are not as severe as those in the health care markets.

Government objectives

If governments intervened in higher education markets what type of objectives would they pursue? These can be divided into three broad categories:

- Economic efficiency objectives.
- Administrative efficiency objectives.
- Equity objectives.

Economic efficiency objectives

The efficiency objective relates to specifying the amounts of education which will maximize net social benefits. Too much will leave not enough resources to provide other services like a health service, and too little will ensure that we are all illiterate. An efficient amount of resources spent on higher education is somewhere in the middle. To reach this amount, we need to identify the costs and benefits of higher education. The costs are relatively straightforward and include expenses like lecturers' salaries and college buildings. But there are problems in defining the benefits. There are the private benefits of consuming or experiencing a course. There are benefits which accrue to the consumer in the future: greater productivity and a relatively higher salary. Then there are the social benefits which, as we have seen, are harder to identify. Governments have tended to focus on productive efficiency objectives like getting value for money from public funds.

Administrative efficiency objectives

These refer to efforts to improve how the system is managed, and might include things like enhancing the levels of accountability and information, and ensuring better integration between different institutions. The problem of provision inflexibility is something which an administrative efficiency objective might seek to remedy. In the case studies, a policy of decentralization has been adopted to improve this type of efficiency.

Equity objectives

These have a number of interpretations in higher education. If a government believes that higher education is a merit good, where consumption benefits one and all, then an appropriate equity objective is one which aims to improve equality of opportunity. This refers to education as being a basic right, and claims that there should be a certain amount of it consumed in society. Equality of access is about people having the same means to higher education. This does not mean that everyone should consume as much education as they want, but rather that, if two individuals have the same qualifications and they wish to consume a higher education course, then they should have the same access.

Government intervention

The issue here is: how can governments overcome the problems of external benefits, imperfections in the information and capital markets, and inequalities of opportunity and access? There are three broad ways in which governments can intervene:

- Provision.
- Taxes and subsidies.
- Regulation.

Provision

As we saw in the previous section, governments are the main sponsors of higher education. Provision is largely through state or independent institutions, and these can take various forms. They can be private universities, but these are rare in Europe, or the institutions can be government agencies or have self-governing status. Their relationship with governments is largely defined through the way they are funded. The relationship with the consumers of higher education, students, is typically that they are offered places on the basis of academic qualifications. Students, therefore, do not have a right to a place. In the UK, the tuition fee is paid out of public funds, although there is now the real possibility of top-up funds being paid by students.

Taxes and subsidies

These can be used for both efficiency and equity reasons. Most countries fund the costs of higher education from tax revenues, although private finance is beginning to play a greater role. Students receive a grant for maintenance, and in most countries this is means tested. This type of intervention helps to overcome capital market imperfections. Students from better-off families receive no grant, and where less than the full grant is allocated, parents are expected to contribute up to the full grant level. Universities receive much of their funding from central government, in some countries through a buffer or purchasing body. The role of the buffer body is to allocate resources among HEIs. This relationship has altered recently, in that HEIs are subject not just to the government's budgetary plans, but also to control over how these funds are used.

Regulation

In higher education this activity refers to two things. There is economic regulation, which relates to government providing the finance and controlling how public funds are used. Many universities are self-governing and regulation by government has, in the past, been an insignificant aspect of intervention. There is also quality regulation, which has become an important aspect of the expansion of higher education systems. Staff, students, employers and governments all have their own opinion on quality. Governments are making inroads into quality by asserting that quality standards and assurances should be undertaken.

Options for reform

Higher education systems are undergoing change, and governments have sought to alter education systems in the light of pressures from both within the welfare state and in the labour market. Reform options will be examined under the following headings:

* Approaches to increase efficiency in finance and provision.
* Approaches to increase student numbers and maintain quality.

Approaches to increase efficiency in finance and provision

Many western European nations face the challenge of how to fund expansion in their higher education systems and at the same time achieve value for public money. There are at least four methods: privatization of HEIs; increasing the level of private finance; altering student grants; and altering the system of financing by creating an internal market. The first option is rather severe and would involve governments having no direct financial stake, but it may have a regulatory role, for example, in making students eligible for public support. A private university system may produce cost efficiencies and be competitive, but there is no guarantee that expansion would take place – in fact, the opposite is more likely to occur.

The second option, increasing the contribution of private finance, is becoming more significant. It involves HEIs attracting funds either for specific learning outcomes or for particular activities, like consultancy reports. The advantages of this approach are that it increases the links between employers and HEIs and forces faculties to capitalize on their competitive advantages. An example of the latter is where an HEI develops expertise on defence and works with local defence employers.

Altering the funding of students has a number of possibilities. If we start from a grant system position, the problem is that expansion will require expensive increases in public expenditure, which is not a political objective at present. There are two broad possibilities: the introduction of student loans or an income-dependent repayment system. The first involves repayment of the loan, with or without interest, over a specific repayment period. With the second system, the repayments take the form of a proportion of the borrower's income and they may continue for life. Space prevents a full discussion of these options, but one of the strengths of these systems is that they meet the benefit principle – that is, those who benefit should pay – but that the costs are redistributed over time. Supporters of these systems also claim that loans may encourage a more responsible attitude among students, and that expansion of higher education systems can take place without reliance on government revenues. Against these strengths, the principal counter argument is that a loan system may increase inequality of access. Potential students from lower-income groups may be deterred from enrolling. In addition, students generally may perceive the consumption of higher education courses as a relatively higher risk. They may be concerned with questions such as: what happens if they fail or choose to work in lower-paid employment? In 1990, the UK introduced a government loan system, but this is not expected to make any public sector savings in the short run and therefore has not freed up any resources for expansion.

The fourth option concerns altering the basis of funding. This can be executed to meet two objectives: increasing the efficiency in provision by allowing HEIs to compete for funds; and providing incentives for the system to expand. This can be referred to as the creation of an internal market. In Chapter 3, we noted that an internal market is more feasible than a normal market arrangement when the goods and services cannot be easily exchanged because of lack of information on the consumers' part and there is a need for an agent on the purchasing side. Internal markets in higher education may have four components: competition for funds from a purchaser or groups of purchasers (a higher education funding body); many differentiated providers (HEIs); student vouchers (loans); and some form of regulation to overcome imperfect information (quality regulation and performance publications).

An internal market in higher education would work like this: the providers would no longer receive a block grant at a standard rate, but this would be replaced with a 'strings attached' form of funding. So, for example, the criteria could include the number of students enrolled, the quality of the courses and the cost per student. The providers, the HEIs, would compete with one another not to sell their services directly to students, but for funding from a purchasing agency, acting on behalf of the students.

The advantages which an internal market may bring, in theory, are the incentives for HEIs to expand student intake, to be cost efficient, to improve quality and to compete with each other. However, for an internal market to be effective a number of conditions must be present. There must be competition on both the purchasing and provision side. It would be ineffective to have only a few undifferentiated providers bidding for money. If there are only a few purchasers, this means that they will have a major regulatory role in monitoring how funds are used. There must be access to information, from the point of view of both the purchaser and the student. If purchasers are unable to monitor the cost and quality of the services they are purchasing, the system may fail through reductions in quality. This is examined in the case studies.

Incentives are an important aspect of assisting the market process. These refer to rewards and penalties given for undertaking the right and wrong decisions. As we saw in Chapter 3 they are a requirement of the proper functioning of an internal market. Incentives can be introduced at the financing level. For example, HEIs can be made to bid for funds from their respective funding agencies. As mentioned above, the bidding process can be based around specific criteria and performance indicators. So funding bodies look out for the cost per student at different institutions as well as additional performance criteria like how long the students stay on the course (retention rates). Universities can be rewarded if they recruit in the numbers which they have been funded for, and penalized by the withdrawal of funds if they overrecruit.

Approaches to increase student numbers and maintain quality

Student numbers can be increased through per capita funding and by setting aside some funding if specific criteria are met. Examples of the latter are changing funding amounts to low-cost HEIs. The cost of expansion is an important aspect to governments because many do not wish to see expansion without due regard to efficiency. The aim of many governments is to expand the system without increasing the cost per student. Is this possible? It might be if there are substantial economies of scale in higher education. This is based on the idea that the more students are recruited, the lower is the unit cost (cost per student). This is difficult to assess because institutions are not normally profit-maximizers and rarely seek to minimize costs. Empirical evidence could help, but it is very sparse. One UK study by Verry and Davies (1976) found that undergraduate institutions could enjoy and exploit economies of scale at the recruitment level of 3000 students per annum. One counterpoint is that many HEIs' assets are unproductive for long periods in the year, and this suggests that there is scope to increase their productive capacities.

Quality in higher education is an elusive subject. For one thing, it is difficult to decide on what a good education is and how standards can be identified if half the benefits of receiving education accrue in twenty years' time. For this reason, assessing the quality factor is very much part of the market-forming process, but it will take time to develop. Quality can be regulated through performance indicators. The economic function of these is that they are designed to monitor, normally on a competitive basis, the performance of higher education institutions in a range of areas which cannot normally be easily assessed. Performance indicators can be used in a number of contexts. Governments can monitor universities to ensure that they are producing the courses and striving to maintain and improve their quality. Students can, in principle, use performance indicators, often presented in the form of league tables, to try and assess which is the better course to attend in terms of their own aims.

Institutional arrangements

The European Commission has had an interest in vocational training and competence development in recent years. However, it is unlikely to introduce directives to harmonize and regulate different educational systems. At present its role is to support and supplement the efforts of member countries, and to help create the conditions for an open market in higher education.

Q1 What factors have caused governments to review their policies and types of intervention in higher education systems? What are the advantages of reforming a system which tries to be more demand orientated?

Q2 How does a measurement problem arise when describing the consumption benefits of a higher education course, and how does this prevent an efficient allocation of resources?

Q3 Discuss the differences between health care and higher education in their emphasis of the following terms: asymmetry of information; capital market imperfections; externalities; and the principal–agent problem.

Q4 In what ways does central planning not foster efficiency in the provision and financing of higher education?

The objectives of the case studies chosen are to illustrate and assess whether market-based approaches can improve efficiency and equity, to contrast different problems being tackled and to describe the changing role of governments in the higher education system.

Case study Sweden: Deregulation in higher education

Objectives

To introduce market principles to the higher education system in order to enhance choice, diversity and quality.

Objectives for the EU

To create conditions for greater mobility of students between higher education systems.

New approaches

Reforms have been introduced in two distinctive periods: 1977 and the early 1990s. This case study concentrates principally on the latter. New changes in higher education were laid down by the Swedish parliament in December 1992, following proposals by the government in its 'Quality through Freedom' bill. The principal reforms can be analysed in the following terms:

- Approaches to increase efficiency in finance and provision.
- Approaches to expand the system.
- Approaches to increase administrative and institutional efficiency.

The background

In order to understand the reforms, we need to understand something of the Swedish higher education system. It has been highly centralized, and national planning dominates the allocation of resources. This means that the government determines the number of places at the universities and colleges, although HEIs are allowed to allocate resources in the area of course subjects. Students who fulfil the qualifications consume the courses free at the point of consumption. The Swedish government provides a study assistance package. The aim, as in most European countries, is to provide higher education supported by the taxpayer and to give students an autonomous choice independent of family income. Students have moderately subsidized loans, there is no expectation of a parental loan and students are expected to bear the costs of living.

In 1977 reforms were introduced. One comprehensive system was created, embracing both the traditional universities and other institutions. There is no distinctive university/non-university education in Sweden. All HEIs fall under the responsibility of the Ministry of Education and Science. Admission to all study programmes had previously been restricted and the system had seen little expansion: the capacity of students had been more or less constant at around 43 000 students per annum since 1975, yet the demand for higher education had been increasing.

Sweden's higher education system continued to suffer from a number of problems in the 1980s, which gave rise to the need for further reform. Despite reforms which brought expansion in higher education and widened the type of education on offer, some gaps remained. The system was very planning based and was not responsive to the demands of consumers. There were too many students engaged on short study programmes and non-degree courses in particular, many of which were related to public sector needs. Two other facts make the system distinctive. There was a great emphasis on adult education (see Table 6.1), and the proportion of people registered for full-time degree courses was below the rate of other countries. In addition, the Swedish system, like that of other western European nations, had more students recruited from the middle classes than from other groups. The Swedish government therefore felt that for the nation to be able to compete internationally, it needed to expand the system of higher education and increase the number of degrees, while maintaining quality.

The latest reorganization of higher education in Sweden is based on the idea that student choice should determine the direction of higher education and it is embedded in a firm belief that students are able to determine the skills they need for future labour markets.

Approaches to increase efficiency in finance and provision

Sweden has embarked on a number of reforms in relation to efficiency. The Swedish government decided to use elements of competition and administrative deregulation. As we saw from the earlier section, efficiency can be increased through changes in financing patterns. The Swedish system of financing has changed. Under the old system, higher institutions would send a budget request to government to perform future activities and the government would approve these budgets and pay up. The old system allocated resources on the number of first-year students. In July 1993 this changed: allocations are now based on proposals from the government.

The total amount of money allocated to an HEI is based on education task contracts, which run for a three-year period and are arranged between the government and the individual HEIs. The contracts set out operating rules governing how allocations will be made. The new resource allocations are now made on the number of students and the quality and effectiveness of teaching. The new funding allocations are based on three grants made on the following criteria:

- The number of full-time students.
- The number of study credits achieved by students.
- Quality performance in predetermined areas.

In the first two cases, allocations are made as a renumeration for results achieved. Results are defined as the number of study credits achieved (about 60 per cent) and the number of full-time equivalent students taught (about 40 per cent). The first type of grant is more or less a fixed allocation, according to the number of students (it is not completely set in advance as some adjustment is made for outcomes). This is called the student voucher. The institutions can decide how to use the resources and the students can take with them part of these resources in a voucher-like arrangement. The second grant is devised to increase the effectiveness of teaching. These are first steps towards the creation of an internal market in higher education. The third grant is a special grant to encourage superior quality, the quality premium. Once the funds are allocated to the HEIs, they can be used in the way that the HEIs see as most appropriate to achieve the long-term goals set out in the contracts. They can specify different performance requirements for different departments, which allow for differing abilities and better use of resources. It is not clear exactly how many funds will be allocated to each of these categories.

The quality premium plays an important role, since resources can be distributed between government and universities on the basis of predefined quality indicators. In other words, there are financial incentives for enhanced quality. The incentives are twofold: on the one hand, there are more finances available, and on the other hand, higher-quality teaching will attract more interested and motivated students.

To maximize funding, institutions of higher education have not only to maximize the student intake, resulting in competition for prospective students, but also to ensure high retention rates. With a national credit transfer system *in situ*, the mechanisms exist for dissatisfied students to transfer from one institution to another. Such an action has financial implications for all institutions. The objective was to bring educational output closer to the market, so that higher education institutions would be forced to respond to changing student demands. The final market-based approach has been the increased use of performance indicators. Previously, external peers played an important role in evaluating quality standards in higher education. The government plans to place an even greater emphasis on evaluation, the idea being that institutions should compete for quality and that the published results of any evaluation would form the basis for differential rewards and thus create an incentive system.

The success of the changes in funding will take time to emerge, but they require at least three conditions for survival: that the quality assurance systems are properly adhered to; that they are fair; and that they have effective penalties for poor quality. Also, it is important that students have access to relevant information, provided by the HEIs on the one hand and publications of a league table type on the other. The latter should show the relative strengths and weaknesses of different HEIs. If these are not present, students will not be able to make informed choices and HEIs will get away with lower quality in service provision.

Approaches to expand the system

The aim of the reforms was to increase the number of students in higher education while maintaining quality. The government has facilitated the expansion by making more money available: for example, more money has been allocated to the humanities, social sciences and law faculties, and more postgraduate research posts have been created. In 1992/93 more than 20000 additional places were made available compared to the year before. Expansion has meant an increase in the number of new places to more than 50000 in the period 1991–95. This represents an increase of 20 per cent. Expansion has largely been achieved through the new resource allocation system.

Approaches to increase administrative and institutional efficiency

The expansion of student numbers is being carried out in parallel with structural or institutional change. Specifically, this means that HEIs have been given more freedom from direct government control. Three approaches have been taken to achieve these aims. The first is decentralization. This began as early as 1989 with more local freedom in defining academic programmes. The government still authorizes the granting of degrees, but course content is the responsibility of the institution. Then the abolition of the Swedish National Board of Universities and Colleges in 1992 was a major step in the process of decentralization. This institution had acted like a buffer organization between the state and the university, it was involved in decision making and was very geared to central planning.

It was replaced with the National Agency for Higher Education, which has a broader set of duties. The outcome is that the system is more decentralized, which allows for greater flexibility in decision making.

The second approach is to give HEIs greater autonomy. From July 1993, HEIs have greater freedom in how they organize their curricula, deal with student admissions and allocate the resources they receive for undergraduate education. The final approach is to offer universities the opportunity to take up the new status of the foundation. This is a form of privatization that would allow them to grant degrees and borrow from broader sources. So far a number of HEIs have shown interest in this proposal.

Old arrangements

The educational system in Sweden was strongly centralized, where the number of students taken in was strictly planned and implemented by the Ministry of Education and Science. There were very few private institutions and no competition between the state institutions either for funds or for students. There were only marginal differences perceived between different institutions. Admission to all programmes within higher education had been restricted, and the demand for places thus had little direct impact on the allocation of resources.

New arrangements

In the 1990s Swedish higher education has attempted to become more stratified. This means that there is a common system which is maintained by the government, but individual institutions have become more differentiated through the operation of market principles. The new degree system has provided greater freedom for students to combine their own studies. Diversity and competition between higher institutions have been introduced, and new incentives for improved quality have been established through the financing system and the national evaluation procedure.

Change of relationships

The government is pursuing its reform strategy through education task contracts arranged and agreed with each HEI. The reforms alter the relationship between the state and the higher education system, but these have yet to develop and it is not clear what their exact nature is, or how the government will influence the system. Government decisions will be more general in nature. Decentralization which gives greater autonomy will alter relationships; one possibility is that lecturers, students and university administrators will assume greater responsibility in articulating the goals and the content of higher education programmes, and local politicians will just ensure that the minimum standards they laid down are being met.

The government has moved from the role of major supervisor of university administration, to that of a contractor: the government's decisions will be made through a higher education law, and it will set guidelines for objectives and resource allocation in higher education.

Q5 The Swedish higher education reforms are aimed at increasing the impact of demand on the system. What approaches have been used to achieve this aim?

Q6 Funds are now only allocated if a number of criteria are met. What is the logic behind having more 'strings attached' to funds?

Q7 One of the ideas driving the reforms is that students should determine the direction of higher education. What are the strengths and weaknesses of this idea in your view?

Case study The UK: Competition in higher education

Objectives

To achieve increased efficiency through competition among the UK higher education institutions, to expand the system and to maintain the quality of service.

Objectives for the EU

To create greater student mobility between higher education systems.

New approaches

A number of approaches have been employed to try and bring about greater efficiency in the provision of higher education. These can be examined under the following headings:

- Approaches to increase efficiency in finance and provision.
- Approaches to maintain quality.

The background

Universities are independent, self-governing bodies; they enjoy considerable autonomy in their academic affairs and, although they receive the majority of their funds from funding councils, they are free to determine the allocation of resources at the institutional level. Until the 1980s, neither market forces nor the performance of HEIs had a role in the allocation of funds. The problems began to emerge in the 1980s when changes in labour markets altered the level and type of demand, but it was felt then that the higher education system did not respond either quickly or flexibly to these changes. In addition to this, the higher education sector appeared reluctant to change itself. The conclusion was that these institutional non-responses were due in part to overdependence on state funding. This case study concentrates on reforms in resource allocation in teaching.

Approaches to increase efficiency in finance and provision

The main approach adopted to improve the allocation of resources is the introduction of a change in funding patterns. Two aspects will be studied: incentives to find new sources of funding and changes in the way public funds are allocated. Table 6.2 shows the sources of funds in the UK. Recurrent income accounts for the largest proportion of funds: these are funds to support teaching, research and related activities, and they are provided in the form of a block grant. The table also shows that dependence on public funding has declined. HEIs now have to find a small but growing proportion of their revenues from other sources. Fees from full-time students, catering and other sources have grown. The aim of the government at the time was to mix the sources of finance for higher education so that expansion could take place without placing any undue pressure on the public purse. During the expansion phase in higher education in the UK, figures presented by the Department for Education suggested that the costs of educating a student in terms of public funding had fallen by 3 per cent between 1989 and 1997. To this extent the policy was successful.

The other approach adopted to increase efficiency in provision and finance was through what economists term the creation of an internal market. This was undertaken by introducing a student loan scheme to cover maintenance costs, imposing an increase in the fee per student which is paid by the local education authority, and laying down specific criteria by the funding council. The body, or the purchasing agent, which allocates funds in England is the Higher Education Funding Council for England (HEFCE), while there are other funding councils for Wales and Scotland. The analysis will consider the role of HEFCE.

The system operates like this: there are two types of HEFCE funds: core

Table 6.2 Changes in higher education funding sources in the UK (% of total income)

Sources of income	1987	1992
Total recurrent income	55.3	32.5
Research grants and contracts	19.2	20.4
Fees from full-time home students	6.8	16.3
Fees from full-time overseas students	5.6	5.1
Endowments, donations and subventions	1.3	3.7
Other fees and grants	1.0	3.9
Residences and catering	. .	6.7
Miscellaneous income	6.5	4.6
Other general income[a]	3.4	5.7
Computer Board Grants	0.7	0.8

[a]Includes provision for depreciation.
Source: 'Higher education statistics for the UK, 1992/93' (1995).

funding and marginal funding. Core funding has subtracted from it an amount which reflects whether HEIs have low or high costs per student. The amount subtracted is less for low-cost institutions. Marginal funding is additional to core funds, and it is allocated competitively across institutions. The criteria used for allocation is, again, cost per student. The lower the cost, the greater the level of council funding in the future. There was a gradual increase in the value of fees, which meant that HEIs could receive partial funding for the additional fee-only students they enrolled. The idea was that there would be an incentive for HEIs to compete with each other to attract fee-only students, who reduce the average cost of educating a student. Fees act as vouchers from the students' point of view, in that fees give them buying power to choose an institution willing to accept them.

The result of these changes was a huge expansion in student enrolment numbers. In 1990 there were 1.2 million students, an increase of 41 per cent since 1980, accompanied by a decline in public expenditure on each student. It would appear that this resource allocation mechanism has been successful in meeting the expansion aims. In 1994 the government slowed down the rate of expansion and introduced penalties by establishing a maximum aggregate student number (MASN) for each HEI. If there are over- or under-enrolments by 1 per cent, funds are withdrawn.

Approaches to maintain quality

There are at least three aspects to quality in higher education. There are those which relate to the procedures of enhancing quality (assurance), there are those which directly inspect provision (assessment) and there is the public disclosure of information. In the first case, the HEIs set up an independent body, the Higher Education Quality Council (HEQC), which helps HEIs develop ways to enhance their internal processes for review and evaluation. There is a strong emphasis on auditing. Included in this are support systems to improve the quality of provision. The HEQC will examine the procedures and management arrangements of HEIs. The second aspect involves the HEFCE. It has a statutory duty to ensure that provision is made to assess the quality of education in HEIs where it funds the activities. Assessment is undertaken by visits and subsequent reports. The reports contain information from the visits and include other useful information for the public. Eleven unsatisfactory judgements have been made, and the institutions involved have been given twelve months to remedy the situation. So far, the five visited have demonstrated satisfactory provision. The third aspect is about the information from Councils being disclosed publicly and included in the Students' Higher Education Charter. The information on performance will include examination results, how many students progress from year to year and how employable graduates are.

There are three weaknesses with the present system of quality regulation. So far, it appears that although performance information is available, few applicants consult it. Even if consumers can be encouraged to use the information more, there is still the problem that all statistics require careful interpretation. Second, the HEIs were more or less self-regulating prior to the reforms, and this has been replaced with external regulation. In a way this represents more intervention by the government rather than less, which might be resented by HEIs. Finally, the finance arrangements are that a uniform price is paid for a uniform quality, but it is likely that, through increasing competition and private funding, this situation may become unsustainable.

Old arrangements

The old system lacked effective efficiency incentives. Providers were very much dependent on state funds and allocation was based on budgets and planning.

New arrangements

The government is in the early stages of introducing competitive elements into the higher education sector. It has attempted to enhance competition among the providers of higher education. There have been changes in the institutional management arrangements and in the funding system.

Change of relationships

The funding council has a strengthened role in the allocation of resources to HEIs. The latter have had to accept, albeit reluctantly, a greater degree of intrusion into their affairs. HEIs have also had to build up relationships with private funders, and will continue to do so.

Q8 *What approaches have been adopted by the UK to meet the objective of expanding the higher education system? Why is quality such an issue at a time of expansion? Why is it that potential students have not consulted perform-ance league tables?*

Q9 *The introduction of an internal market in higher education has begun. In what ways do you, as a student, think that you might benefit from this particular approach?*

Discussion

This section attempts to evaluate the reforms in the UK and Sweden from the point of view of how they have contributed to increasing efficiency and equity. In most cases, it is difficult to evaluate the reforms because they are part of a process and take time to develop. Nevertheless, some strengths and weaknesses can be raised. The UK objectives aimed at expanding the system, encouraging efficient use of public funds and maintaining quality. As we saw from the case study, the first two objectives appear to have been met, in that the higher education system has expanded and this has been achieved with lower public funds and with a lower cost per student. Also, expansion of the system means that the absolute number of students from lower socioeconomic groups will have increased, although this needs qualifying in that what matters more is how the relative proportions have changed. These gains have to be weighed up against a number of weaknesses. The new system is a complicated one and the government has changed its emphasis and hence funding basis more than once. Such changes incur costs. Also, there is a concern about the potential for quality to decline under the present mechanisms. Given the nature of higher education and the presence of imperfect information, there is much more scope for students to be receiving a poorer education compared with ten years ago. They cannot be sure of the quality. So far, efforts to ensure that information on the quality and performance of HEIs has been used by potential students have been disappointing.

The Swedish higher education reforms are at a more embryonic stage than in the UK, which makes them difficult to evaluate and compare, but there are some aspects which can be questioned. The 1991 reforms were aimed at changing the resource allocation mechanism for public funds, the decentralization of institutions, giving greater autonomy to HEIs and expanding the system. Expansion has taken place, although this has also occurred as a result of a higher level of state spending, in addition to changes in funding arrangements. The likely efficiency gains are that movements away from central planning (the abolition of the buffer organization) will bring greater flexibility to the system, as will greater freedom for HEIs to decide on curricular and quality issues. The rationale behind the creation of foundations, which amounts to a form of privatization, is unclear. The aim appears to be to allow HEIs freedom to generate funds from other sources and through other activities. This can be done without privatization, but through deregulation, as we have seen in the case of the UK. There are more likely to be equity losses rather than efficiency gains under a system of more private HEIs. Sweden emphasizes evaluation and the allocation of funds on the basis of quality. Under the present proposals and in the light of the UK experience, there is likely to be a need for further refinement. For example, care needs to taken in deciding on the exact proportions of funds allocated among the three funding criteria: the fixed institutional funding, the student voucher and quality-related funding. This is an important aspect, given the government's wish for student choice to determine the direction of higher education. On balance, there are clearly efficiency gains to be had through the new market-based approaches, but these will have to be weighed up against the way the present mechanisms implement, monitor and enforce quality regulations.

Further reading

Introductory level

Begg, D., Fischer, S. and Dornbusch, R. (1994) *Economics*, 4th edn, Maidenhead: McGraw-Hill, chs 12 and 16.

Griffiths, A. and Wall, S. (eds) (1995) *Applied Economics: An Introductory Course*, Harlow: Longman, ch. 12.

Le Grand, J., Propper, C. and Robinson, R. (1992) *The Economics of Social Problems*, 3rd edn, Basingstoke: Macmillan, ch. 3.

Intermediate level

Barr, N. (1993) *The Economics of the Welfare State*, 2nd edn, London: Weidenfeld and Nicolson, ch. 13.

Bartlett, W., Propper, C., Wilson, D. and Le Grand, J. (eds) (1994) *Quasi-Markets in the Welfare State*, Bristol: School for Advanced Urban Studies, ch. 5.

Griffiths, A. and Wall, S. (1996) *Intermediate Microeconomics*, Harlow: Longman, ch. 11.

Jenkinson, T. (ed.) (1996) *Readings in Microeconomics*, Oxford: Oxford Economic Press, ch. 15.

Roper, B. and Snowdon, B. (eds) (1987) *Markets, Intervention and Planning*, Harlow: Longman, ch. 9.

Other sources

Adia, E., Stowell, M. and Higgens, T. (1994) *Higher Education Sans Frontières: Policy, Practice and the European Student Market*, Leeds: Heist and UCAS.

Bottani, R. (1995) 'Comparing educational output', *OECD Observer*, no. 193, April/May.

Colardyn, D. and Durand-Drouhin, M. (1995) 'Recognising skills and qualifications', *OECD Observer*, no. 193, April/May.

Duguet, P. (1995) 'Education: face-to-face or distance?', *OECD Observer*, no. 194, June/July.

'University challenge', *The Economist*, 20 June 1992.

Gellert, C. (ed.) (1993) *Higher Education in Europe*, Higher Education Policy Series, London: Jessica Kingsley.

'Annual report and accounts 1994–1995', Higher Education Funding Council for England, March, 1995.

'Introduction to the Higher Education Funding Council for England', Higher Education Funding Council for England, January, 1996.

'Council briefing', Higher Education Funding Council for England, 3 July 1996.

'A guide to funding higher education in England', Higher Education Funding Council for England, July, 1996.

'The challenge of audit', Higher Education Quality Council, update, no. 9, April 1996.

'Higher education statistics for the UK, 1992/93', Higher Education Statistics Agency, Cheltenham, 1995.

Hildebrand, M. (1994) 'Swedish higher education', National Agency for Higher Education, June, Stockholm.

Miller, R. and Wurzburg, G. (1995) 'Investing in human capital', *OECD Observer*, no. 193, April/May.

National Agency for Higher Education (1993) *A Guide to Higher Education in Sweden*, Stockholm: The Swedish Institute.

Reviews of National Policies for Education: Sweden, Paris: OECD, 1995.

Scott, P. (1995) *The Meanings of Mass Higher Education*, Buckingham: Society for Research into Higher Education and Open University Press.

Swedish Ministry of Education and Science (1993) *Knowledge and Progress: A Summary of the Swedish Government's Bills on Higher Education and Research*, Stockholm.

Swedish Ministry of Education and Science (1995) *The Swedish Education System*, Stockholm.

Swedish Ministry of Education and Science (1995) *Strategies for Education and Research 1995*, extract from Swedish government bill, 1994/95:100, appendix, Stockholm.

The Swedish Institute (1995) *Study Abroad: Study in Sweden*, Stockholm.

Verry, D. and Davies, B. (1976) *University Costs and Outputs*, Amsterdam, Elsevier.

Part 3

National industry themes

Chapter 7

Postal services

Key words used: state ownership, licences, statutory monopoly, universal service obligation, uniform price

This chapter is about a very specific segment of the communications industry: postal services, and letters in particular. Everyone has posted and received letters; it is part of our daily life. It is also part of an industry which is changing faster than you can read this page. Technological developments have produced substitutes to the letter, once the only means of transmitting information throughout a country, in the form of electronic mail and facsimile. This, along with increasing competition in segments of the mail market, has raised the question of why we need to continue protecting the letter. At present it is legally safeguarded. Many postal service organizations are currently being deregulated, and at the heart of the debate is the question of whether postal services need to be provided by a monopoly. Economics has a valuable role to play in this debate. The subject can provide an analytical framework from which it is possible to evaluate the need for government intervention, and also to assess possible roles for the market in overcoming and meeting the new competitive challenges this industry faces.

Background to the problem

Postal services can be viewed as serving at least three distinct markets: the communications side, which is concerned with the transmission of information; distribution, which relates to the carriage of goods; and the retail business, where things are sold at post offices. This chapter focuses on the letter mail segment of the market, and this will be referred to as postal services. This is an interesting and unique organization in which to study new directions in public policy. In most countries, it is a public monopoly, with a long and close association with the government. It stands out from other sectors examined in this book, in that it is a trading organization, but unlike the energy and railway sectors, the postal service operates in a market which cannot be definitely described as either a natural monopoly or a competitive one. Privatization, therefore, is not an obvious or straightforward solution.

The postal services in western European countries are undergoing reform. Why is this so? The reasons can be grouped into the following: the present market structures are inadequate to meet the changing demands of consumers in the rapidly developing communications industry; postal performances have been mixed; and there are moves towards both deregulation and harmonization of postal services at the EU level. The first point is about problems with the existing market structures. Until recently, postal services have operated under various forms of state ownership and have typically been monopolies. In many cases, the structure has emerged as a result of the statutory monopoly. This is a monopoly defined by a statute (Act). It legally permits a specific supplier, usually the public monopoly, to forward mail exclusively, so that no one else can legally provide this service. These legal rights do not extend to all types of mail: most countries define their letter monopoly by weight. This is called the threshold level and varies between 500 g and 7 kg in different countries. In the UK, all items charged at a minimum of £1 and weighing at least 500 g are allowed to be carried privately. As we shall see later, the threshold level is an important idea in terms of deregulation of this market.

Why are these market structures inadequate? The monopolies are under pressure from competition. The growth and success of private carriers has demonstrated that competition is feasible. Another reason is the change in markets and technology. The communications market as a whole has expanded rapidly and has experienced technological advances, especially in electronic technology. Postal services now have substitutes. This very fact weakens the traditional reason for the public and statutory monopoly. There are at least two further implications of an expanding communications market. First, the communications market has become international: there are now lucrative overseas markets and these need developing. Second, the internationalization of the market has brought a greater need for collaboration and partnership: for example, cable and television companies are offering telephone services. Post offices have an opportunity to collaborate and encourage advertising material through their mail systems. It is not clear how the public monopoly form of control will be able to facilitate these opportunities. If the public monopolies are constrained, competitors may take a growing share of specific segments of their market. For all these reasons, there is pressure for postal services to become more independent of the public sector and to be given greater freedoms in their commercial operations. The present monopoly structures do not necessarily allow such freedoms.

Besides inadequate market structures, postal organizations have had very mixed performance records and, given the pressure on governments to reduce expenditure, many are seeking to improve performances through the introduction of competitive forces. On the whole, postal services have been perceived as being inefficient, suffering from high prices and a lack of innovation. Many postal services around the world have been criticized for being slow and inflexible to changing business demands. Although this charge is difficult to prove, many would say that the cause of their problems is the monopolistic and bureaucratic administration they operate under, some with political interference, and others with financial and operational constraints. Table 7.1 shows huge differences in letter traffic, employment, costs and prices among European nations. Germany handles a few more letters than the UK, but employs twice as many postal staff. Italy handles about a third of the UK traffic, but does so at roughly the same cost. Also, subsidy levels differ between countries: the UK has been subsidy free for nineteen years, while the French have generous postal subsidies.

A final factor for change is the moves being made at the EU level. The European Commission is keen to encourage greater deregulation in specific segments of postal markets. Specifically, it wishes to see more competition for courier services and private operators. It proposes two stages for reform: the immediate liberalization of all mail that weighs more than 350 g; and from 2001, the liberalization of direct 'junk' and cross-country mail. On the other hand, the Commission also wishes to see a more harmonized postal service, where there is one stamp price across the EU. However, there are some real obstacles to these wishes: for example, Table 7.1 shows the wide variations in how post offices operate. We can see that there is no typical postal service, and this is likely to make harmonization a difficult objective to achieve.

Postal services are in different states of deregulation. The UK and the Netherlands are the most liberated systems, while Ireland and Italy are very closed markets, and Germany and France lie somewhere between the two. Sweden Post lost its monopoly in 1993 and remains profitable and efficient.

Current system of allocation

This section explains the uniqueness of postal services, the rationale for intervention and the types of approach which may be adopted.

Table 7.1 Postal features of European nations, 1994

	Number of postal staff	Domestic letter traffic (bn)	Costs (US $bn)	Revenues (US $bn)	Letter tariffs up to 100 g[a]
Germany	342 413	18.32	n/a	12.55	138
France	289 156	23.87	n/a	n/a	105
Italy[b]	221 534	6.62	5.63	4.13	130
Britain	189 000	16.75	5.83	6.29	84
Spain	65 355	4.06	0.92	0.87	32
Netherlands	53 560	n/a	2.03	2.26	109
Sweden	52 251	4.21	1.78	2.01	n/a

[a]EU average = 100.
[b]1993 figures.
Source: The Economist, June 1996.

The market

Postal services are unlike health and education: the post is not a merit good, there are no information problems, capital market problems or insurance problems, but there are industry structure problems. Chapter 2 described types of market failure, and in relation to the postal services these are as follows:

* The presence of market structure imperfections
* The presence of inequalities.

The presence of market structure imperfections

These are economies of scale and scope which give rise to a natural monopoly in part of the postal services industry. Economies of scale mean that the lowest cost per unit of handling a letter occurs when there is one supplier. Economies of scope refer to a situation when there are cost advantages of having many services being provided by one supplier. How do economies arise in the postal services? It helps to think of the industry as being made up of a number of distinct phases: collection, sorting, transport and delivery. Albon (1991) has argued that there are moderate to high economies of scale in collection and delivery of mail respectively. This is where, in the case of the UK, the postman empties the postboxes and delivers letters. It would be a wasteful duplication if two postmen from different companies emptied boxes and delivered letters – volumes would be halved and therefore costs per letter would rise.

There are no significant economies of scale in sorting and transport. There are many postal sorting offices spread all over the country, and each represents a local or regional supplier, so the activity does not require one single national sorting centre. Empirical evidence on economies of scale in postal services as a whole does not indicate that they have a strong presence. Therefore we conclude that, although there might be some economies of scale in some of the postal activities, the traditional argument that postal markets are natural monopolies because of the presence of scale economies is not clear-cut.

To this we must add the economies of scope issue. These economies are said to occur in postal services where post offices typically provide other services, like handling parcels and government transactions. When these services can be jointly provided by one supplier, this can give cost advantages. Again this argument seems to be open to interpretation. There is evidence from the growing independence of parcel, courier and postal bank businesses, which all have their own networks and retail outlets, that they can operate independently of the postal network. This suggests that any economies of scope are not significant enough to have made an impact. The economic implication of the presence of some economies of scale and scope is that there are some cost advantages which mean that a monopoly structure may be desirable, but it is not truly a competitive market nor is it truly a natural monopoly situation. There is some scope for monopoly power and it is possible that a private market will produce an inefficient level of output in the absence of government intervention.

The presence of inequalities

To these two arguments we must add the argument that a free market in postal services would neglect important social and equity issues. There are two assertions to this. The first relates to the wider social benefits of a post office. In a rural setting, people have claimed that the post office represents more than a place to purchase a stamp. It is part of the community, like a social centre. This argument is tied in with the idea that some services in life have special properties, and the ability to have access to transport and communications enables people to participate in society. A private operator may ignore this aspect when deciding to close a post office. This is called the universal service obligation. The second assertion is about equity and argues that it is not fair to charge people different prices for the same service, which is considered basic to participating in life. This is called the universal charge. Intervention may be required to ensure that everyone pays the same price for the same service irrespective of location and of income.

Both these assertions have counterarguments. The common one is that there are many other basic services provided to rural consumers, such as food and buses, which are not subsidized. Why, then, should postal services be? There might be a stronger argument for the universal service if it could be proved that there was a transfer of benefit from higher-income to lower-income groups, but this is something quite separate from allowing rural users to be subsidized by urban users. Also, there is a difference between having a postal service as a means of income distribution and having a postal service because it is considered necessary for participation. At present there is a need for further research to quantify the benefits of a national postal service.

To conclude, postal services have special properties. They operate in a market which is neither a natural monopoly nor a competitive one. A free market is unlikely to produce a competitive market in the long run, with a universal service. There are market imperfections, but there is no clear evidence that these are substantial. Intervention may be justified on the grounds of improving the natural monopoly activities and setting obligations to operate socially important services.

Government objectives

Governments intervene in postal markets to overcome the imperfections described above, and in doing so, they will have a number of objectives. These were discussed in Chapter 3, and in relation to postal services are as follows:

- Economic efficiency objectives.
- Meeting the wishes of the European Commission.
- Social and equity objectives.

Economic efficiency objectives

We have indicated that market structure imperfections may lead to monopoly structures. An example of an economic efficiency objective is one that ensures that the natural monopoly activities are undertaken at the least cost for a given level of output. Allocation efficiency objectives include ensuring that the price reflects the consumers' willingness to pay based upon the benefits they derive. In theory, we say that prices should equal the marginal cost of production. In practice, this is a difficult aim to achieve for a postal operator. Many postal costs are called joint costs, which means that they are shared with other services. It is very difficult to identify marginal costs in this instance; they are all tied up with other costs.

Meeting the wishes of the European Commission

This has become an important aspect of postal reforms. The wish is twofold: for liberalization of certain parts of the postal service and for harmonization of letter prices. The Commission has a desire to see an EU-wide uniform letter price. There is both opposition and indifference from nations and from postal organizations towards these aims. Governments and postal organizations have been focusing principally on changing their internal structures.

Social and equity objectives

An example of a fair objective in postal provision is for everyone to have access to postal service and for the same price to be offered for the same service.

Government intervention

We have considered the reasons why a free market may not bring about socially efficient outcomes and the objectives of governments. The next two sections describe the type of intervention which has taken place, and the options for reform. The types of intervention are as follows:

- Provision.
- Taxes and subsidies.

Provision

Governments can directly control provision through public ownership or nationalization. They can form a public monopoly by passing an Act conferring the rights to deliver mail on one supplier. In theory, public ownership ensures that the potential monopoly abuses are controlled and equity concerns can be met by governments stipulating the aims and objectives of the organization. However, there are problems with this form of intervention. First, there is the age-old problem of the potential for too much government intervention. This occurred in the UK, when the Post Office had pricing and investment constraints put on it during the 1970s, when there were concerns about the macroeconomy. This effectively impacted on commercial decisions – in particular, pricing and investment decisions. Another problem was that, under public ownership, the majority of finance for investment was provided by the government. This meant that investment plans were dependent to a degree on the public finance system. Finally, there was the problem of what to do with surpluses earned. The UK government set surplus targets, which stated how much money had to be paid back to the government. These types of arrangement are claimed to be a constraint on the operations of the organization and untypical of how private markets operate. An alternative to public ownership is private provision with regulation. This is less common in Europe, but can be found in the USA. This form of intervention will be discussed in the next section.

Taxes and subsidies

Explicit taxes and subsidies are not used in the UK. In France direct subsidies are given to the postal services. There are also implicit subsidies and taxes. A publicly owned monopoly means that the monopoly will operate cross-subsidies. The advantage of this system is that, in theory, everybody pays a universal charge and has access to a national service. In Germany, there is an implicit subsidy, in the form of a transfer of money from the telecommunications to the postal business. The disadvantage is that no one knows how the subsidy is used, and hence how much it costs to provide a service to a distant location. Also, a universal charge means that people cannot express their preferences; some consumers may wish to have a better service and be prepared to pay for it. The ability to have different charges gives scope to have a greater variety of service. Under public monopoly, some consumers pay an implicit tax. This generally implies that those in urban areas are paying more than the actual costs of delivering, so that the costs of providing to loss-making, often rural, consumers are covered.

Taxes and subsidies can be used in other ways. Governments could charge a levy on profit-making operators which would be placed in a fund and used to pay out to the operators of loss-making services. The problem with this form of intervention is the skill required in pitching the levy: too much and margins will be cut, too little and the funds will be inadequate. Alternatively, rural services could be funded not through the user, but through local authority funding schemes. The tax could be added on to a local tax or community charge. This might bring greater efficiency as prices would still be universal, but there would be no cross-subsidy. Or, subsidies could be funded nationally. The European Commission has talked about funding from Brussels so that depressed areas can be directly financed. The problem with this is that it smacks of increasing bureaucracy. How do we evaluate the different types of intervention – taxes versus subsidies and national versus local funding? In the first instance, a very simple approach might be to say that, if the costs of setting up a local or national postal tax scheme exceed the costs of having a system run with implicit taxes, then the latter must be retained. Alternatively, if the benefits of local and national subsidy schemes exceed the costs of using implicit cross-subsidies, then the former hold. The answer would depend on the empirical evidence and on the weight attached to the different objectives.

Types of intervention vary across Europe. The Post Office in the UK is a nationalized industry, it is in the public sector, it acts like a commercial organization, but it receives a universal service obligation from the Secretary of State for Trade and Industry. In Germany, France and Italy, postal services have a high level of government involvement in the form of regulation, ownership and subsidy.

Options for reform

Now that we have described the pressures to reform postal services, the next question is: what approaches can be adopted by governments and industry to meet those challenges? This will be examined through the following:

- Approaches to increase efficiency without privatization.
- Approaches to increase efficiency with privatization.

Approaches to increase efficiency without privatization

Efficiency can be increased in two broad ways: measures taken to improve the existing arrangements and deregulation measures. Beginning with the first approach, if a public monopoly exists, it is possible to enhance efficiency by commercialization and restructuring. The first refers to any action which seeks to make the public monopoly more like a private company, but it does not necessarily introduce incentives for competition. Restructuring might involve separating out the individual businesses within the postal industry and giving each division separate profit and loss accounts. Creating corporations is part of this process. It involves incorporating organizations as companies: for example, splitting postal from telecommunications services and placing each on a more business-like basis. Rationalization is part of the process of increasing commercialization and is about streamlining resources and having sharper management practices. It might also include allowing greater flexibility in operating, commercial and financial arrangements. All these means are aimed at making postal organizations more able to respond to changing demand and market factors.

The second measure to enhance efficiency is deregulation. A government might do this as a preparation for privatization. A common method of increasing the level of competition in the postal services is by reducing the monopoly threshold. So, for example, Germany aims to reduce its threshold for mass mailings from 1 kg to 250 g. This will allow private operators to enter the market and deliver letters addressed in bulk. Lowering the threshold can be applied to different segments of the letter market: for example, light-weight parcels, bicycle couriers and unaddressed advertising mail.

Competition can also be increased through franchising. This can be done by granting licences to provide a specific service. There are two broad aspects. First, franchising may require all potential operators to apply for a general licence to provide a specific service. The franchise could be awarded, after a bidding process, on the basis of specific criteria, such as the least call on the public subsidy or the most extensive services for a given level of costs. The second aspect of the franchising process is that it would require regulation to ensure that consumers are being served in all areas and at a reasonable price. Franchising means that the competitive process takes place more *for* the market rather than *in* the market. The idea is that the cost advantages of a single supplier are retained, the natural monopoly elements are not broken up, and the universal service obligations could be contained in the franchise. So far, we have seen much development of the former aspect, especially in the UK.

Approaches to increase efficiency with privatization

This could be executed by two possible routes, either preserving or not preserving the statutory monopoly. The former would involve the organization being sold off, and would be accompanied by market restructuring and regulation. The statutory monopoly would be dissolved. This approach would be adopted if it could be proved that a natural monopoly in postal services was insignificant and if the interest of consumers could be protected. The advantages might be the efficiency gains from having many competitors. Costs would be reduced, thereby reducing the level of subsidy and making it more transparent. The market, not the government, would determine the number of operators the market could sustain. Also, this approach moves the organization out of the political arena, it facilitates access to financial markets not available under state ownership and it offers scope to diversify, to collaborate and to initiate partnerships with other operators. The disadvantages, as we have seen, are that some areas are not as lucrative as others, and there may be limited opportunities for effective competition. Open competition and uniform pricing are not possible in an unregulated market. Regulation would be required to ensure that distant locations were served.

Privatization without competition – that is, where the statutory monopoly is retained – would be appealing to investors. This would involve the postal organization being sold off intact, and it would be accompanied by regulation, but there would be no accompanying change in the market structure. This method would be chosen if it were believed that a significant natural monopoly existed in postal services and that the possibilities for cream-skimming the market were large. The advantages would be those listed above but with some exceptions. There would be no efficiency gains from competition and much would depend on the subsidy arrangements.

Institutional arrangements

These are important in relation to postal reforms. The European Commission has taken a long time to produce its Green Paper on the future of European postal services; it came out in 1992 and was later revised in June 1993. Surprisingly, there is no obligation to remove the statutory monopoly. The Green Paper wishes to see more competition in some areas, but it is clear about wanting a uniform letter price and quality throughout the EU. This is significant, and bad, for some countries like the UK, where the Post Office wishes to see less rather than more regulation.

Q1 What factors have forced governments and postal industries to rethink how they organize their respective roles and activities?

Q2 Do postal services have economic features which are radically different from those of a private good? Is it efficient and equitable for urban postal users to subsidize rural postal users?

Q3 Who should subsidize the provision of a national postal service: other services, the government, the postal user, the general taxpayer or the postal operators?

Q4 Outright privatization of the postal services has not been widely adopted. Why is this, and what are the alternative approaches which might be adopted?

The objectives of the case studies chosen are to contrast different stages of postal deregulation, to illustrate the issues of an organization which cannot be defined as operating in either a natural monopoly or a competitive market, and to illustrate the changing role of the government.

Case study The UK: Deregulation of postal services

Objectives

The government's objective has been to increase steadily the dividend paid to it by the Post Office. The industry's aims are to meet competitive challenges, invest for growth and reduce costs.

Objectives for the EU

Since the inception of the single market, the European Commission has been keen to encourage liberalization of parts of Europe's postal services. Its Green Paper aims to open up markets to competition and to establish a universal service to all.

New approaches

The UK postal services are relatively well deregulated compared to other countries. The process began in the late 1960s, and since then a number of

---

deregulation approaches have been adopted. The most recent of these will be discussed in relation to the following objectives:

*   Approaches to increase efficiency through restructuring.
*   Approaches to increase efficiency through competition.

The background

The Post Office is a public organization; it is owned but not managed by the government. The Post Office Corporation is a legal body created by an Act of Parliament and it is required to publish separate accounts. There are four businesses under the corporation: the Royal Mail, Parcelforce, Post Office Counters Ltd and the Subscription Services Ltd (which is responsible for telebusiness). The corporation employs 161000 people. The Royal Mail, which principally delivers letters, is the largest of the businesses, accounting for about three-quarters of the group's total turnover in 1996. It operates in a wider communications market, competing with electronic mail and facsimile.

Approaches to increase efficiency through restructuring

There have been a number of reorganizations, deemed necessary by the Post Office, to respond to new competitive challenges. In 1981 the Post Office was split from telecommunications. Following this there was a further split: businesses were formed by dividing the organization up in terms of different products, such as letters and parcels. These businesses were then given separate profit and loss accounts, their own staff, management and industrial relations. Finally, these businesses had to contract with Post Office Headquarters for central services. Previously, the Post Office had a hierarchical structure. This meant that managerial and financial decisions were made at the top, and there was less decision making at the level of the different businesses. What the new structure did was to break down the size of the businesses, give greater financial and managerial independence, and allow each business to focus more on its consumers' needs.

Rationalization also occurred with the streamlining of resources, particularly in the workforce. The hierarchial management structure was replaced with one which was orientated towards customer needs. After this restructuring, two other changes occurred: the (partial) privatization of Girobank and decentralization. The latter approach made nine geographical divisions of the Royal Mail in 1992. More recently, allowance for greater flexibility in operating practices has been approved by the government. The Post Office is pressing the government for changes in its operating framework. It is not against the idea of becoming independent from the government. The President of the Board of Trade has promised greater freedom in capital spending and more sympathetic consideration of the idea of partnerships with the private sector and making full use of the government's private finance initiative (see Chapter 10).

These measures have contributed to the overall performance of the corporation. Table 7.2 shows selected performance data. Over the eleven-year period, the financial performance of the Post Office has improved dramatically. Profits, return

Table 7.2 The Post Office: selected performance figures

	Profit before tax (£m)	Return on capital employed (%)	Self-financing ratio (%)	1st-class letters delivered next day (%)	Total letters posted (m)
1985/86	99	10.8	117	87.6	11 200
1986/87	133	9.7	176	87.7	12 019
1987/88	121	10.6	129	88.7[a]	12 991
1988/89	163	7.9	117	74.5	13 204
1989/90	47	3.7	43	78.1	14 719
1990/91	47	1.5	44	85.5	15 306
1991/92	247	11.8	113	89.8	15 379
1992/93	283	13.1	106	91.9	15 745
1993/94	306	13.5	117	91.2	15 960
1994/95	472	18.1	153	92.0	16 751
1995/96	422	14.5	133	92.3	17 529

[a]1987/88 and earlier figures are 'ready for delivery' next day. Figures for later years are for 'delivered' mail. Therefore the figures are not directly comparable.
Source: Post Office, *Annual Report and Accounts*, various years.

on capital employed (returns to investment) and ability to finance operations have all improved. There have also been improvements in the standard of service in the first-class letter post, and the volume of traffic handled has increased. The latter point is important because this has occurred against a background of increasing competition. Although it must be recognized that there are a range of factors which have contributed to these improvements, there is little doubt that managerial, financial and organizational restructuring have played an important role.

Interestingly, it can be argued that these improvements weaken the arguments for privatization. If such gains can be made within the public sector, why should they not continue? Also, it may be that the bulk of the potential gains have already been made, and that privatization may only bring relatively small gains. Unfortunately, without knowing the actual benefits from privatization, it is not possible to evaluate these assertions.

Approaches to increase efficiency through competition

These approaches involve introducing competition without actually privatizing the Post Office. Competition has been introduced by reducing the monopoly threshold and by the use of licences. Postal services have been exposed to private operators for letters which have a value of more than £1. Above this threshold there have been increasing signs of competition, particularly in parcel delivery and courier services. Franchising and licensing operates across postal services. Many of the post offices are franchised out to individuals. The Post Office has an exclusive right to deliver letters charged at less than £1. In July 1996 the government decided on a trial basis to remove the statutory monopoly: that is, to allow mail priced below £1 to be carried by other operators. Already, in several cities private operators are beginning to move into the monopoly area. In Portsmouth, one company is now charging 17p for next-day delivery in the city; another operator is charging 19p for first-class letters and it handles 7000 letters a day. In London some courier companies are charging 25p for same-day deliveries. Although these are only city-based operations, there are some serious economic implications. First, these activities increase the level of competition that the Post Office faces. Second, they represent cream-skimming; they will undermine the Post Office's profitability. The corporation argues that, if it is to keep to its duty of making daily deliveries to every address in the UK for the same price, it must retain its monopoly. Clearly, if these activities were to expand, a new type of arrangement would have to be considered.

Old arrangements

The Post Office was a centrally organized industry, with decisions being made from the top. It had a hierarchical structure with no separate business definition; it was not product based and there were no separate cost and profit accounts.

New arrangements

Postal services are increasingly becoming more like a private business. The Royal Mail has set its own agenda to compete with other forms of competition, such as electronic mail. Much of the change has come from internal adjustments. Top management have devised strategies in operations and management structures in order to ensure that price and quality targets are achieved. The process of commercialization and the introduction of competition have combined to improve the quality of service.

Change of relationships

The formal relationship between board and government has not altered, but internal relationships have changed in that new managers have been appointed with greater and specific responsibilities for resources. They have responded to the need for greater employee focus in managing change. What the organization wishes for now is greater freedom to be able to compete with other forms of communication.

Q5 How does restructuring help an organization more able to meet consumer needs?

Q6 Do you think that making efficiency improvements within a public sector trading organization is a substitute for privatization? If the Post Office were privatized, what measures do you think would be necessary to ensure that there was an accessible and equitable postal service?

Case study Germany: Postal liberalization

Objectives

The aim of the German government is to liberalize the postal market by 1998. The chairman of the postal business stated his aim as listing a privatized and profitable postal business with shares on the German stock exchange by 1998.

Objectives for the EU

Since the inception of the single market, the European Commission has been keen to encourage liberalization of parts of Europe's postal industries. Its Green Paper aims to open up markets to competition and to establish a universal service to all.

New approaches

The steps for postal liberalization are as follows:

- Approaches to increase efficiency through restructuring.
- Approaches to introduce competition without privatization.

The background

Germany's postal monopoly is not in as liberated a state as that of the UK. Recently the federal government has announced plans to reform the industry radically, and it is these proposals which will be analysed.

Approaches to increase efficiency through restructuring

The German government wishes to privatize its postal services. At present, postal services have a poor financial record and consumers face relatively high prices, which they have continually protested against. Table 7.1 showed that, for an EU average letter price equal to the index number 100, Germany charges the highest tariff compared to other countries. This case study illustrates the process of moving a public corporation towards commercial viability. In order to privatize such an industry, a number of preparations need to be undertaken. These include developing an appropriate organizational structure through corporatization, and introducing commercial practices and, eventually, competition. These preparations have been made and reforms have begun. The organizational changes came in 1990. Figure 7.1 shows the organizational structure before and after this date.

Deutsche Bundespost had an unusual structure: it was simultaneously a ministry and a self-governing enterprise providing postal and telecommunications services. After 1990 postal services, telecommunications and postal banking were split into three independent enterprises, with a stake-holding company called Deutsche Bundespost. In 1995 there were further organizational changes and the three public enterprises were made into separate joint stock companies, Deutsche Post AG, Deutsche Telekom AG and Deutsche Postbank AG. The major

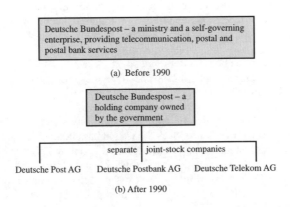

(a) Before 1990

(b) After 1990

Figure 7.1 Organizational changes in the German postal industry

shareholder (over 50 per cent) is the government. In the case of the new postal organization, Deutsche Post AG, the government will be the only shareholder for five years.

These changes do a number of things. They make each business self-standing. In becoming a stock-holding company, postal services will have issues of equity finance. The presence of equity finance means that some part of its operations must be undertaken along commercial lines if it is to make a return to investors. The repackaged post business has so far produced mixed financial results, with a turnover of DM28.6 billion in 1994, following a loss of at least DM150 million in the previous year. However, in 1995 it made a net loss of DM2.9 billion.

An important aspect of preparing an organization for privatization is the rationalization of resources. The labour force has been reduced with the elimination of 46 000 jobs in the early 1990s, and a further 35 000 are to disappear by 1999. Postal debt has been transferred out in order to make the business look more attractive to would-be investors.

Approaches to increase competition without privatization

The German postal market has been subject to increasing competition in specific market segments. Private operators have entered the market, first in the courier services and then in the international letter segment. The postal monopoly is under pressure to change both from new substitutes coming on to the market and from increasing competition. Postal services are divided into monopoly services, mandatory services and competitive services. All three services are subject to price regulation, which takes the form of price caps.

The statutory monopoly is made under the Postal Law called the *Postgesetz*, and this states that an item including a written message is to be carried by the Deutsche Poste. Unaddressed advertising mail, books or small packages do not fall under the monopoly (or reserve) area, but these have until recently been forwarded

137

by the public enterprise. There is price regulation on the letter, on some competitive services mentioned above and on letters delivered by private firms. The introduction of competition has taken three forms:

- The lowering of the postal letter monopoly.
- The relaxing of price regulations in specific areas.
- The introduction of franchising.

The letter monopoly is decided by weight: it currently stands at 250g and it is planned to be lowered. In other services the weight has already been lowered: mass mailings for certain companies have been lowered to below 1 kg through the issue of special licences. Price regulations are to be relaxed in the items delivered by bicycle courier. The Federal Ministry of Posts and Telecommunications has been examining the possibility of opening up the market of addressed advertised mail by the granting of licences. The plans are that operators would be allowed to enter lucrative segments of the market. How would the implicit subsidy be handled? The proposals are that a fund would be set up which would pick up the difference if open competition failed to provide a basic service to all, at a reasonable price. Companies granted a licence would have to pay into the fund to cover the deficits on the universal service obligation. Since the end of 1994, private licence holders have been allowed to deliver addressed mass mailings weighing more than 250g. Fifty licences have so far been granted. The plan is for private mass mailings to be permitted down to a weight of 100g by 1996.

There is a problem with economies of scope. The government has separated Postbank from Deutsche Post and plans to sell off the latter in 1996, but to sell off the former business much later when it looks more attractive. The government believes that it can raise more money by selling the businesses separately. Recent developments have seen Deutsche Post looking to buy 40 per cent of Postbank's shares. The latter claims that unless banks do more business through the post offices, it will close down 4500 of its 17000 post offices. There are four issues here: there are large cross-subsidies between the two businesses; the two businesses are heavily dependent on one another; Deutsche Post is a loss-making business; it would be undesirable if a majority shareholder in Postbank used the business in a way which disadvantaged the post offices. The government needs to find a way in which the two businesses can mutually operate and benefit as private companies. This is an example of where political considerations are overruling economic considerations. A more appropriate approach would be to delay privatization and allow both businesses to improve their performances under the current cooperative agreements.

Old arrangements

Deutsche Bundespost provided postal, postal banking and telecommunications services all under one roof with an objective of covering costs with revenues. The postal service was organizationally bound with telecommunications, a state mail monopoly with little incentive for efficiency and not run on a business-like basis. It suffered from high prices and overmanning. There was a transfer of money from the telecommunications to the postal services.

New arrangements

Restructuring has allowed the different businesses to develop at their own pace and in response to market conditions. Changing market conditions brought about structural changes and a reduction in the reserve area. However, the company is to keep its monopoly on letter delivery until the end of 2002.

Change of relationships

The Postal Ministry so far has authorized the lowering of the letter weights and the granting of licences. It will be replaced by the Economics Ministry which will regulate the licensed private operators.

Q7 The German government proposes creating a fund to cover deficits made by the private postal companies. Contrast this method with one of retaining the organization in the public sector and continuing to allow the practice of cross-subsidization.

Q8 Economies of scope are said to exist in traditional postal organizations in Germany. The government appears to be planning a separation and eventual privatization of postal and postal banking businesses, but allowing the cross-subsidies to continue. In what way could this be deemed an unfair proposal?

Discussion

This section analyses the two broad approaches from the point of view of how they have increased efficiency and met the wishes of the European Commission to liberalize postal services. In the case of the UK, the approach has been to restructure radically, involving the separation of business units, and to lower and temporarily suspend the monopoly threshold. There is evidence that the corporation has made efficiency gains through these changes, in terms of both its financial performance and its quality of service. A relatively free regulatory structure is in place, where the government has laid down targets for reducing real unit costs and for return on capital employed. So far the suspension of the postal monopoly has attracted competition, mainly within cities, and it is likely that this trend will continue. It is not yet clear whether private postal services might extend to rural areas. The government is now faced with a choice. It can either privatize the industry or allow it to have greater commercial freedom within the public sector. The latter would appear a more appropriate approach if the Post Office could be allowed to diversify into other lucrative areas and continue to cross-subsidize its loss-making activities. Privatization is not an obvious solution because of the unique features of the industry. Given the already substantial gains made by the industry, it is unlikely that the costs of setting up a regulatory body to ensure a universal service would be outweighed by any significant benefits. In terms of meeting the wishes of the European Commission to introduce private competitors, the UK has more than complied. Ironically, the problem for the Post Office is that the universal tariff proposal is not in its interests; it is already heavily deregulated and it wants less regulation and more commercial freedom.

In the case of Germany's post office, the approach is about ten years behind the UK. The German government has focused on restructuring and the encouragement of new operators in very specific market sectors. It wishes to privatize the separate businesses and overcome the postal cross-subsidy problem with a pay-in fund from profit-making operators. The postal business is a chronic loss-maker and unless it can use the banking profits to offset its mail losses, it is unlikely to improve its performance in a way which will make it acceptable for privatization. In this instance, it would be more appropriate to allow both businesses to develop within their mutually beneficial agreement, and to delay privatization plans. It is likely that the EU proposals will be better suited to Germany than the UK, given the current state of postal deregulation.

The two approaches are difficult to compare because they are at different stages of deregulation. On the one hand, the UK government has abandoned the idea of outright privatization and has instead opted for a suspension of the postal monopoly on a trial basis. The German government seeks privatization, but at an unrealistic speed in relation to the current performance of Deutsche Post. Neither has given serious consideration to funding the loss-making services by means other than public monopoly. In addition, both governments have opted for difficult strategies without due regard to the long-term implications.

Further reading

Introductory level

Begg, D., Fischer, S. and Dornbusch, R. (1994) *Economics*, 4th edn, Maidenhead: McGraw-Hill, ch. 18.

Griffiths, A. and Wall, S. (eds) (1995) *Applied Economics: An Introductory Course*, 6th edn, Harlow: Longman, ch. 8.

Intermediary level

Albon, R. (1991) 'The future of postal services', Institute of Economic Affairs, Research Monograph, no. 47, July.

Crew, M. and Kleindorfer, P.R. (eds) (1995) *Commercialization of Postal and Delivery Services: National and International Perspectives*, Boston, MA: Kluwer Academic Publishers.

Vickers, J. and Yarrow, G. (1988) *Privatisation: An Economic Analysis*, Cambridge, MA: MIT Press.

Other sources

Centre for the Study of Regulated Industries (CRI) (1993), 'Franchising network services – regulation in post, rail and water', London: Chartered Institute of Public Finance and Accountancy.

'Development of the single market for postal services', Commission of the European Communities, Green Paper, Brussels, 1992.

Denny, N. (1993) 'Racing for the post', *Marketing Week*, vol. 16, no. 31.

Duff, L. (1987) 'Policies and performances of the UK nationalised industries', unpublished thesis, UMIST, Manchester, ch. 6.

'Privatising Britain's Post Office', *The Economist*, April, 1994.

'German banking: post boxing', *The Economist*, October, 1995.

'Return to sender', *The Economist*, June, 1996.

'The Post Office: monopoly game', *The Economist*, August, 1996.

'Privatised post office to gear up for global competition', Embassy of the Federal Republic of Germany, press release, October, 1994.

'Postal monopoly under fire', *German Brief*, April, 1994.

'Private postal services: a new era', *German Brief*, July, 1995.

'Postbank AG: a complex privatisation', *German Brief*, February, 1996.

Hastings, P. (1992) 'Postal harmony: can the Community deliver?', *Accountancy*, vol. 109, no. 1182.

Heller, R. (1993) 'How the Royal Mail rode out its shame and found a culture', *Management Today*, April.

'The future of postal services', HMSO, Cmnd. 2641, 1994.

Parker, D. (1994) 'The last post for privatisation? Prospects for privatising the postal services', *Public Money and Management*, July/September.

Post Office Annual Report and Accounts, 1994/95 and 1995/96.

Visco Comandini, V. (1995) 'The postal service in the European Union: public monopoly or competitive market?', *Annals of Public and Cooperative Economics*, vol. 66, no. 1.

Warwick, M. (1993), 'Germany – DBT: hung up on terms for privatisation', *Communications International*, vol. 20, no. 8.

Chapter 8

Railways

Key words used: rail infrastructure, public service obligation, restructuring, franchising

How many times have you weighed up the cost of going to London by car or by rail for a weekend, and found that driving there by car is a fraction of the apparent rail cost? How often do you read about government subsidies to the railways rising at the same time as rises in rail fares? In an old-fashioned economics textbook, the railways would be described as well loved and supported, but in decline. Now railway systems all over the world face changes, not just from competing modes of transport, but from changes in government policies towards them. Many railways are being faced with commercialization, deregulation, franchising and privatization. The questions that governments have to ask themselves right now are: how much do they value their railways; in what ways they are going to support their railways in the future; and is there a greater role for the market? This is a unique area in which to study new directions in public policy because the issues surrounding deregulation of the railways are complex and there is much debate about the effectiveness of various approaches. Economics has a useful contribution to make towards these debates, through a framework of analysis that explains the rationale for government intervention in the railway industry and provides a basis upon which to evaluate possible new roles for governments and for markets.

Background to the problem

The railway industry's principal function is to transport passengers and freight using trains (which are part of the rolling stock assets) on a network of rail tracks with stations and signalling equipment (which are part of the infrastructure assets). This chapter concentrates on the passenger rail business. Most railway systems in western Europe are undergoing change, and part of this change involves a process of deregulation of the railways. A number of factors have brought about the need for governments to change their role in the railway industry. These factors include the desire to make better use of the railways and in some countries to expand the industry; to improve the quality of railway

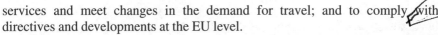

services and meet changes in the demand for travel; and to comply with directives and developments at the EU level.

The desire to make better use of the railways stems from the belief that railways have some specific strengths over other transport modes. They offer better access to national and other European cities. They are a faster form of transport over long distances. They are relatively safe forms of travel. There are, on average, 65 000 fatal road accidents compared with 500 railway deaths per annum across Europe. Railways are also an environmentally cleaner transport mode. They emit far less pollution than road transport and have higher energy savings. Railways allow for combined transport arrangements which gives greater overall efficiency in travel. Finally, developments in technology, such as the advent of high-speed trains, mean that there is the potential for winning back market share from other forms of transport, especially air transport. In other words, changes in technology have opened up the potential for fundamentally improving the quality of rail service, in terms of time and comfort.

Despite these advantages, we can see from Table 8.1 that rail has a significantly low share of passenger traffic. The Austrians have the highest passenger kilometres per head in rail travel, while the UK has less than half that level. If governments wish to increase rail's share of travel, then they will need to find ways of valuing the benefits of railways to an economy, and they will need to devise policies which create incentives for railways to expand and for people to use them more.

Related to this last point is the fact that, in order to make better use of the railways, improvements must be made to the quality of services. Modern living means that people more than ever demand fast, efficient and reliable transport

Table 8.1 Passenger traffic by mode: country comparison, 1993 (thousand km per head)

	Cars and taxis	Buses and coaches	Rail[a]	All these modes[a]
Austria	8.4	1.7	1.2	11.4
Belgium	8.6	0.5	0.7	9.8
Denmark	10.9	1.8	0.9	13.5
Finland	9.8	1.6	0.6	12.0
France	11.0	0.7	1.0	12.7
Germany	8.8	0.9	0.7	10.3
Great Britain	9.6	0.7	0.5	10.9
Italy	10.6	1.5	0.8	12.9
Luxembourg	–	–	0.7	–
Netherlands	9.2	0.8	1.0	11.0
Portugal	7.7	1.2	0.5	9.4
Spain	5.3	0.8	0.4	6.5
Sweden	10.4	1.2	0.7	12.3

[a]Excluding metro systems.
Source: Social Trends (1996).

modes. Reductions in travel time are paramount. On the supply side, railways have not always been able to respond quickly to these changes. One of the problems is that many of the western European railways are public monopolies and are financially supported by government. One criticism of these types of arrangements has been that the organizations have had a tendency to lose sight of the needs of consumers and have had limited scope to diversify into related service areas. For these reasons, governments have begun to consider ways in which changes in structure and greater commercial freedom can be used to improve the quality of service and levels of efficiency.

Besides pressures to improve the quality of service, there have been pressures to improve on the mixed financial performances of railway industries. The financial situation of the railway reflects partly the declining share of the transport market, and partly the obligation to maintain public services on a national scale. An example of the financial position of some of the European railways is the French public railway monopoly SNCF, which made a loss of FF11 billion in 1995, despite subsidies of FF30 billion. It has a long-term debt of FF175 billion. In Belgium, the SNCB reported a loss in 1995 of 13 per cent of its operating revenue and had long-term debts of 120 per cent of total revenue, despite substantial subsidies. In Germany, the Deutsche Bundesbahn made its first operating profit in 1994, DM88 million on revenue of DM24 billion, although this was after the government took over the debt of the company.

There are three challenges for governments here. First, many wish to see a reduction in the level of public subsidy. Second, many wish to see greater value for money in the way that public subsidies are used. Third, many wish to expand their railway industries. With these objectives in mind, many governments have looked to the market for solutions. The approaches adopted and being experimented with include deregulation, the introduction of private finance, and giving greater commercial freedom to form joint ventures with other transport companies. For example, the Channel Tunnel rail link between England and France has largely been privately funded, Italy has just introduced the world's first public–private high-speed train, and beyond Europe, Argentina, Brazil and Mexico have planned to privatize a number of major train routes.

The Commission of the European Union has played a role in promoting change. It sees a need for greater integration among EU railway networks as a way of strengthening industry and trade in the Union. In its plans for an internal market, it presented a common transport policy. This is seen as supporting the free market and encouraging competition. These aspirations are rather ambitious, and so far they have had little success in being implemented. One reason for this is that great diversity exists among transport systems within EU countries. There is much variation in terms of integration (between transport modes) and the size and degree of state aid. These facts make it difficult to harmonize policies. The Commission is also interested in the idea of a community railway network. This would require the development of high-speed trains and improvements in services. It might also require changes in how railways are controlled. At present, most railway systems are controlled by governments and have been restricted to national markets. Finally, the Commission has stressed the need to strengthen the accountability of railway management and to make clear the basis of investment decision making between the railways and roads. This is a worthy aim because at present many countries adopt different approaches to evaluating roads and railways.

In summary, the challenge facing governments is to improve the financial and operational efficiency of their railway systems, in order to alleviate the strain on public finances and arrest the railways' declining share of the transport market. The industry, on the other hand, faces pressures from a more demanding consumer, who wants reliability and greater savings in time. These pressures have prompted many governments to reorganize and deregulate their railway industries.

Current system of allocation

Why is it that most of the railway networks in the world are state owned or have substantial levels of government involvement? Why is it that so few railway systems are able to make a profit? The answers to these questions can be partly explained with reference to the specific features of railways.

The market

This section asks what a free market in rail travel would look like and what are the special properties that railways have. Failures of the market were discussed in Chapter 2, and in relation to railways these are as follows:

- The presence of externalities.
- The presence of market imperfections.
- The presence of inequalities.

The presence of externalities

These arise from the wider costs and benefits of a nation using the railways. There are positive consumption externalities in the form of safety, because travelling by rail is safer than travelling by road. If more people used the railways, the nation would benefit from a lower national health bill. Externalities arise from other sources. Trains emit smaller quantities of air pollution than vehicular transport. This has a value in a world increasingly concerned with the state of the environment. Ideally, we would like to see more people using trains rather than cars because of these wider benefits to society. But private operators would be unlikely to take these external benefits into account and train service provision would not be at the socially efficient level.

The presence of market imperfections

These may be explained from two angles: from the distinctive nature of rail costs and from the presence of economies of scale. The first refers to the fact that trains operate on tracks and other assets which need to be in place before the service can take place. These are called the infrastructure assets. Not all industries require infrastructure assets specific to that service. So, for example, in order to run a taxi service, roads are the infrastructure assets, but roads can be used for other transport services. Trains need tracks, and tracks have few alternative uses. The rail infrastructure part of the railways industry is a natural monopoly. Second, once these infrastructure assets are in place, we can say something important about the nature of the costs associated with them. They are typically very high: that is, they account for a large proportion of total costs. Moreover, once installed they take a long time to be recovered. These costs are often referred to as being fixed or indirect, which means that they do not vary with changes in the level of service in the short run. In addition, these costs are shared by all train services. For example, think about the costs involved with a passenger sitting in a train carriage: there may be a small amount of wear and tear on the seats, but basically the use of the assets and hence the costs associated with that particular service do not change much with that passenger. The implication of this is that it is difficult for this industry to identify the marginal costs of providing a service. It is very difficult to separate out indirect and shared costs between different services.

Economies of scale are present in railway industries but, as we have seen, they do not exist in all railway activities. They arise generally because of the scale of production required to set up the rail network and because of the way various activities have to integrate with each other. Railways are complex industries where production is linked to operations, which in turn is linked to the network (the infrastructure). Central coordination of these activities brings cost advantages. This is also true for related functions such as advertising, marketing, R & D and the procurement of equipment. The industry has different degrees of monopoly within the provision of a rail service. So for example, infrastructure is a natural monopoly: it is not feasible or desirable to have more than one set of train tracks. The operation of trains is a monopoly in the sense that it is desirable to have only one company offering a train service to a particular distant location, but this monopoly does not necessarily have to be a national monopoly. It might be possible to have local or regional monopolies.

It is likely, given the nature of rail costs, the natural monopoly element and the cost advantages of integration, that a monopoly structure would prevail in a free market. This would be socially inefficient if there were monopoly power. This refers to setting prices above the marginal costs of production and reducing the quality of service. How severe is this condition in railways? It can be argued that the scope for monopoly power in the railways is limited. In the UK, the only source of real monopoly power comes in the commuting segment of the market; for most of the other services, trains compete with other modes of transport.

The presence of inequalities

This relates to the idea that having access to transport is part of being able to take part in modern society. If individuals could not access transport in a rural area and they did not drive, their ability to participate in business and society would be limited. There is an argument, therefore, which states that a minimum level of some goods and services is required to allow individuals to participate in society. Everyone should be able to have access to basic transport services. It is unlikely that a private rail company would put these considerations at the top of their agenda. It is likely that train operators would either charge relatively high prices or not provide the service at all. There is little doubt that if a railway industry had no government intervention, the total rail network would be smaller than most railway systems are today.

Government objectives

If governments intervened in private railway markets, it would be to try and overcome the market features and special properties described above. Governments will develop a set of objectives to guide them. From Chapter 3, these are as follows:

- Economic efficiency objectives.
- Administrative efficiency objectives.
- Equity objectives.

Economic efficiency objectives

An example of a production efficiency objective is one which ensures that, for a minimum set of costs, the maximum output is produced in terms of society. Railway production costs fall into three categories. First, there are the private costs: the capital and operating costs, such as the tracks and the train carriages, fuel and tickets. Then there are costs to the train user which are imposed by other users: these might include the costs of overcrowding in carriages. The third category are those costs imposed by the operation of train services, such as air pollution. These costs have to be weighed up against the benefits of rail travel, which include the private benefits to individuals and the wider social benefits, discussed in the first section. From the point of view of society, when these costs are minimized and the benefits maximized, there will be economic efficiency. This has implications for the level of rail investment and is a contentious area in the UK, as critics have claimed that the railways have been underfunded and thereby have been unable to meet the changing demands of their customers. One of the claims is that investment decisions have not been made on the same basis as investment for other transport modes, such as roads.

Allocation efficiency objectives focus on ensuring that the marginal benefits derived from using trains equal the prices that consumers are willing to pay; or, put another way, that the net benefits (costs minus benefits) from consumption are at a maximum. The demand for transport is a derived one, which means that people consume it so that they can reach another goal, like going on holiday. Within this idea, it is true to say that people derive different types of benefit from rail use, for business, for social and for commuting purposes. Allocation efficiency means that charges should be structured to reflect different levels of benefit derived from the consumption of these services. Meeting the require- ments of consumers has become a prime objective for railway companies.

Administrative efficiency objectives

Examples of these objectives in railways might include anything which enhances the way the system is run: for example, coordination between services, or information systems which provide data on the costs and revenues of individual services. Improvements in administrative efficiency might involve better communication between different activities and, in the case of government, better relationships with the industry. More accountability can improve the way public funds are used within the system.

Equity objectives

An example of these is ensuring that a minimum level of service exists – for example, in a rural area – at a cost which is not beyond the average income- earner. Concessions for the unwaged and the elderly may ensure that they have equal access to using train services. The UK government imposes a public service obligation on the railways, which means that they must, among other things, maintain rural services and have subsidized fares.

Government intervention

Governments intervene in railway industries to overcome the market failures and to achieve a set of objectives. We now turn to the types of approach that governments might adopt:

- Provision.
- Regulation.
- Taxes and subsidies.

Provision

This can take a variety of forms: public provision or mixed provision or totally private provision. The majority of railway systems in western Europe are publicly owned and they are public monopolies. Unlike health care, however, railways are rarely wholly publicly financed. The bulk of revenue comes from user charges. Monopoly structures prevail for the reasons explained earlier, and they are predominantly public for historical reasons and to maintain public services on a national scale. State ownership or nationalization means that the industry is under government ownership and control. Possible arrangements might include a minister being responsible for ensuring that the public interest and other objectives are met. A board would agree those objectives and translate them into operational objectives. There are problems with this form of intervention. Governments have not been able to refrain from constant interference in the policies and management of national railways. This has led to many decisions being made which are of a political and not of an economic nature. Also, the public monopoly structure plus the dependence on state funds tend to dampen the drive for innovation. On the train service side, as we have seen, this structure and form of control tends to make the organization less responsive to consumers' needs, which can lead to a perceived or actual decline in the quality of service.

Regulation

This may take the form of economic regulation, and regulation to specify minimum standards, in train safety, for example. In the first case, if we assume that a private monopoly exists, governments might regulate its economic activities. This would involve ensuring that the public service obligation or duty to service all geographical areas was being undertaken. This could be built into formal licences administered by the government or a government agency. Regulation could be used to ensure that prices were not being set at a level which exploits the consumer. The advantages of this form of intervention are that the industry would be free to access capital markets, it could diversify into related areas, and the industry would be free from direct ministerial intervention. The disadvantage of this form of intervention is that there would be large costs involved in setting up and operating the regulatory regime, and these costs would have to be weighed up against the benefits of having a competitive railway industry.

The other type of regulation refers to governments setting legislation to ensure that minimum standards are met with regards to driving safety, installation and health.

Taxes and subsidies

Taxes and subsidies can be used to finance the railway operations and they can be used to alter the prices of rail travel. In the first instance, if there is a public service obligation to provide a national service, at prices which are fair to one and all, most railway systems will require a subsidy. As we saw earlier, substantial rail subsidies exist in France and Belgium. Governments can raise revenues through general taxation and transfer a lump-sum subsidy to the railway to ensure that the public service obligation is met. Public monopolies typically have an implicit cross-subsidy, where revenue is transferred from profit-making services to loss-making ones. This arrangement also helps to meet the public service obligation. Also, subsidized prices can be offered to the disadvantaged and funded from other activities. The problem with public subsidies in situations with limited competition is that the industry may become dependent on them and have few incentives to try to reduce the size of the subsidy.

Governments can also provide finance for investment purposes, which can take the form of capital loans and grants. The problem with this form of intervention is that the railways might be dependent on government annual expenditure plans for a proportion of their investment, and a situation can arise whereby the railway investment projects are curtailed by political considerations.

Options for reform

So far we have discussed the pressures facing governments to change the existing arrangements in railway industries, the objectives they might pursue and the types of intervention. This section considers the types of approach open to governments in the light of the following objectives:

- Approaches to increase efficiency without privatization.
- Approaches to increase efficiency through privatization.
- Approaches to encourage the expansion of railways.

Approaches to increase efficiency without privatization

There are two broad ways of increasing efficiency: to improve existing arrangements and to introduce deregulation. The first approach may or may not involve changing the incentives in the industry. Such an approach might include the reorganization of activities so that there are greater levels of accountability at regional and local level. This might in turn involve better cost-accounting methods: for example, breaking down costs, so that there is more information about how costs vary with changes in the level of services. This can improve the decision-making processes. Another option is improving the environment in which relationships are conducted between government and industry. This was attempted in the UK, when a major review by the National Economic Development Office (NEDO) was undertaken in 1977. The aim, among other things, was to come up with methods of improving the nature of relationships. It proposed a third tier, an independent authority to be responsible for the economic control of the industries. This proposal was never adopted, on the grounds that it would add to the burden of bureaucracy.

The second approach involves efforts to change incentives within the rail industry, such as deregulation. Such measures might include restructuring, commercialization and franchising. The first two are more about preparing the business environment for competitive processes to proceed; the other, franchising, is about the competitive process itself. Rationally, any move towards improving the performance of the rail industry must involve at an early stage the streamlining of activities. Commercialization involves making the industry a corporation, which means having it run along the lines of a private enterprise with similar management structures. This might include the reorganization of activities into self-standing units by making them self-financing. Also, individual activities or businesses can be allowed to purchase or procure services not just from the other public businesses, but from private companies: for example, buying railway-signalling equipment from a foreign or private company. This represents an effort to increase efficiency because it forces the established public business to try and become more aware of its costs and their relationship with levels of service.

Restructuring is an important method being adopted by many nations. It refers to changing the way the various activities relate to one another. It might involve restructuring on the basis of regions or on the basis of business sectors: for example, services between cities. Specifically, it could involve making regional managers responsible for selling their services rather than this being done by a central unit. The key aspect of restructuring is that it begins the process of unbundling. This is about separating out costs and revenues associated with different services. It is a move away from averaging out costs. It therefore makes it more clear which costs are associated with individual train services.

How does this increase efficiency? When a public organization moves into the private sector, all revenues and costs must be clear, otherwise it is difficult to make commercial decisions, such as when to close a service. Under public ownership many of the costs are shared out among different services in an arbitrary manner. The problem with this is that no one knows how the public funds are being used and whether the level of subsidies should be increased, reduced or eliminated. Restructuring was implemented in British Rail in 1982. Five business sectors were formed, each responsible for the costs and revenues of its own services. Staff and assets were made specific to each business, although the responsibility for operating the services was left to a larger body. This can be seen as an effort to increase efficiency as it makes the lines of managerial control clearer.

Franchising goes one step further from restructuring in that it is a method which introduces a competitive process. It may be used with or without outright privatization. It introduces competition not *in* the market, which would be impossible because of the presence of subsidy and natural monopoly in the railways industry, but competition *for* the market. One way to think about franchising is that it is about what happens before the market exchanges begin. It refers to the selling of the right to supply a service where revenues will be generated. The idea is executed through the granting of a franchise to the most appropriate bidder. The appropriate bidder is the one which meets the criteria set down by the government or by a regulatory agent. The criteria might include the lowest use of public subsidies, the lowest expected prices, the number of services which will be run in addition to the minimum required, or the best quality of service.

Franchising retains the monopoly nature of services, in that there is no competition within the service as defined, so cost gains can be retained. The activity generates competition for the monopoly as an alternative way of achieving cost reductions. It is a suitable method of introducing competition when monopoly is the best market structure for the provision of the service. The franchise can take different forms and the franchise type chosen should reflect the market conditions. How do consumers benefit? Depending on the specifications, if prices are important, they might face lower prices. If subsidy is important, they at least have the knowledge that their tax is being reduced and it is being used more effectively, as franchising encourages cost effectiveness. The problem with this approach is that franchising takes a lot of resources to set up. Moreover, for there to be effective competition, there must be more than one bidder and there must be some financial incentive, such as profit, for the potential operator. The UK reforms involve franchising and privatization.

Approaches to increase efficiency through privatization

This approach involves a change of ownership. This could take two forms: either retain the monopoly structure and use regulation to ensure that consumers are not exploited through higher prices or reduced services; or change the structure of the industry in order to promote competition. The former approach has been adopted by New Zealand and Sweden. It is often referred to as privatization on a vertically integrated basis, since there is no division between the rail operations and the ownership of the track. Alternatively, the industry structure could be broken up and a franchising process put in place, as is the case in the UK. This might involve splitting the natural monopoly assets (the track) from the non-natural monopoly activities (rail operations). The latter are then made up into separate companies which bid to run the services, and they pay the natural monopoly company for using the infrastructure. A regulatory body would be required to ensure that the payments were not too high and were related to costs.

The disadvantage with this approach is that privatization plus restructuring, plus franchising, plus regulation, involves many transaction and set-up costs. Transaction costs, discussed in Chapter 2, refer to the costs involved in making an exchange: for example, search and negotiation costs. In terms of the railways, the new market structure would mean that the train operators would have to negotiate access charges to use the tracks. The set-up costs are those used in setting up the regulator and the conditions for competition, overseeing the charges and making sure that the new train operators provide a good service.

Approaches to encourage the expansion of railways

Many western European nations have adopted expansionist policies towards their railways. There are a number of ways in which expansion can be supported and achieved, such as increasing railway investment levels, either by greater public contributions or by getting the private sector to fund specific programmes.

The setting up of a national policy framework, which has clear objectives and plans for a national transport strategy, is one way of ensuring the expansion of the railways. This framework can be reinforced with regional and local policy frameworks which can be set up with public authorities and coordinated with development and land-use planning. Developing different ways of assessing the value of railways in terms of the economy, the environment and other transport modes is an important part of demonstrating the benefits of promoting the railways. Finally, setting up specific programmes for rail development and ensuring greater integration of the railways with buses, trams and metros can bring about a better and bigger railway system.

Institutional arrangements

The European Commission is calling for an administrative split between rail infrastructure and operations. This means that it would like to see nations trying to provide separate profit and cost accounts for these two activities. The reasoning behind this is that it makes it much clearer what the size of the subsidies are, and for what purposes they are being used. In addition, the Commission wishes to see the opening up of the infrastructure assets. What this means, in theory, is that any train operator would be able to use the rail tracks. It is unlikely that this wish will be met in the near future.

Q1 The role of government in railway industries is currently undergoing change. What factors have led to the need to change, and what types of change are required?

Q2 Railways have important economic features which justify government intervention. How strong do you think the case is for public ownership?

Q3 Privatization of the railway industry is one approach seen as offering solutions to the problems faced by governments and the railway companies. There is a great difference, in practice, between privatization of the railways and privatization of, for example, the electricity industry. Discuss what you think these differences might involve.

Q4 How do the following increase the efficiency of a publicly owned railway industry: the adoption of commercial practices; restructuring; unbundling; and franchising?

The objectives of the case studies chosen are to contrast different approaches to rail deregulation and to illustrate the role both governments and markets have played in facilitating these changes.

Case study The UK: British Rail (BR)

Objectives

To privatize or partly privatize BR in order to improve services by increasing the level of competition, and to reduce the subsidy support.

Objectives for the EU

The principal aims are to strengthen the accountability of railway managements and achieve a level playing field for investment decisions with road.

New approaches

The privatization of BR has many elements of change to it and will be discussed in relation to the following:

- Approaches to increase efficiency through privatization.
- Approaches to maintain the size of the railway system.

The background

BR has been subject to extensive deregulation for at least a decade, but now the government is privatizing it. There are a number of aspects to this approach. However, space prevents a comprehensive discussion, so this case study concentrates on the role of franchising. The plans are contained in a series of government papers: the 1992 White Paper, 'New opportunities for railways' (Cmnd. 2012), set out the policy reforms, while the Railways Act 1993 laid down the duties of the regulator, which include, in the short run, preparing the industry for privatization.

Approaches to increase efficiency through privatization

The approach adopted to increase efficiency involves splitting the industry into different operations and companies, each of which will be sold or franchised in the privatization process. It has four characteristics: the infrastructure ownership and operation are separated from train operations; infrastructure assets are vested in Railtrack; passenger rail services are supplied primarily through a franchising process; franchised passenger rail service companies have to pay Railtrack access charges (payment for using the tracks). Finally, the subsidy payment from the government will be injected through the franchising process. This means that when rail passenger companies prepare to bid for a franchise to supply passenger rail services, their bid will comprise the total costs, which will include Railtrack charges less the expected passenger revenue. If their costs exceed revenue, then the government will pay the difference to them in the form of a grant.

The changes in the passenger rail services after the 1993 Act are shown in Figure 8.1. There are four key players. The aim of the Office of the Rail Regulator

(ORR) is to promote and protect the public interest. Its running costs are planned to reach £7 million in 1996/97. The Office of Passenger Rail Franchising (OPRAF) is responsible for, among other things, giving out the franchises. The ORR also has a relationship with Railtrack, overseeing that track access is given and that appropriate charges are made. OPRAF has a relationship with the train operators, by deciding who receives the franchises. Each franchise gives details of service obligations, prices and how much grant the franchisee will be paid. Its running cost plans for 1996/97 are £4 million. The regulator will also allow independent operators to gain access and compete with franchised operators: these are the open access passenger operations.

What does the franchising process mean? In attempting to maximize the amount of competition, the natural monopoly element, rail infrastructure, is separated out, and then the competition process is meant to take place in the trains services side of the industry. The point is that there is little or no price competition in train services because prices are more or less fixed, so the competitive element takes place for the market. What is actually being auctioned is the minimum subsidy, which reveals the level of subsidy associated with individual services. In theory, the costing out of a bundle of services should improve. There will be competition among potential operators, which will raise productivity and improve the quality of service. Also, franchising means that, where losses occur, these will be revealed, and this in turn means that the pattern of financing loss-making services will become more rational. Previously, there was less clarity and accountability in how these resources were used.

The effectiveness of franchising rests on three conditions: the bidding must be competitive; track charges must be pitched at the appropriate level to encourage potential bidders; and there must be close monitoring of the contract (the

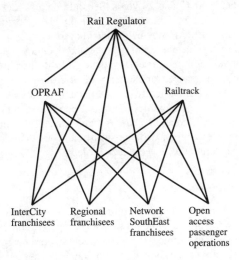

Source: Harrison (1993).

Figure 8.1 Changes in BR's passenger service

franchise). In the first case, bidding has been slow and in some instances a distinct lack of interest has been shown. So far, there have been few instances of collusive bidding. The problem with the second condition is that setting up competition and ensuring that it will be effective is contingent on the track access conditions and charges. If track charges are set too low, there may be too many operators and overcapacity. Set too high and companies may lack incentives to undertake investment.

Approaches to maintain the size of the railway system

The railway is undergoing a process of being sold to, and operated by, private companies. Railtrack, responsible for the infrastructure, is planned to be privatized. There are clearly incentives for the railway to become a more efficient system, but will this occur at the cost of a reduction in the size of the industry? What approaches have been installed to ensure that the system is maintained? The functions of OPRAF relevant to this question are: to promote railway investment; to form a view on closures; and to provide support for loss-making rail services. The relevant objectives are to secure an overall improvement in the quality of railway services. There are clearly safeguards in place to ensure the maintenance of the railway, but there are some indications that these incentives may not be strong enough to maintain the system alone.

There are three possible areas of weakness. First, the length of franchise periods will be around seven years. It can be argued that this is an insufficient time for franchised companies to undertake necessary new investments, and there is no guarantee that they will be able to renew the franchise after the seven years are up. It terms of investment in new trains, it would be more appropriate to award franchises for between 15 and 20 years. Second, the loss-making services will be supported by OPRAF, but this will depend on grants being available, in any specific year. Also, OPRAF may be inclined not to set the service levels very high for a given contract, so as not to put off potential operators. The problem with this is that as the private companies seek to make a profit, there may be a tendency to reduce the quality of service: for example, by offering fewer train services. Third, investment in the rail infrastructure is undertaken by Railtrack. No provisions have been made for how investment decisions will be made and how the current level of investment may be increased. There is some concern that the revenue Railtrack will make from user charges will be insufficient to maintain the infrastructure assets, improve quality and carry out new projects.

Old arrangements

The old model was run on a single command structure: that is, directions came from the top down. It was a public monopoly and it was operated on a vertically integrated basis. Grants were paid from central government to core operating businesses, but there was limited knowledge about how individual services performed.

New arrangements

The new arrangements involve a restructuring of the industry into smaller units. It is a rule-based system in which different organizations have contractual obligations to each other. More information will be revealed in the franchising process: in particular, which services are chronic loss-makers. The government will enforce standards of service and see that the public service obligation is met.

Change of relationships

Prior to privatization, BR was a monolithically structured industry, tied to the public finance system and open to ministerial intervention, and although there was some scope or incentives to respond to customer needs, political considerations played a part in commercial decisions. The nature of relationships between state and industry have changed. Activities have been broken down and each organization now has a relationship with the others according to what its objectives are. It is an unusual privatization in that two bodies, Railtrack and BR operations, will remain in the public sector in the near future.

The government will still play an active role in setting objectives and budgets and in paying subsidies. It will have a role in monitoring the functions of both the ORR and OPRAF, and overseeing the rules in which the contractual obligations are made. But the government will not be as directly involved with the industry, as relationships will be conducted by more government-independent organizations.

Q5 Explain the structural changes which have occurred in BR since 1993. What is the economic rationale for using franchising in the railway industry?

Q6 Although safeguards have been introduced to ensure that the quality of services will not fall under privatization, in what ways do you think that these new approaches will undermine the role of railways in the economy?

Case study The Netherlands: The Netherlands Railways (NS)

Objectives

The government's objectives are to develop a more commercial approach towards passenger services, and the industry aims to make the necessary preparations to meet those objectives.

Objectives for the EU

The principal aims are to strengthen accountability of railway managements and achieve a level playing field for investment decisions with roads.

New approaches

The Dutch railway industry has been going for over 150 years. In 1989 a combination of increases in demand for train services and increasing congestion in cities forced the government and the industry to rethink their plans for the future, and the approaches adopted will be discussed in relation to the following:

- Approaches to increase efficiency without privatization.
- Approaches to expand the railway system.

The background

The Dutch railways, NS (Nederlandse Spoorwegen), became a limited liability company in 1938. Although it is a commercial company, all its shares are held by the state. The company is headed by a board of directors who are appointed by trustees. These trustees are in turn appointed by the Minister of Transport. The relationship between industry and government is that the government gives instructions, but it has no direct involvement in the running of the railways. Financially, the industry relies heavily on the government. Every two years the government and industry enter into a contract whereby the railway subsidy is fixed in advance. Before the plans in 1989, the industry generated a total income of £1 billion; some £0.4 billion, just under half, was in subsidies. Total expenditure was £0.9 billion, operating profit was £86 million and there was a net profit of £22 million. The approaches developed in this case study contrast with the UK because they do not involve privatization and are principally aimed at improving arrangements within the industry. The Dutch are very environmentally conscious. They are a nation with much to lose from global warming because so much of their land lies below sea level. The government has agreed with NS a substantial expansion in rail passenger services throughout the Netherlands, which will include new and expanded lines funded by the government as part of its policy on the environment.

Approaches to increase efficiency without privatization

The approach adopted to improve efficiency in the railway industry is contained in a five-year commercial contract set up between the government and the industry. The idea is to give NS management autonomy and financial independence, which will allow it to decide its own investment and price levels. Three specific measures have been introduced to improve the efficiency of the Dutch railways, and this case study describes the reforms to date. The measures are restructuring, the introduction of competitive tendering and rationalization. The restructuring of the industry is seen as a necessary means of preparing for privatization. It involves the separating out of individual business operations. This approach was adopted following the work of the Wijffells Committee, which looked at the relationship between industry and government. Its suggestions included the separation of freight and passenger services and the direct funding of infrastructure by the government. The industry responded by producing 'Tracks towards 1996', a strategy document which aims to turn the railways into an independent, commercially focused business.

Restructuring means that two distinct groups will be formed, task organizations and commercial business units. The former will be in charge of the natural monopoly element, infrastructure, with subdivisions being in charge of traffic control, infrastructure management and Railned. The latter will decide what is needed in terms of tracks. Passenger services do not have to pay track charges. The task organizations will work within a budget of £1.5 billion (1995 prices), will stay in the public sector, will perform the 'public services' and will be directly funded by the government. The company is to own all its own assets (unlike BR). The industry has made substantial progress in meeting these plans, by creating self-standing companies and separating out the non-commercial units.

Competitive tendering has been introduced as a method of improving efficiency. It works by allowing the newly formed passenger business units and the non-commercial task organizations to shop around for services at the best price, and this will include purchasing from the private sector. Business managers buy from supply services, but these prices are regulated in the sense that they have to be lowered by a certain amount each year. There are no guarantees that the old NS service providers will obtain the contracts. The aim is to use competitive tendering in order to make the railway more cost effective. The non-commercial (task) organizations too will be able to put more than 25 per cent of their maintenance work out to tender. The idea is that this should reduce maintenance costs.

The third efficiency measure is rationalization. This is about streamlining the industry. The plans are to increase industry productivity by reducing its 28000 workforce by 4800. The target level of 23200 by 1998, if achieved, will save NS about 450 million guilders (£1 = 3.40 guilders). Other cost reduction objectives have been set: for example, a target to reduce infrastructure costs by 20 per cent. This will be done by the tendering process and by better cost control. The important point is that the industry has set up these targets in response to the government's plans to eliminate the subsidy by 1998; at present it is 400 million guilders a year.

There have been problems of implementation with this contract: essentially, the government has got cold feet. The details of the contract, which took two years to negotiate, proposed the transfer of full commercial powers to the railway. This was deemed a necessary move as the railway's operating subsidy for passenger services is scheduled to be phased out during the next five years. The industry plans were contingent on the commercial businesses gaining commercial freedom and increasing passenger fares. Political factors have intervened in these hopes. In 1996 the government forbade any fare increases up to the year 2000. The logical response of the industry was that it would have to make service closures. Ministers have intervened and decided that the industry is not to have its commercial freedom as agreed. NS will only be allowed to make reductions through shortening the length of its trains. Remember that this is against a background where the annual subsidy is to be reduced and eliminated by the year 2000.

This is an example of where political concerns interfere with economic decisions. What the government wants is a reduction in the public subsidy, but without dramatic service closures; at the same time, the industry feels it can only achieve this by being a fully independent and commercial operation. This setback has reduced the prospects of privatization because the industry will be unable to produce a profitable track record.

Approaches to expand the railway system

Rail 21 is a long-term investment strategy presented by the industry in response to the government's environmental and congestion concerns. In 2005 the number of passenger kilometres is planned to be 18 billion compared with 9 billion in 1987. It has been realized that traffic demands will increase by up to 100 per cent over the next two decades. In the absence of large increases in investment, the railway's share of traffic would decline, thereby increasing congestion and pollution. The industry has proposed improvements to the existing services and infrastructure, and offered a strong set of arguments for an increase in the overall level of investment. It plans extensive investment, about £100 million more, to be spent per annum over the next two decades on infrastructure and operations. The NS has strengthened its arguments by demonstrating the potential environmental benefits to be had with this expansion. No allowance is to be made for increasing the subsidy levels in real terms. In practice, NS has in the past maintained a policy of keeping passenger fare increases below the rate of inflation, thereby making rail travel a relatively cheap way to travel. The commercial contract would give the industry the opportunity to increase prices where it sees fit.

These plans would appear optimistic, and in relation to the restructuring more work needs to be done. Passenger Services has an annual turnover of 2.3 billion guilders, about 50 per cent of total turnover, but it had only a 4 per cent return on investment in 1994, compared with an earlier target of 10 per cent. It is not clear at present how the industry can fulfil its ambitious investment plans without either greater levels of support from the government, or the government granting greater commercial and financial freedom to the industry.

Old arrangements

The old NS structure was based on central decision making, with vertical lines of communication from the top. Bureaucratic problems meant that the organization was unable to meet changing customer needs, there was little flexibility and this prevented productivity improvements being made. There was no unbundling of costs, resources and services.

New arrangements

The new arrangements are about breaking up a monolithic structure, fine-tuning finances and reducing costs. Rail transport has become part of a national policy framework. Specific programmes exist for national and regional line development. The government has agreed with NS to expand its network, with new lines being funded by government as part of its policy on the environment. The government initiated the process of commercialization by establishing that the subsidy was to be eliminated; NS responded by breaking down its operations in preparation for management autonomy and financial independence, and critically deciding what aspects no longer needed replacing.

Change of relationships

Prior to reorganization, the government had a direct involvement in the commercial, financial and managerial decisions of NS. The railway operated within strict government guidelines. With the establishment of the five-year commercial contract, the nature of this relationship was supposed to change. As we have seen, government rejection of the contents of this contract has dealt a blow to the industry and possibly upset the balance of relationships between the board and government.

Q7 How is economic efficiency increased through separating business units into self-financing and government-financed ones?
Q8 Why is commercial freedom, as agreed between the government and the industry, seen by the latter as paramount to achieving its goals?

Discussion

This section analyses the strengths and weaknesses of each approach adopted in terms of increasing efficiency and meeting other objectives, and contrasts the two approaches adopted. In the case of the UK, considerable innovation has been shown in terms of maximizing the degree of competition. This has been done by separating out the natural monopoly element, infrastructure, and then promoting competition for the market rather than in the market. In the first instance, the approach adopted, franchising, is a logical one given the conditions in the railway industry. This process ensures that there is competition for the bundle of services defined, through auctioning the minimum subsidy. It means that the natural monopoly is retained and that cost advantages are kept. On the positive side, this approach has the potential to produce benefits in terms of better management, improved productivity and reduced costs. However, effective competition is contingent on the nature of the franchises, among other things.

The length of the franchises will be around seven years. This seems a little short, given that the government hopes that private companies will undertake much needed investment. The private companies will clearly rely on price increases, but these have now been limited by OPRAF to the rate of inflation until the year 1999. With both these restrictions, it is difficult to see where the financial incentives will be. A better solution might be to have longer franchises with more pricing freedom on services which compete directly with other transport modes. It is easy to see how private companies may be forced to provide only the minimum services required in the franchise and to press for service closures.

Alternatively, the government could improve the revenue-earning prospects of

161

the companies by making car use more expensive and hence encouraging a shift of traffic to passenger services. Much depends on Railtrack's charges. These have to be pitched at a level which encourages private operators, but not to the extent that open access (non-franchised operators) can cream-skim the market. Pitched too high, as they were claimed to be in 1995, they may have dampened potential interest. The final consideration is that the restructuring of the industry is complex and involves high transaction and development costs. There have been many consultancy reports, lawyers' fees and set-up costs involved with the two bodies, ORR and OPRAF, relative to the size of the operations. It is not clear that these costs will necessarily be exceeded by the benefits.

The Dutch approach has been less concerned with ownership and it is taking the whole process at a much slower pace. This is a strength. The other strength is in the objectives set and, in particular, the aim to expand the industry. This directly recognizes the environmental externality. The approach taken to increase efficiency is through restructuring, in which the industry has made significant progress. Clearly, although financial independence is seen as an industry requirement, political concerns are preventing the industry making further inroads on its agreed plans – in particular, reducing costs. This is a prerequisite for any real deregulation. Another problem is that the targets set were too ambitious: one cannot expect to eliminate a relatively large public subsidy in four years.

Comparing the two approaches, the UK has gone for privatization and restructuring for competition, with pressure on bidders to use the least amount of subsidy. The Dutch have adopted restructuring by dividing up the commercial and non-commercial units, but have used a blanket subsidy reduction threat to bring about cost savings. The UK government would have benefited from taking a longer time over the restructuring process, particularly the franchise specifications, from being less concerned with ownership and from building a real commitment to expansion in the proposed mechanism. The Dutch government would have benefited from agreeing a contract which it was fully committed to; instead, it has broken the flow of progress that the industry was making, by not allowing full commercial freedom. Otherwise this could have been a very sensible, realistic and noble set of reforms.

Further reading

Introductory level

Begg, D., Fischer, S. and Dornbusch, R. (1994) *Economics*, 4th edn, Maidenhead: McGraw-Hill, ch. 18.

Griffiths, A. and Wall, S. (eds) (1995) *Applied Economics: An Introductory Course*, 6th edn, Harlow: Longman, ch. 11.

Le Grand, J., Propper, C. and Robinson, R. (1992) *The Economics of Social Problems*, 3rd edn, Basingstoke: Macmillan, ch. 7.

Sloman, J. (1996) *Economics*, 2nd edn, Hemel Hempstead: Harvester Wheatsheaf, ch. 11.

Intermediate level

Bailey, S. (1995) *Public Sector Economics: Theory, Policy and Practice*, Basingstoke: Macmillan, ch. 13.

DeSerpa, A. (1988) *Microeconomic Theory: Issues and Applications*, 2nd edn, Boston, MA: Allyn and Bacon, ch. 11.

Griffiths, A. and Wall, S. (1996) *Intermediate Microeconomics: Theory and Applications*, Harlow: Longman, chs 4 and 7.

Other sources

Centre for the Study of Regulated Industries (CRI) (1993) 'Franchising network services – regulation in post, rail and water', London: Chartered Institute of Public Finance and Accountancy.

Department of Transport (1992) 'New opportunities for the railways', HMSO, Cmnd. 2012.

Department of Transport (1995) 'The government's expenditure plans for transport, 1994–95 to 1996–97', HMSO, Cmnd. 2506.

Duff, L. (1987) 'Policies and performances of the UK nationalised industries', unpublished thesis, UMIST, Manchester, ch. 5.

Glaister, S. and Travers, T. (1993) *New Directions for British Railways? The Political Economy of Privatisation and Regulation*, London: Institute of Economic Affairs.

Harman, R. (1993) 'Railway privatisation: does it bring new opportunities?', *Public Money and Management*, January/March.

Harrison, A. (ed.) (1993) *From Hierarchy to Contract*, Newbury: Policy Journals. *Social Trends* (1996) HMSO, ch. 12, series 26.

'Utility regulation: challenge and response' (1995) Institute of Economic Affairs, Readings, no. 42.

'NS seeks a guilder in every corner', *International Railway Journal (IRJ)*, January, 1995.

'NS sets ambitious cost-cutting targets', *IRJ*, February, 1995.

'Jury still out on rail privatisation', *IRJ*, March, 1995.

'Privatisation means higher subsidies', *IRJ*, November, 1995.

'The Privatisers', *IRJ*, November, 1995.

'NS fails to win commercial freedom', *IRJ*, February, 1996.

Ison, S. (1995) 'Rail privatisation', *British Economy Survey*, vol. 24, no. 2.

'UK passenger sell-off edges closer', *Passenger Railway*, May/June, 1995.

Swift, J. (1995) 'Regulatory relationships between key players in the restructured rail industry', in *Utility Regulation*, London: Institute of Economic Affairs, ch. 5.

'Travelling leaner: Dutch and British transport policy compared', Transport 2000, 1992.

Violland, M. (1996) 'Whither railways?', *OECD Observer*, February/March.

Waller, P. (1990) 'Towards 2000 in the Netherlands', *Modern Railways*, April.

Chapter 9

Electricity

> Key words used: natural monopoly, privatization, universal service obligation, structural change

This chapter is about an important sector of the energy industry, the electricity industry. When we think of electricity, most of us recall images of grid lines, complicated account bills and, in the UK, news headings about mergers between regional electricity companies. This is a remarkable industry; it affects the lives of all of us, it is a central part of the EU's plan for an internal market in energy, and it has had a long association with government. This is an interesting and unique area in which to study new directions in public policy; it is different from other areas presented in this book because it is principally a trading organization which has been publicly owned, but recent changes have brought about the need for deregulation and privatization in many western European countries. Economic analysis provides a framework from which it is possible to see how the market fails to give an efficient allocation of resources. Economics has a valuable role in that it suggests how governments can work with markets in ways to overcome some of the resource, environmental and international pressures which this industry currently faces.

Background to the problem

Governments in all western economies have been involved with their energy industries; the form of this involvement has varied, but the level of involvement has typically been significant. France, Greece, Ireland, Italy and Portugal have outright nationalized electricity sectors, with the state holding the monopoly on generation, transport and distribution. Here the sectors are marked by the strong influence of the state on energy policy, price setting and distribution. In Germany, while a formal state monopoly does not exist, the state controls significant stakes in the equity of the private utilities and the national market is inaccessible to new competitors. The UK is unique in that it has privatized the electricity supply industry, which is now regulated.

There are two broad sources of change which explain why there has been a need to alter the role of government in electricity markets. There have been changes within electricity markets and changes in the rationale for government. Western European electricity markets currently face a number of challenges. The eastern European countries, having broken with command economy principles, need western companies to invest in new plants as they begin to modernize their industries. There are likely to be large investment opportunities. Second, internationalization means that, as western countries find their domestic markets saturated, they will be increasingly seeking new opportunities elsewhere. For both these reasons, many European electricity companies will be seeking to help develop these markets, and it is likely that they will require a different and more flexible type of arrangement with their respective governments than exists at present.

Costs play an important role in electricity markets. Consumers and nations alike wish to see lower electricity tariffs. Figure 9.1 shows that great differences in industrial and commercial electricity prices exist across nations. This reflects diversity in practices, regulation and subsidy. In Germany, industrial and commercial users face electricity prices which are up to 30 per cent above those of its competitors. This suggests that there is scope for profitable trading.

Costs are also an important aspect in terms of competing with other trading blocs. In European countries, energy costs are 30 per cent above those in the USA. The problem with this is that changes in energy costs feed back into the costs for other industries. There are wider advantages, therefore, of keeping energy costs as low as possible. One way to put pressure on costs is to increase

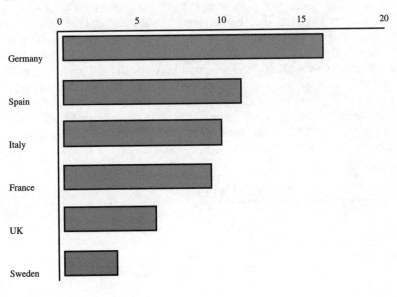

Source: *The Economist*, June 1995.

Figure 9.1 Electricity prices: international comparison of industrial and commercial electricity prices, April 1995 (cents/kWh)

the level of competition and this may be encouraged through deregulation policies.

Electricity markets face growing concerns about environmental damage from electricity generation. This is an example of a negative environment externality, and it provides a very strong case for governments to intervene in electricity markets. Power stations are one of the main causes of air pollution in Europe. They emit relatively large quantities of carbon dioxide, nitrogen oxide and sulphur dioxide. Table 9.1 shows the proportion of carbon dioxide produced in electricity. A number of measures have been used to curb this pollution, but many governments are reluctant to impose regulations without neighbouring countries doing the same. The European Commission is keen to progress the idea of the EU-wide carbon tax, but so far the proposals have been stalled because of worries about the impact on international competitiveness.

Deregulation is also driven by the European Commission's wish to see a single European market, beginning with the creation of an internal market in energy. What this means is that countries would be able to trade and supply electricity across national borders. Consumers would be able to choose their electricity supplier. A number of directives have been introduced aimed at liberalizing electricity markets. The Commission believes that there are immense economic benefits to be had from an internal market in electricity, in terms of lower prices and ability to compete with other trading blocs. The implication of these directives is that government intervention in electricity markets will be as much influenced by national objectives as by developments at EU level.

The other broad area that has created a need for change is the role of governments. The enthusiasm in most industrialized countries for public ownership has waned. There have been difficulties with governments intervening in electricity markets, and a recognition that the old indicative planning from governments in energy markets, which characterized the middle part of the twentieth century, was full of flaws. We are all too familiar with the claims that there has been too much ministerial interference in the operations of the industry. Besides this, the traditional arguments for government intervention have declined in importance. The natural monopoly argument has now weakened:

Table 9.1 Air pollutants, by source, 1993 (%)

UK	Carbon dioxide	Carbon monoxide	Sulphur dioxide	Nitrogen oxides
Road transport	20	91	2	49
Electricity supply	31	1	66	24
Domestic	16	5	4	3
Other	34	4	29	24
All air pollutants (= 100%) (million tonnes)	151.0	5.6	3.2	2.4

Source: Social Trends (1996).

changes in technology have favoured smaller units, where the costs have lowered, and small natural gas combined cycle units now operate at relatively lower cost levels. Also, the costs of renewable technologies in wind, hydro and solar are falling. The implication is that private ownership, with governments regulating the natural monopoly elements of electricity, is a preferable form of control to the public ownership model.

In summary, there are two broad forces for change: changes in electricity markets and the changing rationale for government intervention. Electricity markets face new challenges abroad and at home. There are some doubts as to whether the old public ownership model can offer the flexibility and political detachment required for this industry to reach its potential. At the same time, there is a new rationale for governments, and the traditional arguments of social equity and natural monopoly have been overshadowed by concerns about the environment.

Current system of allocation

The electricity industry can be divided into four types of activity – generation, transmission, distribution and supply – and these will be described in relation to the UK situation. Generation involves power stations, which are powered by steam turbines, which in turn can be powered by coal, nuclear power, oil or gas turbines. Transmission is where electricity is dispatched along high-voltage lines around the country. Distribution involves putting the electricity into lower voltages for consumers. Part of the distribution system are the electricity lines we see on our streets, and there are also underground cables. The final activity is supply or the retailing of electricity, and this involves billing and collecting payment from customers.

The market

A market allocation in electricity supply needs to be considered in relation to the specific economic features that electricity markets possess, which give rise to market failure. Market failures were discussed in Chapter 2, and in relation to electricity they are as follows:

- The presence of externalities.
- The presence of market imperfections.
- The presence of inequalities.

The presence of externalities

These arise from a number of sources. There is a negative environmental externality in electricity generation. Mentioned in the first section, carbon dioxide and sulphur dioxide are two principal pollutants which contribute to acid rain, eye and skin irritations, and damage to plant life. Markets fail to take full account of the associated environmental effects. This occurs because, as we saw in Chapter 2, air is a common property resource and there are opportunities to free ride. Private solutions are very limited. Bargaining is unlikely because there are a large number of generators and affected parties. In the case of the particular pollutants which have global impacts, such as global warming, property rights are impossible to define. A free market in electricity is likely to lead to an inefficient allocation of resources.

Externalities arise from the spill-over effects of research and development (R & D). Again the problem is getting the market to recognize the wider benefits of R & D to society. There is a need for R & D in a number of areas, including renewable energy sources, more environmentally friendly production and consumption, and better use of energy resources (energy efficiency). The problem is that a private electricity company may undertake R & D, particularly in potentially commercial areas, but it may need specific incentives to research in those areas which benefit one and all.

An example of a positive externality in electricity is the security of supply concept. This refers to the benefits of having continuous and secure supplies of electricity to meet the expected demands of the economy in the foreseeable future. In a free market there is no such guarantee: such wider benefits may be overlooked by a private company. Some have claimed that security of supply could be achieved if free markets were able to diversify into other energy sources, but the problem with this is that it may require a large proportion of imports, and if these are imported from unstable economies, it could lead to exploitation.

Short-termism is said to be a failure of the market. This is where the interests of future generations are neglected. For example, electricity can be generated from burning fossil fuels, and a private company may make use of these inputs with little regard to the amount of supplies left for future generations. If the sources of non-renewable fuels are declining, this needs to be taken into account. In the absence of incentives, there is likely to be an inefficiency in the production and consumption of electricity.

The presence of market imperfections

In the electricity industry, these arise from market structure imperfections and, in particular, the presence of natural monopoly. This is where the average production costs fall over the whole area of market demand, and perfect competition is neither feasible nor desirable. A natural monopoly with a single supplier is then in a position to make excessive profits. By dividing the electricity industry into stages of activity, it can be demonstrated that natural monopoly does not necessarily apply across all activities: for example, generation and supply are naturally competitive activities. However, it has been argued that natural monopoly exists in the distribution and transmission of electricity, since it would be too expensive to build duplicate networks. The presence and significance of natural monopoly in electricity, compared to natural monopoly in, for example, the computer industry, is that it is inefficient from society's point of view to allow companies to exploit consumers through high prices in a fundamentally necessary service. It is likely that these considerations would not necessarily be taken into account by a private company.

As we saw from the first section, the enthusiasm for this argument has waned. The focus of regulation is now more towards separating out those aspects of the industry which do, and those which do not, contain natural monopoly. Regulation is then aimed at protecting the consumer in the former and encouraging competition in the latter.

The presence of inequalities

These are said to arise because electricity has special properties in relation to modern living. The access to electricity supply allows people to participate in society. If you did not have a warm home or lighting, your quality of life would be very low. In a free market, a private company may not extend the electricity lines to your home if the additional costs outweigh the revenues. The company would also be able to charge consumers different prices for the same service. Given that most governments believe that energy is something which benefits one and all, and that no economic sector can function without it, this situation would be unfair. Formally, this is referred to as the universal service obligation. There is a counter argument to these points: electricity has substitutes like gas, coal and oil, and therefore the presence of these make electricity less unique. Whether governments should intervene in electricity markets to use them as an instrument of social equity appears to depend on the stance of the government. The case studies illustrate this idea.

Government objectives

We need to state what aims and objectives governments are likely to pursue in relation to electricity markets. This is an important aspect of public policy reforms because, when objectives change, this implies that different approaches should be adopted:

- Economic efficiency objectives.
- Administrative efficiency objectives.
- Equity objectives.

Economic efficiency objectives

An example of a production efficiency objective is where electricity is supplied at the lowest possible cost per unit for a given level of output. Production efficiency objectives for the UK nationalized industries became the more important concern in the late 1970s. For example, the electricity industry was

169

given a target of reducing its unit costs over a three-year period. Allocation efficiency objectives in the electricity industry might include efforts to make the final price reflect the marginal costs of production. This was one of the objectives for the UK nationalized industries, contained in the 1967 White Paper. The industries were encouraged to set prices equal to marginal costs of supply. In practice, this was very difficult to achieve, as confirmed by the NEDO Report of 1977, which stated that few industries operated marginal cost-pricing principles. The electricity industry operates a national network which involves a large proportion of fixed costs and, under these conditions, it is very difficult to identify the marginal cost of supply.

Administrative efficiency objectives

These refer to the relative expense of implementing different policy approaches. Specifically, these objectives may focus on such aspects as improvements in the information-collecting systems, the levels of accountability and the nature of the relationships within the industry, and with government. The latter was an important aspect of electricity under UK nationalization. Relationships had at times been strained between the government and industry. The problem with poor relations is that it affects the quality of information disclosed, the levels of accountability and ultimately the quality of the decisions made. Too much and inappropriate ministerial interference was a common criticism made about the UK government and how it handled the nationalized industries.

Equity objectives

An example of an equity objective in electricity supply is to ensure that all reasonable demands for electricity are satisfied. Further examples are ensuring that consumers are charged the same price for the same service, if they live in the same area, and ensuring that the same quality of service is provided to one and all.

Government intervention

We have now described the types of objective a government may pursue, and the special properties of electricity. We now need to ask what types of intervention can be used, and these can be viewed as follows:

- Provision.
- Regulation.
- Taxes and subsidies.

Provision

This can take the form of a public monopoly. This has been the most common form of government intervention in Europe. Public ownership or nationalization means that governments can, in theory, control monopoly abuses and meet equity concerns. Governments have an economic role to ensure that the objectives of the industry are in place – for example, that guidelines are set on pricing and investment – and that the industry is made accountable to government. There are problems with public ownership. In particular, it can be argued that the incentives for efficiency and innovation are relatively weak, and there are lots of incentives for governments to interfere with commercial decisions. With the first point, in the absence of cost-reduction targets, the monopoly may not be producing at the lowest possible cost. Also, in segments of the market where there is little competition, consumers may face price increases which are not related to costs, and quality of service may not be given as much attention as in a private and competitively structured market. Ideally, government should intervene to instruct the industry to behave efficiently. This occurred in the UK when the government set cost-reduction targets. But in practice, problems emerged because there were few incentives incorporated into the setting of these targets and there was no penalty for their non-achievement. In other words, controls were present, but they were not particularly effective.

Regulation

An alternative to nationalization is where governments regulate private monopolies. Regulation is required to prevent monopoly abuses, especially in areas where competition may be restricted, and to meet equity considerations. Regulation to bring about economic efficiency might include setting targets to control the monopolist's profit or prices. This could be undertaken by determining reasonable rates of return or by setting price-increase limits. Rate of return regulation restricts the company's profits to a defined proportion of its capital. This is a method favoured in the USA, but there have been problems. Rate of return regulation encouraged companies to overuse capital, so regulators became involved in defining what capital could and could not be included. This approach has incurred large litigation costs. Recently, there has been a move in the USA towards a more deregulated form of control.

Direct control of prices is a form of regulation which allows the monopolist to make profits, but only by reducing its costs. The idea is that the monopolist will seek out the least-cost inputs. In practice, regulation can take the form of price caps. These act by putting a limit on annual price increases in relation to the change in overall prices and how much the regulator thinks costs can be reduced. This approach can be relatively cheap and easy to implement. The drawback is that a monopolist may reduce costs so much that the quality of service falls, and consumers are unable to do much about this because of the lack of alternative suppliers.

In addition to economic regulation, governments can have a regulatory role in ensuring that specific standards are met in relation to things like safety, installation and health. Governments can also regulate by giving incentives to direct the level and types of R & D activity.

Taxes and subsidies

These are both used in the electricity industry. Under public ownership there are implicit subsidies: that is, governments can allow cross-subsidies to be used to ensure that equity concerns are met. Governments can also provide capital subsidies in the form of cheap loans in order to ensure that electricity is provided at an affordable price. In France the industry is heavily subsidized by the government. Capital loans at cheap rates are frequently used. Taxes can be used for a number of purposes. In the UK, in order to ensure that electricity supply companies use a proportion of non-fossil (mainly nuclear) fuels, a fossil fuel levy is charged. This acts by compensating supply companies for the additional costs of this power, and the levy is ultimately borne by the consumer. The EU-wide carbon tax proposal is an example of recognition of the costs of damage done to the environment by carbon dioxide emissions. The tax would act by increasing costs to the supplier, and would ultimately result in higher prices to the consumer. It would, in theory, encourage consumers either to use fuels with less carbon content or to use electricity more efficiently.

Options for reform

The challenges facing electricity markets in the industrialized countries were discussed in the first section of this chapter. Countries, whether they have a public monopoly or a private regulated market structure, must find ways of improving the efficiency of electricity supply along with meeting social objectives and taking into consideration directives at EU level. The types of approach open to governments can be discussed in relation to the following:

- Approaches to increase efficiency.
- Approaches to protect consumers.

Approaches to increase efficiency

There two broad ways in which efficiency can be increased. Efficiency can be improved either within the public monopoly or by transferring it to the private sector. First, improvements can be made to the existing arrangements. This could involve efforts to tighten up procedures or administrative arrangements, but it would not necessarily change incentives within the organization. Another option is liberalization or deregulation. This approach would involve changing incentives or freeing up anti-competitive practices. Many western European countries are embarking on this strategy in the first instance. Deregulation within the public monopoly or within a heavily regulated utility sector can be achieved in a number of ways: for example, approaches which are aimed at prohibiting price-colluding practices. In Germany, the government is looking into cartels and collusive practices among its principal electricity companies. The French are adopting similar approaches. The aim is to improve existing resource allocations: for example, by improving planning techniques. A government might decide to keep the monopoly intact and in the public sector if it places greater emphasis on its social and regional aims than on the efficiency benefits emerging from outright privatization.

Another form of deregulation involves making the role of subsidies clearer and setting limits on annual public subsidies. The former is called increasing the level of transparency. This might include an independent organization requesting the public monopoly to provide information on how it uses a public subsidy, or to identify those services which are uneconomic and those which are profit making. This forces the monopoly to provide information which it may not have produced before; it shows the public how subsidies are being used and the extent of cross-subsidy between services. These actions tend to make a monopolist relatively more aware of its costs.

Deregulation can also take the form of unbundling costs and revenues. Unbundling is about making it clear how costs and revenues relate to different services. This would involve breaking down costs to the local service level, or the smallest operational level, or by type of cost. In some cases, it might involve moving to a more sophisticated cost-accounting system or changing the organizational structures within the company.

Other deregulation methods include getting an independent review of practices and policies. An independent reviewer can comment on market-distorting practices. For example, Germany has for many decades had a coal penny levied on all electricity users to subsidize the coal industry, and this practice is currently being investigated. Also under scrutiny are the pricing arrangements between the large private electricity companies. A recent review by the German Monopolies Commission, entitled *More Competition in All Markets*, found that within the energy industry as a whole extensive price cartels operated. The German government has begun legislation for the abolition of protection of local monopolies. The French government has just had a major review of its electricity industry.

The other main approach to increasing efficiency is to privatize the industry and set incentives to increase the level of competition. Within this approach there are two options. The first is to privatize the industry and keep the market structure intact; the second is to alter the market structure. The potential efficiency gains from the first option are that the organization gains independence from a government's public expenditure system, as it can decide how much to invest from profits without the constraint of paying back the government; that international capital and equity markets can be accessed; that an organization can

173

compete outside its national boundaries; and that the organization has greater freedom to diversify into other areas.

This approach would involve selling the industry intact and regulating all activities to ensure that the universal service obligation and anti-monopoly practices were controlled. Cross-subsidies would probably be retained. It is not clear how efficiency would be greatly increased, as there would be incentives to suppress competition and because of this there might be few incentives to be innovative. There would also have to be substantial regulation.

Privatizing the electricity industry and changing the market structure can potentially bring even greater efficiency gains. This is the approach adopted by the UK government. Changes in structure, after privatization, were thought necessary to bring about increases in the level of competition. Generally, this can be done either at the time of privatization or gradually through the intervention of a regulatory authority. For example, generation, distribution and supply can be separated out. On the supply side, local electricity companies can be set up to serve their designated areas, but they can also be allowed to compete in each other's areas. Within different segments of the market, more competition can be encouraged in a number of ways. First, through the granting of licences, potential suppliers could be allowed to bid to supply a particular area in addition to the existing supplier. A related method of encouraging competition is to extend the licence. This can be done by the gradual lowering of the threshold limits. Threshold limits specify what size of consumers can be supplied by the dominant company. In the UK the latter is called the public electricity supplier. It has a sole right to supply consumers with a specified maximum demand. The idea is that its contract to supply will gradually be reduced, thereby allowing other suppliers to enter the market.

Approaches to protect consumers

Amid the debate about deregulation and increasing competition in electricity markets, there is still a role for governments to ensure that consumers are protected. This is because it takes a long time for a market to shift from a monopoly to a competitive structure. Electricity regulation, therefore, is not only required for the promotion of competition, but also to protect the consumer and achieve social and national objectives. The former would be undertaken by the methods described above, while consumers' interests, in particular, could be protected by profit or price controls and the setting of quality of service standards. Licences could contain specific requirements to meet national objectives, such as a code of practice on the efficient use of electricity. Changing the market structure is undertaken, in theory to assist in the promotion of competition. The idea is to separate out generation from distribution and supply. Regulation can be set so as to create incentives to be cost efficient, to lower prices and to provide conditions for competition in supply. A government might embark on this approach if it felt that the benefits of the market could promote a better allocation of resources than previous government arrangements, and if it felt that the interests of consumers could be adequately assured under a regulatory framework.

The problem with privatization plus regulation is that the success of this policy is contingent on a number of things: for example, getting the market structure changes right in the first place, so as to allow effective competition to take place; getting a regulatory framework in place which is tough and will not suffer from regulatory capture (where the regulator loses some of its independence and gets caught in the interests of the strongest pressure group); and ensuring that there are mechanisms which channel the benefits of privatization to consumers and not just to shareholders and managers' pay packets.

Institutional arrangements

As we saw in the first section of this chapter, the European Commission wishes to achieve greater transparency in the setting of prices and subsidies, and greater access for suppliers to use the national transmission and distribution networks, so that consumers can choose any supplier they wish. The Commission has produced a number of directives. The transparency directive focused on making more information available on prices and on the conditions of sale of electricity. The transit directive aims to allow companies to use the national transmission grids of other countries. Both these directives are forms of deregulation: they are aimed at freeing up the particular aspects of the electricity markets where it is believed that both inefficiencies and little competition exist.

The second stage of liberalization is that operations should be conducted along commercial principles, charging should be fair and transparent, and activities should be unbundled. The latter term means that the costs and revenues associated with a service should be made clear to everyone. The issue which is causing the most controversy and debate at present is third party access (TPA). This refers to consumers of electricity having the right to choose their supplier irrespective of which country is supplying the electricity, and to suppliers having the right to transport electricity via grids which are owned by another company in return for payment.

Implementation of these policies has been slow. On the one hand, there are a group of countries which support the TPA idea: that is, allowing both producers and distributors to sell across frontiers by using other member states' networks. On the other hand, there are countries which want total control over their own networks, such as France. The most recent proposal is that only large users of electricity should be allowed to shop around for cheaper deals between countries. This idea could then be extended to smaller users after a certain period.

Q1 The appropriate role for governments in electricity markets is currently a major issue. What are the factors which have brought about the need for a change in their role in electricity markets?

Q2 What would a free market in electricity look like?

Q3 What approaches are open to governments to improve the level of efficiency in electricity markets?

Q4 What is the role of regulation in a privatized electricity industry?

The purposes of the case studies chosen are to compare different objectives and different approaches adopted, and to consider the changing role of governments in the electricity industry.

Case study The UK: The Regional Electricity Companies

Objectives

The government privatized the Regional Electricity Companies in order to bring about greater efficiency and competition.

Objectives for the EU

Energy deregulation to end the state monopolies over the production, supply and distribution of electricity by 1996.

New approaches

This is a case study about the privatization and regulation of the English and Welsh electricity supply industry. It will be discussed in relation to the following objectives:

- Approaches to increase efficiency.
- Approaches to protect consumers.

The background

The UK electricity industry was a set of state monopolies in generation and supply, with the Central Electricity Generating Board (CEGB) owning the power stations and the higher-voltage transmission system (transmission), and the Area Boards owning the low-voltage local distribution system (distribution and supply).

Approaches to increase efficiency

The privatization plans were set out in a White Paper in 1988. Twelve Regional Electricity Companies (RECs) based on their old Area Boards were established to generate, distribute and supply electricity in England and Wales in December 1990. Included in the sale was the National Grid Company, which is jointly owned by the RECs through a holding company. The government retained a special share with no voting rights in each of the RECs.

Privatization was accompanied by market structure changes. The aim was to increase efficiency through the promotion of competition. Privatization divided

---

activities into transmission, generation and supply. It put each of these specific activities under a different organization. For example, on the distribution and supply side it established the twelve regional companies. There was to be a separate transmission company, the National Grid, which was to be floated in 1996. On the generation side, it created two nuclear power generators, and it is intended to privatize these companies eventually.

The problem with the market structure changes was that they did not go far enough. Some critics have claimed that this was a product of the privatization process, which was trying to achieve other objectives at the same time, such as increasing share ownership and raising revenue. Economists would say that the ideal situation was that the regulator should regulate the natural monopoly elements and that competition should take place through the introduction of an appropriate market structure. What happened in practice was that a duopoly was created in generation – hardly a prerequisite for effective competition. Remember that generation is not a natural monopoly activity. Now a situation has arisen whereby the regulator has to regulate generation. There was a split of transmission from generation, which was needed because transmission is a natural monopoly, but then the RECs ended up owning the transmission grid. It might have been more appropriate if electricity supply had been totally separated from transmission. This would have made it easier to regulate.

Approaches to protect consumers

The duty of the regulator, the Office of Electricity Regulation (OFFER), is not just to increase competition, but also to protect the consumer. It would be incorrect to judge efficiency gains in the privatized industry without taking into consideration whether consumers had benefited from them too. The whole point about promoting competition is to create choice and to ensure that consumers pay prices which are related to both the costs of production and any efficiency gains. So one way of assessing the former is to consider the movement of electricity prices. One reasonable expectation is that after privatization there would be downward pressure on prices, *ceteris paribus*. The results of electricity privatization in terms of prices have been disappointing. In the non-competitive, regulated market, electricity prices have outstripped increases in other domestic fuel prices since the late 1980s. It is useful to distinguish between market segments: that is, considering consumers as large, medium-sized and small in relation to their maximum demands for electricity. Drawing on the work of Robinson (1995), price increases of up to 46 per cent were experienced by large energy-intensive consumers between 1989 and 1994, medium-sized consumers enjoyed smaller price increases, and small consumers experienced large increases, against only small price increases in other domestic fuels.

These figures are very much a snapshot of the post-privatized industry, and the price increases are products of many things, including the lack of competition in generation, so they are somewhat limited in their interpretation. One of the problems with the regulatory approach adopted was that the government focused on production efficiency objectives, but failed to put in place ways in which the accruing benefits could be passed on to consumers. Criticisms such as these have led the regulator to take a firmer stance on electricity prices, and tighter price increase controls have been proposed from 1996 onwards.

Old arrangements

The UK electricity supply industry was a nationalized industry where fuel choices (to produce electricity) were under the influence of the government, and there were constraints under the external financing limits to pay back money to the government.

New arrangements

The electricity supply industry has been changed from a group of state-owned monopolies into a largely privately owned, and partially competitive, industry.

Change of relationships

The government previously had an involved role in the allocation of resources in this industry: it exercised control over prices, investment and borrowing. Through the sponsoring minister, the industry had to seek approval for investment plans and price increases. The minister appointed the chairman, and set financial targets and external financing limits (i.e. on how much the industry could borrow from the Treasury). Relationships have changed: rather than the government dealing with matters directly, there is a third organization, the regulatory body, headed by a director responsible for regulating prices, setting quality standards and creating the conditions for long-term and effective competition.

Q5 How are equity and social objectives met under a system of regulation compared to one of public monopoly?

Q6 To what extent has transforming the public monopoly into a regulated, privatized and partially competitive industry increased or decreased the level of government involvement? What are the advantages of this form of intervention compared to nationalization in terms of relationships between government and industry?

Case study France: State monopoly in electricity

Objectives

The French government opposes privatization and wishes to maintain its public monopoly. It has embarked on a strategy of liberalization of parts of the electricity industry.

Objectives for the EU

Energy deregulation to end state monopolies over the production, supply and distribution of electricity by 1996.

New approaches

The French electricity company is called Electricité de France (EdF). It is one of the largest generators of electricity in the world and the largest power exporter in Europe. Although there has been much resistance to deregulation, some measures and proposals have been made:

- Approaches to increase efficiency.
- Approaches to maintain equity and other objectives.

The background

EdF has a near monopoly in generation, transmission, distribution and supply to consumers. It is a public company and employs 120000 people. In 1946 the Nationalization Law created EdF, and gave it the monopoly for distributing electricity. Today almost 95 per cent of electricity is produced by EdF. There is a small private generation sector, where independent companies are allowed to produce electricity for their own use, but any they do not sell is bought up by EdF and sold through its network. At the end of the 1960s and for a further twelve years, EdF began to build a series of nuclear power stations. Approximately 78 per cent of its electricity is generated from nuclear power. In the 1980s there was a great increase in the importance of commercial strategy. The company became more customer orientated. It is run on the model of *dirigiste* (direct) state intervention and long-term planning. This is where the government determines, through forecasting and the formulation of plans, future trends of electricity consumption and investment. The French have no fossil fuels and so are very eager to protect their principal energy industry, they have therefore made only small changes to its structure.

Approaches to increase efficiency

The first question to ask is: is EdF inefficient? This is difficult to answer accurately because information about the company is kept very secret. However, a number of estimates can be made. There are five indicators which can be discussed: prices, subsidies, profits, investment and planning outcomes. EdF prices are about average compared to other European nations (see Figure 9.1). Given that this is an industry using a high-cost means of production, nuclear power, prices would appear competitive. However, the industry has a policy of keeping electricity tariffs low. A situation has arisen where a state-owned French aluminium company negotiated a 0.75 pence per kilowatt-hour with EdF, but British companies have to pay a lot more than this for imported French electricity. The problem is that the French import rates are about 30 per cent below UK energy-intensive industry, but considerably above what French businesses have to pay. A report by the Commissariat à l'énergie atomique (CEA) in 1987 revealed that EdF was earning 22.4 centimes per kWh on exports to the UK, compared with a production cost of 22.5 centimes per kWh. This can be construed to be distortive to trading.

This fact was recognized when the CBI filed a complaint to the European Commission about EdF's dumping practices. It claimed that French companies which enjoy relatively low electricity costs were gaining a competitive advantage. The EdF charges domestically based industry unusually low prices and then dumps electricity across its borders at higher prices. There is much concern about this exporting policy. To the French, it appears to be a profitable way of using the plentiful supplies of power produced from nuclear plants. Recent estimates have shown that the exporting business costs between £650 million and £4 billion, taking into account the maintenance, investment and transmission costs of exporting, against export earnings of about £1.6 million. It is unclear how it can be seen as a profitable and sustainable policy.

However, we must add to this state of affairs the electricity subsidies. The French government gave £3.05 billion at 1987 prices in subsidies between 1979 and 1985. Also, there is an extensive system of cross-subsidies. (The UK RECs are not allowed to use cross-subsidies.) Against this, we must set the fact that profits have been mixed and not substantial. The CBI estimated that by the end of 1990, the company had profits of £279 million against cumulative losses of £3.12 billion. Comparing ratios with the UK, EdF had a net income of 2 per cent of turnover, whereas the twelve RECs had an average rate of 10 per cent of turnover. Besides this, the industry enjoys investment loans at a cheap rate from the government. On the planning front, the French use exports as a profitable way of using the plentiful power produced by their nuclear plants. France exports about 13 per cent of its output and, in 1992/93, exported 5.4 per cent of the UK's total supply.

In summary, there is some evidence to suggest that this is a company which is not operating as efficiently as it could. It has anti-competitive practices, receives much support from the government and has accumulated large debts. With these considerations in mind, how has the industry sought to improve operations?

The EdF has made some efforts to become more liberalized, but these do not include privatization. The measures adopted, which include initiatives from the government, are debt reduction, rationalization, the commissioning of independent reports, and the single buyer approach proposal. The industry is in debt because of its nuclear building programme, and the government guarantees all its debt. The government has intervened directly by asking EdF to reduce its net borrowing, and in 1989 EdF agreed to reduce it by £1.91 billion by 1992. The government also asked it to reduce its debt, which was £22.25 million in 1989, by more than half by the year 2000. The company expects little or no borrowing in the future, until it starts to finance nuclear power construction after the year 2000. The debt reduction programme took place in February 1993 when the company made a public offer to buy back £0.8 billion of Eurodollar debt. In addition, the French government expanded the dividend required from EdF from 30 to 50 per cent of company profits. These measures represent efforts to try and tighten up the financial arrangements of the company.

Rationalization means reorganizing to improve efficiency. EdF announced in

1994 that it will shut down 2000 megawatts of coal-fired and 3000 megawatts of heavy fuel oil-fired plant over the next five years. It has done this because there is growing competition with cheaper production coming from the private generation sector.

The French are having an energy review for the first time in decades. This is an indication that some need for change is recognized by the government. The Institut d'évaluation des stratégies sur l'énergie et l'énvironment en Europe (INESTENE) is undertaking the review. This is a very well-respected, independent group of energy consultants which operates for governments, economists and the European Commission. They are looking at how nuclear power could be phased out in France without closing the plants immediately. The report could help alter how energy is organized in the future. Much depends on how receptive the government is to the contents of this and any other reports; the International Energy Agency (IEA) recently tried to publish a report on French energy policies and the government prohibited its publication.

Finally, the French have proposed a form of liberalization in response to the Commission's directives. It is called the single buyer (SB) approach. They do not want transmission grids to be open to other suppliers. However, they are happy with the public monopoly ending its control over the production, import and export of energy, provided the organization retains its control over the purchase of electricity from all producers, and over selling electricity to consumers. In summary, efforts to promote efficiency in EdF can be described as peripheral in nature and involving little effort to increase competition.

Approaches to maintain equity and other objectives

We have to ask: why do such protective policies exist in France? The French government states that it is committed to its social and regional objectives. The best way, it claims, to meet the universal service obligation is with a state monopoly. It places great emphasis on equity objectives and claims that these justify its policies to subsidize French industry.

The government feels that the present industry structure best meets the strategic objective of security of supply and uniform prices. So it aims to enhance existing arrangements. It sees a number of advantages with state-driven nuclear power: it provides employment in rural areas, it arms the workforce with a valuable set of skills in the workforce, and there are high technological spin-offs and value-added export opportunities. Hence the decision in France to concentrate a high proportion of the nation's resources on nuclear power development. Another wider benefit to the economy of a public monopoly is that services can be provided to all consumers at the same reasonable cost, whether they are located in the cities or in the countryside where the infrastructure costs are highest.

A final argument recently put forward in favour of the single buyer approach is that it is an essential instrument of national energy policy: since France has no other energy sources, it firmly believes in defending its electricity monopoly and thereby safeguarding its defence. Moreover, in the interests of the environment, the single buyer can opt for more expensive but cleaner fuels; nuclear power does not produce carbon dioxide.

181

Old arrangements

Effectively, France has resisted pressures to change its electricity monopoly. There is much support for the nuclear power industry and much opposition to change. Its workers went on strike in 1996 over suggestions of privatization and the loss of its monopoly. The changes have really been only marginal in nature.

New arrangements

The French have avoided privatization and have followed a policy of planned liberalization of parts of the monopoly and strengthening its financial position by introducing more equity shares, better debt management policies and rationalizations.

Change of relationships

EdF enjoys an intimate relationship with the government. There is a mutual support system in operation and it looks as though there will be few changes to this relationship.

Q7 How does retaining a state monopoly in electricity help the French to meet their equity and industrial objectives?

Q8 What are the disadvantages of the French retaining their preferred form of government intervention, a public monopoly, rather than complying with the intentions of the European Commission? Who are the gainers and who are the losers?

Discussion

This section considers the potential of the measures to increase efficiency and protect the consumer in both countries, and contrasts the different approaches adopted. The UK measures to increase efficiency involved privatization plus changes in market structure to promote competition. Efficiency gains will be achieved only if there is sustained and effective competition. This has occurred in the highly competitive industrial markets, where electricity competes with oil and gas. In the small user market, it is going to take time and careful regulation to develop competition. One of the problems is establishing how much potential electricity suppliers should be charged to use the national grid. Regulation appears to be very dependent on information supplied by the RECs. Prices within the regulated small user market remain high against a background of rising profits. While there are provisions to ensure that productive efficiency gains are made, there are some weaknesses with the regulatory system. So far, there has not been adequate provision to ensure an even distribution of the benefits. Managers and shareholders have been the principal beneficiaries, while consumers have been placed further down the list. On the positive side, the UK is very well placed to meet the Commission's directives. It now has open access on its grid and is in a strong position to supply to other countries.

The French have undertaken a number of measures to increase efficiency. These include injecting more private finance, allowing independent reviews of policy and practice and rationalization. So far, there have been very few attempts to bring in major deregulations or encourage competition. These measures appear mild compared to the UK. The question is: do the arguments about achieving national social and industrial objectives justify the continued exporting practices and the current market structure? Also, how are these national benefits reconciled with the EU-wide aim to have an internal market in energy? On the one hand, in the absence of any substantial evidence of inefficiency, the public monopoly structure does justify the stated French objectives. However, these benefits must be weighed up against the potential benefits to be had from increasing competition at national and EU level. In this instance, the French are least well placed to meet the Commission's directives. They are likely to experience much upheaval and unrest eventually, if they are to comply with the wishes of other member states in achieving an internal market in electricity. In this respect, the UK has made better deregulatory and structural provisions for the inevitable changes in the future.

Further reading

Introductory level

Bailey, S. (1995) *Public Sector Economics: Theory, Policy and Practice*, Basingstoke: Macmillan, ch. 13.

Begg, D., Fischer, S. and Dornbusch, R. (1994) *Economics*, 4th edn, Maidenhead: McGraw-Hill, ch. 18.

Griffiths, A. and Wall, S. (eds) (1995) *Applied Economics: An Introductory Course*, 6th edn, Harlow: Longman, ch. 8.

Intermediate level

Griffen, J. and Steele, H. (1980) *Energy Economics and Policy*, New York: Academic Press.

Griffiths, A. and Wall, S. (1996) *Intermediate Microeconomics: Theory and Applications*, Harlow: Longman, ch. 7.

Pindyck, R. and Rubinfeld, D. (1992) *Microeconomics*, 2nd edn, Basingstoke: Macmillan, ch. 7.

Other sources

'Regulatory policy and the energy sector', Chartered Institute of Public Finance and Accountancy, 1993.

Cooke, S. (1993) 'Nods, winks and subsidies' and 'Iniquities of the French connection', *Management Today*, January.

de Bony, E. (1995) 'Energy deregulation: a change of course', *EIU European Trends*, 2nd quarter, Economist Intelligence Unit.

Duff, L. (1987) 'Policies and performances of the UK nationalised industries', unpublished thesis, UMIST, Manchester.

'Energy market report: electricity', *Energy Economist*, no. 159, 1995.

Green, R. (1994) 'Electricity privatisation: coal and gas', *Economic Review*, February.

'European electricity: battle for power', *The Economist*, June, 1995.

'Electrifying news from Paris', *The Economist*, May, 1996.

'How the French get power', *The Economist*, May, 1996.

'Nationalised industries: a review of economic and financial obligations', HMSO, Cmnd. 3437, 1967.

'Privatising electricity', HMSO, Cmnd. 322, 1988.

Jaccard, M. (1995) 'Oscillating currents: the changing rationale for government intervention in the electricity industry', *Energy Policy*, vol. 23, no. 7.

Jackson, P. and Price C. (eds) (1994) *Privatisation and Regulation: A Review of the Issues*, Harlow: Longman, ch. 4.

Lederer, P. and Bouttes, J. (1991) 'Electricity monopoly v. competition?', *Utilities Policy*, vol. 19, no. 3.

Littlechild, S. (1991) 'Electricity: refereeing the contest', *Economic Affairs*, September.

Mittra, B., Luccas, N. and Fells, I. (1995) 'European energy: balancing markets and policy', *Energy Policy*, vol. 23, no. 8.

National Economic Development Office (NEDO) (1977) 'A study of UK nationalised industries', HMSO.

Robinson, C. (1992) 'Making a market in energy', Institute of Economic Affairs, Current Controversies, no. 3.

Robinson, C. (1993) 'Energy policy: errors, illusions and market realities', Institute of Economic Affairs, Occasional Paper, no. 90.

Robinson, C. (1995) 'Utility regulation: challenge and response', Institute of Economic Affairs, Readings, no. 42.

Thomasson, K. (1995) *The Energy Industry in the UK*, London: Key Note.

Part 4

Environmental themes

Chapter 10

Roads

Key words used: road finance, road infrastructure, earmarked funding, shadow tolls, user charges

Roads are becoming a costly and scarce resource. As the demand for transport steadily rises across western Europe and is likely to continue to rise into the future, pressures mount on the limited resources available to fund and provide new road building and maintain the existing road network. The problem is that, for most of us, driving is such a pleasurable activity that the demand for roads is likely to continue. Most roads have been built largely from public funds with a small, but growing contribution from the private sector. Various pressures have forced a change in the balance between the two, and governments are intensifying the use of the private sector, both as a means to fund road building and as a way of collecting revenues through road use. For a long time, road use has been free at the point of consumption, but it looks as though this is going to change for specific segments of road networks. Economic analysis provides a rationale for government intervention in a market economy by identifying a number of areas where the market fails to work in road provision. It also offers solutions to those market failures and provides an analytical framework within which it is possible to identify and evaluate possible new roles for governments and for markets.

Background to the problem

Road traffic was a subject rarely discussed with any anxiety twenty years ago. Today, politicians right down to village shopkeepers have all become more aware of its presence. Roads can be usefully studied by economists from two broad angles: the supply side, which relates to the finance and provision of roads; and the demand side, which relates to our need for vehicular transport and the costs we impose on ourselves and others. On the demand side, there are current debates about the use of road pricing, seen as an arguably valuable instrument in deterring road use through increasing the costs of driving, but it is at a very experimental stage in most countries at present. The interest in this chapter is on the supply side and, in particular, how finance for road infrastructure is being raised in different ways. Public authorities have become quite innovative in efforts to change the way finance is raised and used for road infrastructure. Infrastructure is an important term used throughout this chapter and it refers to assets fundamentally required to drive on a road. These include road foundations, road surfaces, banks, motorways, junctions, roundabouts and bridges.

Roads can no longer be taken for granted. They are expensive assets to construct, they take a long time to build and yet, for the large majority of roads, they are free at the point of consumption. Governments are looking for ways both to use their funds with greater effectiveness and to use more private funds. A number of factors have contributed to the changes taking place in financing roads. These changes are: concerns about the environment, pressures on public finance, growth in road use and a shift in transport mode.

The first is about growing environmental awareness. Road transport was responsible for 19 per cent of carbon dioxide emissions in the UK in 1992. Other pollutants from road use can damage the quality of the air, natural vegetation, animals and human lungs. Concern about pollution is beginning to be expressed in changes in policy intervention. For example, one approach is to increase taxes on fuel or passenger cars. Also, increasing awareness of environmental problems has made many governments actively expand public transport, such as railways. Another approach has been to generate additional revenue from road user charges and to use these for investment in both road and public transport. Finally, road design and construction can be made to take into consideration the likely effects on the environment.

Constraints on public expenditure are at the centre of most transport policies, and while public money has a continuing role to play in road finance, this role is beginning to change. There are two aspects to this. Finance for road building needs to keep up with the increases in the demand for transport, but at a time of slower economic growth and budget deficits, there is an even greater need for private funds and for better use of public funds. Second, funds are increasingly being taken up not in new investment in roads, but in maintaining existing road infrastructures.

Road traffic, in terms of cars and lorries, has grown significantly in western Europe. For example, traffic in terms of car vehicle kilometres grew in some countries by as much as 82 per cent (the UK) and 85 per cent (Italy) between 1970 and 1987. Table 10.1 shows that road infrastructure has also increased in many western European countries, whereas rail infrastructure has seen a decline between 1982 to 1992. It is likely that the trend in traffic growth will continue to put pressure on the size and quality of road networks.

In addition to the increase in road use, there has been a shift towards using vehicular transport, across all the transport modes. People's preferences have increasingly favoured the motor car and lorries rather than rail transport. This has raised concerns about the impact on the environment, but while this subject is debated at the EU level, the trend is unlikely to be reversed, which means that more, and more efficient, infrastructures will be required.

In summary, the traditional ways roads have been financed and provided are

Table 10.1 Road and rail infrastructure, 1982–92

	All roads (000 km)			All rail network (000 km)		
	1982	1992	% change	1982	1992	% change
UK	367	387	+5	17.6	16.9	−4
Belgium	127	128[a]	+1	3.9	3.4	−12
Denmark	70[b]	71[b]	+1	2.5	2.3	−6
France	804	811	+1	34.1	32.7	−4
Germany	520[c]	550[b,d]	+6	45.6	40.8	−10
Ireland	92	116[d]	–	1.9	1.9	–
Italy	298[b]	305[b]	+2	16.1	16.1	(−)
Netherlands	95	105	+11	2.9	2.9	−4
Portugal	19[b]	19[b,c]	+1	3.1	3.6	−16
Spain[f]	154	327	–	14.6	15.8	−8
Sweden	129	136[d]	+5	12.4	10.2	−18

[a] 1989 data.
[b] Excludes urban roads.
[c] Estimated.
[d] 1991 data.
[e] 1990 data.
[f] Excludes local roads prior to 1992.
Source: International Comparison of Statistics (1995).

under pressure to change. Governments can no longer sustain their financial contribution at levels seen twenty years ago. A combination of increases in traffic demand, expenditure constraints and environmental concerns have forced many governments to seek new sources of finance for road building, to use public funds more effectively and to build better roads.

Current system of allocation

This section explains why governments intervene in the financing and provision of roads, and what the outcomes might be if this activity were left wholly to the market.

The market

A free market in road provision is likely to produce an inefficient level of output. This is because roads have important market failure characteristics. Market failures were introduced in Chapter 2, and in relation to roads these are as follows:

• The presence of public goods and externalities.
• The presence of capital market imperfections.

189

The presence of public goods and externalities

Public goods have two features. The first is that consumption of a good by one person does not detract from the consumption of a good by another person. If a road is not full of drivers, the presence of one extra driver does not stop others from using it and consuming it at the same time. However, this classification changes with circumstances: as more drivers use the road, all users will suffer, until congestion is so great that drivers will have to wait until someone leaves the road. At this point, the road space has become a private good. The second feature of public goods is non-excludability. In the case of roads, it is difficult to exclude road users. This is significant for a provider of roads. Road-building companies would construct roads only where they could recoup the finance and charge road users directly. This may not be possible where roads converge or where there is no practical place to locate a road-charging scheme. Much depends on the degree of excludability. Where exclusion is impossible and a price cannot be charged, there will be limited provision or none at all. In the case of smaller roads, it is not practical to have a charging system at the entrance or exit of every road, so excludability is difficult. Roads have elements of non-excludability and non-rivalry, but as we saw, they can change when circumstances change. We therefore say that roads are semi-public goods. It is unlikely that the market will provide an efficient allocation of resources in road construction. For this reason, there are grounds for government intervention.

Roads have positive and negative externalities. These arise from a number of sources. A national road network gives wider benefits to society; it enhances economic development and improves communications. A private operator might ignore these wider aspects. For these reasons, resources are likely to be underallocated in a private operation. Negative externalities arise from road safety being neglected. In a free market, roads could be designed in a dangerous way: for example, they might be too bendy or narrow, or have a cheap road surface. Proper safety requirements lead to fewer accidents and a lower national health bill. Private operators would not necessarily recognize these values. Externalities such as pollution, noise and congestion all come from road use. These create a spill-over effect on the community and are generally not taken into account by the road user, who is concerned with the private costs of travel like petrol and car maintenance. Intervention can be justified to bring about a more efficient allocation of resources.

The presence of capital market imperfections

This refers to problems with attracting finance to build roads. There is a problem with getting lending institutions to invest in roads. Under a free market, finance for roads would have to compete with other investment projects. Roads would be built only if a private company believed that the demand would be sufficient to generate a profit on the capital investment. The problem, as we saw earlier, is that road builders would find it difficult to charge road users; it is therefore likely that capital funds will not be forthcoming. In addition, roads are peculiar assets in that they require a large initial outlay, and in some cases they may have low and delayed returns with high risk because of the problem of charging users. Even if it were possible to have a road-charging system – for example, on a motorway – there is scope for a private road operator to set charges which may exploit road users. This could lead to exclusion for those on low incomes. These problems could be overcome through public financing.

Government objectives

If governments are to publicly finance and provide roads they will have a range of objectives to meet and these can be grouped into the following broad categories:

- Economy efficiency objectives.
- Administrative efficiency objectives.
- Equity objectives.

Economic efficiency objectives

In relation to roads, an example of an efficiency objective is where a government seeks to build a road network or makes extensions to it, at a quantity and quality which will provide the maximum social benefits. Decisions about whether a new road project is given the go-ahead will depend on the costs of the road scheme and the benefits to road users. The costs might include the construction and preparation costs of the road, plus maintenance costs, which will depend on traffic forecasts; the benefits to road users might include the amount of time saved, savings in terms of accidents, and savings in vehicle operating costs. An efficient level of road provision could be said to be that where the given level of output is met with the minimum level of costs.

Administrative efficiency objectives

These refer to the decision-making processes involved in road finance. Examples are better accountability systems, stricter planning and forecasting procedures and, more debatable, the adoption of private sector management techniques. Clearly, any scheme which involves the private sector more will have an impact on administration costs. For example, if a government wishes to use a greater proportion of private funds, this will involve more negotiations, contracts, legal work and monitoring activities. These costs would have to be weighed up against the costs of alternative in-house schemes.

Equity objectives

It is possible to think of equity objectives in the financing of a road scheme. In devising a financing structure, governments have to decide who should pay for roads. Should it be the taxpayer, all road users or a combination of the two? Clearly, there is a case for everyone to contribute because everyone benefits from economic development and a better transport system in a country. Increasingly, road users are being charged for road use. While this has efficiency consequences, it could also be argued to be fairer. Why should those who do not impose a cost on the environment, by not driving, have to pay towards any damage caused? The problem with this idea, as many governments are learning, is that road users dislike being charged for something which was once 'free' to them at the point of consumption.

Government intervention

Governments intervene in the provision of roads to overcome the market failures outlined above. The types of intervention can be grouped as follows:

- Provision.
- Taxes and subsidies.
- Regulation.

Provision

Governments intervene by directly providing roads. Provision has a number of dimensions. It involves the planning, designing and construction of roads. In addition to construction, the maintenance of roads is beginning to account for a growing proportion of road finance. Local authorities often have the duty to provide roads, but they contract out the actual construction of roads to private companies.

Taxes and subsidies

These can be used in two ways: to finance road-building programmes and to change the prices which road users face. Taxes are used to assist the financing of road construction, maintenance and expansion. In the UK, road revenues are generated from driving licences, VAT and import duties. These are specific taxes and are not directly related to use. Governments can raise additional revenues from user charges. These are imposed only when a part of the road network is directly used. User charges take many forms. There are road tolls, which are usually a fixed price and are typically used to make a contribution towards the funding or maintenance of a road. If governments wish to increase awareness of the environment, a levy can be imposed on fuel, as was done by the Swedish government. Road pricing, on the other hand, is a form of intervention often used to manage traffic congestion. In this case the function of the charge is not principally to raise funds for road infrastructure, but to reduce traffic at specific times. Subsidies can be used for road-building purposes. They can be transferred to road construction companies. Operating subsidies act by reducing the total costs to a provider. These can be paid in the form of a block grant, or they can be tendered for on the basis that the successful bidder is the one which requires the lowest public subsidy.

Regulation

Governments typically have a large regulatory role in roads. Examples of areas where governments regulate are: driver testing and licensing; road haulage licensing and transporting of dangerous goods; vehicle testing; and the collection of car taxes. In many cases, the governments will lay down the requirements and private operators will undertake to carry out the specifications, as with the private MOT testing stations in the UK. Governments also have responsibilities for road safety, securing improvement in the safety of vehicles and encouraging better behaviour by road users.

Government intervention in western European countries is largely publicly funded, with some variation in sources of funds and road user charges. In continental Europe, direct motorway charges are commonly used, on the basis of both managing congestion and raising additional revenue to support national road programmes. The Netherlands is proposing that revenue collected by users be placed in a fund and used for investment on roads. France uses road tolls and the private sector to finance its inter-urban highways. The UK has proposed introducing electronic tolling on the motorway network and has undertaken a road pricing experiment in Cambridge.

Options for reform

As we saw in the first section, governments need to improve the supply-side arrangements of roads to keep up with road traffic demand pressures. There are two broad policy options: governments can either tighten up existing arrangements within the public sector or intensify the involvement of the private sector. These two approaches are discussed below:

• Approaches to increase the efficiency of road finance within the public sector.
• Approaches to increase efficiency by using the private sector.

Approaches to increase the efficiency of road finance within the public sector

It is easy to fall into the trap of believing that all the solutions to the mounting pressures on resources lie with the private sector. It is also important to appreciate that improvements can be made within the public sector.

Improvements can be made to decision-making processes in road finance and provision. These relate to ways of improving the handling of resources within the public sector. Possible approaches include: better accountability procedures; changes in financial reporting; and organizational changes. The UK has attempted to bring in such changes: executive agencies in central government have been set up to bring about greater financial reporting. These are public bodies and they must produce an annual report and account and be accountable for expenditure against budget. The idea is that commercial-style accounting will strengthen the quality of financial reporting. In 1994 the Highways Agency (HA) was established. It is responsible for delivering an efficient, reliable, safe and environmentally acceptable motorway and trunk road network within England. It has its own performance targets and it may eventually become self-financing. The HA improves the road network by managing the design, purchasing and construction of road schemes. The HA contracts with the private sector on road financing and construction. The benefits of these internal changes are that commercial-style accounting, sharper organizational responsibility and the strengthening of financial reporting can all contribute towards enhancing the decision-making process.

Earmarked finance is an interesting idea which has the potential to improve the efficiency of road financing in the public sector and has long been advocated by economists. This refers to the specific raising of finance for a specific project. From the public point of view, there is evidence to suggest that voters and taxpayers are keen to see a direct relationship between their road taxes and expenditure on transport. Revenues raised from general and specific taxes are often allocated to a basket of transport projects, with little linkage between the two. This is different from the idea of raising specific finance for a specific project. The economic rationale behind earmarking is that people who want the good or service have the choice to make a contribution towards it, and they specifically benefit eventually.

So, for example, a local authority could set up a road charge for entering a city centre by car. Revenues collected from this activity would be specifically used to improve the city centre's roads. People who do not drive a car and who would never benefit from improved roads obviously would not pay the charge. Car drivers can choose to pay the charge or use other forms of transport. If they pay the charge, this in part represents their willingness to pay for something from which they are going to receive a direct benefit. Hence the idea is based on willingness to pay. The advantage of this method is that it allows for better accountability between revenue and costs. One of the main problems lies with getting it accepted by the road user. The strengths and weaknesses will be examined in the case studies.

Approaches to increase efficiency by using the private sector

There are a variety of ways in which the private sector can be utilized to assist governments in meeting some of their problems. Privatization would be an extreme option, involving selling off the entire road network and leaving the private sector to raise the finance to install road-tolling equipment and to fund a road-building programme. The German government has announced plans to privatize its autobahns, with road users facing an annual charge. Such a policy would require government regulation to ensure that the private companies met safety standards and expanded the road network in conjunction with other social and environmental considerations. The problem with this approach is that road users may revert to secondary roads, thereby adding to the congestion and pollution in those areas.

Contracting out refers to selling the right to provide a good or service, often where no revenues are generated directly from the use of the good. In the case of roads, contracting involves private construction companies bidding for road projects and the public subsidy which goes with it. In the UK, subsidies used to be allocated in the form of a block grant, but now this arrangement has been tightened up so that there is greater control over the amount of subsidy applied for and the purposes for which it is used. Many of the contracts are awarded on the basis of how much or how little public subsidy is required. The aim is to provide some competitive pressure among potential suppliers of public services. This may encourage all bidders to look closely at the costs of provision and find ways to reduce costs. The advantage of tightening the contract arrangements is that governments have better control over the level of the public subsidy.

Private sector investment is a different approach because it involves private sector investment, as opposed to provision. There has been a growing interest in this approach from many countries. Private sector investment has two aspects. The first is that finance for the investment in road infrastructure is provided by a private sector company, either for the whole project or as part of a joint funding arrangement. In the UK, private investment has been used in the Dartford Bridge and the second Severn Bridge. The rationale behind it is that investments in new road infrastructure can be undertaken at a much faster rate in the private than in the public sector.

The second aspect is one step on from the situation described above, and involves both private sector investment and management. Private companies have a more extensive role in that they are maintaining the assets throughout their economic life. This is a recent development in the UK. Rather than just provide the finance, a private company will design, construct, maintain, finance and operate the road project. The public sector still retains a duty to deliver the services, but it is no longer the provider. It is effectively buying the services from the private sector, which will both own and operate the road assets. The rationale behind this is that every road project has risks associated with it: for example, going over budget or construction risks. By conferring more responsibilities on the private company, there is effectively a transfer of risk. Private companies will be invited to tender for specific work and the government chooses the bidder which fits its specifications. The advantages, in theory, of this approach are that private companies are selected through a process of open competition, there is better control of public expenditure at the level of individual projects, and risk is transferred. In effect, the capital and management skills are provided by the private sector, but the service remains a public one. The strengths and weaknesses of this approach will be considered in the case studies.

User charges are an approach which can be used in a number of ways to meet different objectives, but essentially they increase the involvement of the private sector. User charges refer to charges being made directly for the use of a particular road or motorway. There are charges which do not vary with the level of demand: for example, downtown area cordon fees, bridge and other toll fees, and mileage-based vehicle fees. Cordon fees, used in many Norwegian cities, are imposed in order to raise revenues or discourage road users in downtown areas. They are typically flat fees and do not vary with traffic congestion. Bridge and motorway tolls are usually flat fees and are imposed to cover the costs of building, maintaining and operating the assets in question. Vehicle charges are used for purposes other than traffic control. These are examples of user charges and, while they may alter road use, that is not their principal objective.

Road or congestion pricing, on the other hand, aims to affect peak demand and is an example of a market-based approach. It has gained support from environmentalists and free marketeers alike. The economic rationale for its use is that road users who impose costs on themselves and on the environment do not contribute towards these costs. In addition, revenues raised can be used to subsidize public transport, which imposes relatively lower costs. One should add a further point to the general interest in the adoption of user charges. Technological advances have produced electronic equipment for use on vehicles, which makes it easier and cheaper for charges to be collected from road users.

Shadow pricing is where the private road builders are paid 'shadow prices' in relation to the use made of the roads. They are called 'shadow' because they reflect what might have been charged under a private market. What happens is that a contract is set up between government and contractor. Under this contract, the operators may design, finance and operate a road, in return for being paid a fixed sum for each vehicle over a specified period of time. Shadow pricing can be applied when two conditions exist. First, it can be applied when it is not possible for consumers to choose: that is, when they cannot reveal the type of service they would like. This is the case with roads because, as we have seen, it is impractical to have a price system at the entrance to every private road, so people cannot reveal their willingness to pay. Second, shadow pricing can be applied where externalities exist: that is, when the price of the good or service does not reflect the value society places on the good or service. Under this condition, the role of price is limited. As we saw earlier, this is also the case with roads. If both these conditions are satisfied, we say that the function of price is limited and it is appropriate to replace prices with a set of shadow prices or accounting prices. Shadow prices can be used to approximate market prices. The government calculates the costs of a particular road scheme, and agrees on a fee per road user, which it will pay the private company. The advantage is that there is an incentive for the company to provide the road and it means that constraints on public finances can be spread out. The disadvantage of this approach is that payment is based on vehicle use, and if this falls or there have been errors in planning forecasts, then the private company could make losses.

Institutional arrangements

The European Commission has a role to play in transport financing: it has taken on an increased responsibility via the transport infrastructure part of the Community Budget, and makes direct transport investments through the Regional Development Fund. Its interest comes from its objective to bring about an open market in trade, and in this context it wishes to see transport costs which reflect true economic costs and subsidies conforming to common criteria. The EU has been directly involved with funding transport infrastructure projects which have importance throughout the Union.

Q1 Explain the economic rationale behind why roads are largely publicly financed and provided. Why is the situation of road construction being largely publicly funded untenable for the future?

Q2 Explain the different economic functions of road prices, shadow prices, road tolls and fuel levies.

Q3 Explain the difference between private sector road provision and private sector investment and management of roads. What are the advantages to governments of the latter?

Q4 Expansion of national road networks is the only way to respond to increased demand for road use. Discuss.

The following case studies have been chosen to illustrate and contrast new approaches adopted in the financing of road infrastructure, and to describe changes in the role of both governments and markets.

Case study Norway: The Trondheim toll ring

Objectives

The aim of the Norwegian government is to involve the private sector more in the financing of new road infrastructure, and public transport infrastructure in general.

Objectives for the EU

Norway is not a member of the European Union, so it is not directly affected by EU directives or legislation.

New approaches

In Norway there is a long tradition of funding road infrastructure from both public funds and user charges. Norway has financed road infrastructures from road tolls, mainly on bridges and tunnels in rural areas. Recently, the emphasis has changed to using this approach in urban areas and altering how the user revenues are allocated. One particular urban project is discussed in this case study in relation to the following:

197

- Approaches to increase efficiency in the use of finance for roads.
- Approaches to improve road use.

The background

In Norway, road infrastructure, bridges and tunnels have long been funded by a combination of road user charges and public finance. Figure 10.1 shows how the composition of funding has changed.

Private revenues in the form of toll income have been increasing, although not at a steady pace. These revenues have been used for investment in national (state) highways. Currently, more than one-quarter of total finance comes from this source. This has been executed by the introduction of toll rings, in Bergen in 1986, in Oslo in 1990 and in Trondheim in 1991. The original idea was that ring tolls (tolls which cordon cities) should be set up to raise additional finance for urban road-building programmes; it was seen as a way of raising finance quickly. This

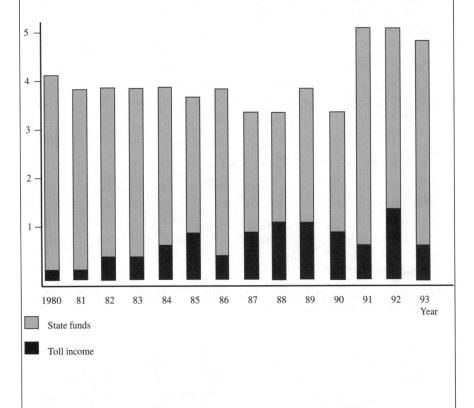

Figure 10.1 Toll and government financing of investments in national highways (NOK billions, 1993 prices)

national objective changed with growing environmental awareness and developments in technology. So with Oslo and Trondheim, the raising of finance was not just for road programmes but also for public transport, cyclists and pedestrians.

Approaches to increase efficiency in the use of finance for roads

The principal approaches described here are the use of earmarked finance and user charges. As we saw earlier, earmarked finance refers to reserving money for particular projects. User charges can be imposed to raise finance for new road infrastructures and to alter the pattern of travel. The Trondheim toll ring has been set up to do both these things: to finance the Trondheim package and to influence car mode and departure time. The idea is that part of the revenues raised from road tolls are earmarked for new road construction and part are to be used for public transport infrastructure. Specifically, the package includes a range of planned improvements in the local transport system which will benefit cyclists, pedestrians and public transport. The package costs approximately NOK2.3 billion (NOK=Norwegian kroner, NOK11=£1) and this is phased over a fifteen-year period. Revenues from the ring are expected to contribute 60 per cent or about NOK90 million a year, with the remaining amount being provided by central government. User charges are imposed on those road users who are willing to pay them, and it these users who will benefit most from the subsequent expenditure. Earmarked funding is also being used for another project within this ring toll. The Randheim toll station, on the main road north-east of the city, also collects revenue for a specific reason: to finance a new motorway east of the city. In this toll station, tolls are levied 24 hours per day, seven days a week for traffic in both directions, and the basic toll level is twice the charge of the other stations.

The Trondheim toll ring came into operation in October 1991, and it is designed so that about 60 per cent of the inhabitants live outside the ring, and mostly shops, commercial properties and public services lie inside the ring. The toll ring operates from Monday to Friday between 6a.m. and 5p.m. and collects revenue from inbound traffic only. Public transport and motorcycle vehicles are exempt. The basic toll charge is about 90p per crossing for light vehicles and about £2 for heavy vehicles. This charge was doubled recently when the latest extension of tolled road was completed.

Drivers can choose from three methods of payment: manual, by automatic ticket machine or using the Q-tag. The latter is a free electronic tag which is placed in the vehicle. This means that when road users pass through the ring, there is an automatic debiting machine which will detect and automatically debit their Q-tag. This charge is paid either through direct debit or through prepayment units. If one subscribes to this method, there are discounts available. For example, the amount deducted falls if the crossing is made after 10a.m. There are no such discounts for cash payers. Also there are limits on the number of crossings allowed: a maximum of one an hour and no more than 75 a month. The scheme relies on people using the Q-tag. This has been promoted and approximately 85 per cent of the local vehicles registered use tags.

This system has brought a number of efficiency gains. The innovative Q-tag ensures that drivers can deposit money in their account and pass through without any delay, thereby benefiting one and all. In terms of meeting the objectives of raising finance, in 1994 approximately 8 million crossings were made, and at an average of NOK15 per crossing, the government has exceeded its target of raising NOK90 million a year. Finally, this scheme has been successful in adapting new technology and getting its support from road users. The advantage of this is that it is a valuable first step towards introducing the concept of road pricing. This could be useful if the Norwegian government ever decided to implement policies to address congestion and environmental problems associated with road use.

Approaches to improve road use

While the principal objective of the toll ring is to raise revenue and the more secondary objective is to alter travel times, the ring has brought about a change and improvement in driving patterns. A travel survey undertaken in 1994 found that the actual number of cars that went through the toll ring was virtually unchanged between 1990 and 1992, but the number of car trips per traveller fell significantly in this period. Total time used for every car trip increased, suggesting that people were organizing more complicated car trips and re-routing because of the toll ring. Its presence also caused people to alter their travel times. More people travelled outside the tolled periods. One of the drawbacks of the ring is that so far only a small number of drivers are paying the tolls: approximately one-third of car drivers in Trondheim pay tolls regularly. Some modification to the system is needed so that a greater number of road users will contribute to the Trondheim package.

Old arrangements

Previously, toll rings were used to raise revenue for new road infrastructure; there was no earmarked finance or provision to raise revenue for public transport. These finances were raised wholly from general taxation.

New arrangements

The new arrangements are that revenues raised through user charges are to be used to subsidize public transport infrastructure and urban environmental improvements.

Change of relationships

The toll ring is operated by Trondelag Toll Road Co. Ltd, which is jointly owned by the municipal and county authorities. There are no changes to relationships with road users, except that there is now an expectation that the government will successfully implement the promised improvements over the next fifteen years.

Q5 Who are the gainers and who are the losers from the Trondheim toll ring?
Q6 What is the rationale of subsidizing the costs of public transport infrastructure through the toll ring?

Case study The UK: The Private Finance Initiative

Objectives

In addition to public sector investment, the government wishes to extend the role of the private sector in the financing and management of road schemes.

Objectives for the EU

To ensure that transport subsidies are used in accordance with common criteria and to fund specific infrastructure projects with EU importance.

New approaches

There are a number of ways in which the government is reforming how it funds, designs, builds and operates roads and motorways, and these can be discussed in relation to the following:

- Approaches to increase efficiency in road infrastructure financing.

The background

The UK has embarked on extending a number of schemes to increase efficiency in road infrastructure financing and a number of local experiments with user charges: for example, road-pricing testing has been undertaken in Cambridge. In February 1994 the Department of Transport began experimental schemes to evaluate electronic technology for motorway charging. This initiative is only at an experimental stage and trials are beginning on the M4 motorway. There is no scope for charging on existing roads, only on new roads and/or new bridges like the second Severn Bridge.

Approaches to increase efficiency in road infrastructure financing

The UK, like Norway, is seeking new ways to raise finance for road infrastructure. The two methods discussed here are earmarked finance and shadow pricing. The first method is employed through the Private Finance Initiative (PFI), which was introduced in November 1992. The aim was to increase the level of private sector involvement in the financing and provision of projects which have traditionally been provided by the public sector. This is a supply-side initiative, in that it introduces greater flexibility in the provision of finance. Unlike other supply-side policies, such as privatization and contracting out, this initiative focuses on infrastructure. The PFI is applied not just to roads, but also to the building of hospitals, prisons and schools.

In relation to roads, the PFI is about introducing finance for road infrastructure. The actual name of the scheme is Design, Build, Finance and Operate (DBFO). The Department of Transport has a duty of service provision. It decides on a road scheme and presents the proposal for public inquiry, which is like asking for planning permission. If approved, it seeks expressions of interest for the contract. Potential bidders must follow procedures, giving details on the design, building, maintenance and operation of the road scheme for a period of 30 years. In essence, the private operator is responsible for the asset over the long term. This type of arrangement is different from injection investment, whereby a private investor might put the money up front and then become independent of the building and operation.

The scheme will be executed through a form of shadow prices or tolls. These will be paid to the companies on the level of traffic and can be adjusted for performance: for example, if there are lane closures due to maintenance work and if it can be demonstrated that the level of safety has been improved. The benefits of this approach are that risks, like construction being on time and to budget, are transferred to the private sector. This should provide incentives for innovation in both design and construction, and increase the level of management and commercial skills.

So far the scheme has been successful, in that the road-building programme has been accelerated. Some £5 billion has been allocated to road infrastructure schemes between 1995 and 1996, and in one month alone £0.25 billion was contracted out.

Old arrangements

Road infrastructure projects were funded either wholly by the public sector or through joint funding schemes. Private investors typically put up the money and this was where their responsibility ended.

New arrangements

The government has made a number of initiatives in organizational arrangements, funding and operations, to try and introduce greater flexibility in the financing of road infrastructure.

Change of relationships

The Highways Agency has been set up to monitor the performance of these private companies. It will inspect for quality and safety standards. The Department of Transport is asking the private sector to provide public services. More generally, the government has become an enabler. It decides on the service it wants and then challenges the private sector to bid for the work.

Q7 How does shifting risk to the private sector improve the allocation of resources?

Q8 Explain the function of shadow prices. What are their disadvantages in relation to addressing problems of road congestion and environmental damage?

Discussion

This section analyses how efficiency has been increased by the two approaches. In the case of the UK, the approach has been to increase efficiency through the greater involvement of the private sector: specifically, using earmarked finance, private sector finance and management, and shadow pricing. There are a number of potential strengths with this approach. The first is that in theory, by using private finance, the government can accelerate its road-building programme. Previously, this was very dependent on the annual public expenditure plans. Second, private sector finance and management have responded well to this initiative. This has effectively moved road building out of the complicated and often delay-prone procedures of the public sector.

In theory, private sector management expertise will be used and, as private companies are using their own money, they have incentives to manage and recoup the cost of capital. Bidding for the DBFO contracts also introduces an element of competition. Besides this, bidders not only will be trying to reduce their costs to win the contract, but they will be doing this with the knowledge that they are responsible for the assets after construction. The advantage of shadow prices is that there is an incentive for operators to ensure that the roads are used by as many road users as possible, otherwise the payments from the government will decline.

The weaknesses of this approach is that this money and the obligation to pay in the future is not counted as public expenditure. The second point is: will private sector investment be maintained? So far, projects offered have been large scale, potentially lucrative and attractive, but what happens to the less attractive and riskier projects? Third, governments can borrow capital funds more cheaply than the private sector, as the government cannot be made bankrupt. This implies that greater savings would have to be found from the private operator in order to justify the initiative. There might be scope for savings in operating costs, but there is also scope to allow standards to fall.

There are problems with shadow pricing. It is an uncertain activity, in that the prices are based on the forecast traffic flows of the Department of Transport. There is scope for potential operators to put in bids higher than the actual cost in order to cover political risks such as higher fuel taxes. Also, what happens if a contractor becomes bankrupt? The taxpayer loses out because the work will still have to be paid for. The final criticism is that shadow pricing does nothing in terms of bringing home the costs to road users of the damage they do to the environment.

In Norway, the approach is to earmark finance for specific local transport projects and to introduce user charges. One of the strengths so far is that finance raised has been on target. Second, the road users have displayed a willingness to pay. They have been given an opportunity to express their preferences for different transport routes and different ways of paying. We know this because many people have purchased the Q-tags, which save them time and money when passing through the toll. The scheme has been well publicized and road users know that what they are paying for is being used directly to make a better motorway for them and to improve public transport generally. Here we see the real advantage of earmarked taxes coming through: those who pay the tax benefit most from the associated expenditure. One positive side-effect has been that people have altered their driving times and trips and, although these have amounted to only small adjustments, this has led to an improvement in road use for one and all. There has also been an 8 per cent increase in the use of public transport.

There have been weaknesses with this approach. The first is that road tolls could potentially be paid by a greater number of car users; at present only a small number pay frequently. This is an implementation problem and could be adjusted with some modification to the toll times. Also, this approach does very little for environmental concerns. Contrasting the two approaches adopted, they have both used earmarked finance, but the UK has adopted shadow prices and the Norwegians have adopted user charges. The advantages of user charges could be claimed to outweigh those of shadow prices because they do two things simultaneously: they raise finance from the private sector *and* improve road use. Shadow prices raise finance from the private sector, but do nothing to ensure better road use. In fact, they constitute an incentive to use roads more rather than less, and this is at odds with policies on the environment. A longer-term argument is that, if road pricing does become a reality for road users, then the Norwegian approach has at least established the 'experience' for road users. This may become an important point, given that one of the reasons why road pricing has not been successful is that people hate having to pay for something which was once considered 'free'.

Further reading

Introductory level

Griffiths, A. and Wall, S. (eds) (1995) *Applied Economics: An Introductory Course*, 6th edn, Harlow: Longman, ch. 11.

Hardwick, P., Khan, B. and Langmead, J. (1994) *An Introduction to Modern Economics*, 4th edn, Harlow: Longman, ch. 12.

Le Grand, J., Propper, C. and Robinson, R. (1992) *The Economics of Social Problems*, 3rd edn, Basingstoke: Macmillan, ch. 7.

Intermediate level

Cullis, J. and Jones, P. (1992) *Public Finance and Public Choice: Analytical Perspectives*, Maidenhead: McGraw-Hill, ch. 6.

George, K. and Shorey, J. (1984) *The Allocation of Resources: Theory and Policy*, Hemel Hempstead: Allen and Unwin.

Griffiths, A. and Wall, S. (1996) *Intermediate Microeconomics: Theory and Applications*, Harlow: Longman, ch. 10.

Other sources

Bayliss, D. (1994) 'Electronic road pricing for public transport', *Economic Affairs*, vol. 14, no. 2.

Button, K. and Rietveld, P. (1993) 'Financing urban transport projects in Europe', *Transportation*, vol. 20, no. 3.

Decorla-Souza, P. and Kane, A. R. (1992) 'Peak period tolls: precepts and prospects', *Transportation*, vol. 19, no. 4.

'Design, Build, Finance and Operate concessions for trunk roads and motorways: a preliminary note by the Department of Transport', Department of Transport, April, 1994.

'Building tomorrow's transport network', Department of Transport, November, 1994.

'The government's expenditure plans for transport, 1994–95 to 1996–97', Department of Transport, Cmnd. 2506, 1995.

'The Private Finance Initiative', *Economic Briefing*, May, 1996.

'New roads: shadowy finance', *The Economist*, 3 June 1995.

'Motorway tools: red light ahead', *The Economist*, 5 August 1995.

Giulliano, G. (1992) 'An assessment of the political acceptability of congestion pricing', *Transportation*, vol. 19, no. 4.

Hayes, S. and Cabrero, K. (1995) 'Generalised and advanced urban debiting innovations: the GAUDI project', *Traffic Engineering and Control*, January.

Highways Agency (1995) 'Roads and DBFO projects: information and prequalification and requirements', Department of Transport, February.

Highways Agency (1995) 'Background note on Design, Build, Finance and Operate contracts for roads', Department of Transport, November.

'International comparisons of transport statistics, 1970–1992', *Transport Statistics Report*, HMSO, 1995.

Johnsson, B. and Mattsson, L-G. (eds) (1995) *Road Pricing: Theory, Empirical Assessment and Policy*, Dordrecht: Kluwer Academic Publishers.

May, A. (1993) 'Road pricing: an international perspective', *Transportation*, vol. 19, no. 4.

Meland, S. (1995) 'Generalised and advanced urban debiting innovations: GAUDI project: the Trondheim toll ring', *Traffic Engineering and Control*, March.

Teja, R. and Bracewell-Milnes, B. (1991) 'The case for earmarked taxes', Institute of Economic Affairs, Research Monograph, no. 46.

Terry, F. (1996) 'The Private Finance Initiative – overdue reform or policy break-through?', *Public Money and Management*, January/March.

Chapter 11

Air pollution

> Key words used: market-based approaches, command and control approaches, voluntary agreements, tradable emission permits

Economics is concerned with activities within the economy, but the environment in which we live is also part of the economy, and everything that happens in the economy affects the natural environment. Production and consumption activities generate waste, some of which can be discharged into the atmosphere. We cannot treat the economy and the environment as separate areas; they are intertwined. This is also the paradox of economic development: on the one hand, it brings a greater quality of living, and on the other, it damages the environment we live and breathe in. In the real world what we want is economic development that is undertaken in a way which uses the least harmful methods and which seeks to conserve our environment. Economics has a useful role to contribute to the problems of air pollution: it can provide an analysis of the impact of economic decisions on the environment, it offers a framework from which to evaluate different responses in dealing with environmental problems and it can offer useful insights into practical policy making.

Background to the problem

The scope of this chapter is air pollution, and greenhouse gases in particular. These are gases which trap heat between the earth's surface and the atmosphere, and the principal ones are carbon dioxide, chlorofluorocarbons (CFCs), methane and nitrous oxides. Global warming happens when the greenhouse effect (ie. the tendency for certain gases to act as solar traps) is enhanced by greater concentrations of greenhouse gases in the atmosphere. Global warming can lead to higher sea levels, flooding, climate changes and increases in the size of deserts. These are some of the estimated consequences, but there may be other effects which are unknown at present. This chapter concentrates on carbon dioxide (CO_2), which accounts for about 56 per cent of the greenhouse effect.

Global warming has become an important issue for most nations. This was evident in the Earth Summit held in Rio in 1992. There were many resolutions made here, including the aim to stabilize greenhouse gas emissions at 1990 levels by the year 2000. The principal contributing gas is CO_2. The main sources of this gas are the burning of forests and of fossil fuels such as coal, gas and oil (in order to convert them into energy). Specific country statistics can illuminate this fact. In Germany, 45 per cent of the annual average CO_2 emissions come from all energy conversion, while in the UK the electricity supply industry alone generated about one-third of the total carbon dioxide produced in 1993. In addition to energy conversion, the transport and domestic sectors (households and other small-scale consumers) are important. Although the latter each emit tiny proportions of CO_2, in total they account for a significant share: for example, in the UK they represent about one-third of total CO_2 annual emissions.

The levels of CO_2 have been increasing in the atmosphere since the nineteenth century. This has been directly related to the growth of economic development. Developed areas like western and eastern Europe, North America and the Soviet Union accounted for 65 per cent of global CO_2 emissions in 1986. Developing countries as yet play a small but growing role in emissions.

At the EU level, significant environmental directives have been introduced relating to water, air and wildlife, and there is now a large body of legislation. However, although it can be argued that the directives helped prevent the deterioration of environmental conditions, so far there is little evidence that they have directly helped to reduce pollution levels. There has been a high level of non-compliance, which could be explained either by the complexities of trying to incorporate legislation into national law or by the evasion strategies of nations. The key point is that this is a complicated business. The EC has produced a number of Environmental Action Programmes, the fifth and most recent of which in 1995, had a new orientation. It focused on the need for greater integration between government, industry and the public, and the need to develop new policy instruments and to use market-based approaches. Examples of new policy approaches include environmental auditing and eco-labelling. Market-based approaches are receiving much attention at present. However, their design and implementation are at an early stage. One specific market-based approach being debated is the EU-wide CO_2 tax. There has been much opposition to this approach from energy conversion industries because the tax would be set on the three fossil fuels – gas, oil and coal – in proportion to their carbon content. The industries involved are likely to face higher costs in the short term with this approach. There are currently proposals for new legislation and extensions of existing air quality. It is likely that the EC will continue to build up legislation on air pollution and influence nations.

Pressures for change in environmental policy are occurring at national level. There are two aspects to this: the targets which each country sets and the instruments used to meet those targets. For example, the UK is committed to a policy of stabilization of CO_2 emissions at their 1990 level by the year 2005. This means that CO_2 emissions will have to be reduced by between 20 and 25 per cent. How is this to be achieved? It is interesting that countries use a range of approaches with different emphasis on particular types of instrument. There are a range of instruments which can be used, often together, to achieve these targets, but governments are increasingly reluctant to use the traditional heavy fiscal or regulatory requirements on companies. This can be explained by the fact that governments face slow economic growth, rising budget deficits and concerns about international competitiveness. These factors mean that there is less money available to continue expensive and often lengthy regulatory procedures, and that a unilateral tax (in one nation) on domestic companies gives overseas competitors an unfair trading advantage. Hence there are some incentives for governments to meet existing regulations in innovative ways and to consider alternative approaches. Two possible ways are examined later in this chapter: working more closely with industry to reach mutually agreed objectives and the use of market-based approaches.

Current system of allocation

Air pollution provides a unique challenge for economists: it is less tangible than the other environmental topics studied in this book, it is produced from many sources and it can cross over borders into other countries. For all these reasons it is likely that it will take decades to perfect appropriate approaches.

The market

Chapter 3 described the various market failures, and in relation to air pollution these are as follows:

- The presence of externalities.
- The presence of imperfect information.

The environment is a very special type of asset: it is something we all use, but it is not something which is directly demanded; nor is it marketed as there is no market for clean air, although there is a market for air cleansing. Why is this so? The market fails to develop because the environment is something which has open access: that is, access is unrestricted and there are no clearly defined property rights. This gives rise to a market failure.

The presence of externalities

These occur because the action of either producing or consuming a product causes a spill-over impact on to a third party. Externalities can be classified in terms of the number of parties causing and suffering from the consequences of pollution. In the case of CO_2 the externality can be classified as a many-to-many case: that is, there are many parties involved in causing pollution, and many suffering the consequences of it. The greenhouse effect caused by CO_2 emissions is global in nature. A global externality brings a set of complexities. It is much harder to identify the key parties. Many people are affected by global warming, and as individuals or as groups of people they are too small a unit to warrant the expense of solving the problem on their own. When a large number of people are affected, it makes it harder to measure the environmental damage and it is difficult to get cooperative action. It is costly to gather information on emissions and it relies on the polluter to provide information. Firms are producing and imposing a cost on society which they are not paying for. This does not lead to the socially efficient level of emission.

One of the challenges for economists is trying to identify what is an acceptable level of pollution. One way is to place a monetary value on the marginal private and social costs, as was done in Chapter 3. The model shows us that the socially optimal level of emissions is where the marginal social cost curve intersects the marginal social benefit curve. The problem is obtaining the monetary values which give the curves. Economists are still learning how to place a value on non-market goods. One approach that has been developed is the contingent valuation method. Broadly, this asks people to state their willingness to pay, for example, to have an unpolluted recreational area. These responses are then used to place a monetary value on the externality. Other approaches are being developed and modified.

The next problem is finding the appropriate incentive or approach which will lead to socially efficient emission levels. We begin with conventional economic solutions. Chapter 2 introduced the idea that individuals could form economic units of sufficient size to take action against the polluter. In relation to air pollution, this is unlikely to work because the damage costs to each party are small relative to the costs of taking effective action against the polluter. Another solution is to make producers pay for the full consequences of their actions. Coase (1960) argued that externalities can be dealt with by assigning appropriate property rights. Once property rights are assigned, all externalities will have been internalized. What this does is give a party the right to control the asset – in this case the environment. The owners will then put a value on their asset and enforce the relevant property rights. The assignment of property rights can be done through the legal system or through the market. However, this again is not realistic because it is impossible to define property rights in the global environment. Given the problems with conventional solutions in dealing with air pollution, there is a strong case for government intervention.

The presence of imperfect information

This refers to the fact that the consequences of increasing concentrations of CO_2 are not fully understood and there are contentious debates about extent and causation. Hence it is likely that the presence of imperfect information means that, even if we knew all the current information about the marginal social and private costs involved with CO_2 emissions, we still would not know about the long-term consequences. The existence of imperfect information tends to lead to uncertainty and 'overproduction' of the pollution. At present CO_2 can be measured and predicted relatively easily, but as yet we do not understand the relationship between it and climatic change. There may be a role for governments to encourage further research.

Government objectives

All governments intervene in the amount of pollution emitted into the environment. It is useful to discuss the possible objectives that governments might pursue. These can be divided into the following:

* Economic efficiency objectives.
* Administrative efficiency objectives.
* Equity objectives.

Economic efficiency objectives

It is a strange idea to think of efficiency and pollution together. How can there be efficiency in the 'production' of something which is undesirable? One approach to this is to think of pollution control as something which has costs and benefits. Control takes up resources and these resources are limited in supply. The starting point, as we have seen, is the determination of the socially efficient level of emissions. This is where the sum of the marginal private and marginal external costs of the activity equal the marginal social benefits. Governments need to choose the most appropriate approaches for achieving this socially efficient level.

Administrative efficiency objectives

These refer to the relative costs of setting up different systems in relation to each other and to the benefits they derive. They might include researching into, designing, monitoring and sanctioning a particular approach. Clearly a solution which encourages companies to produce the socially efficient level might be very desirable, but it does not make economic sense if the costs of implementing the approach outweigh the benefits. Also, what happens in a situation where the benefits of one approach exceed the costs, but compared to an alternative approach both the costs and the benefits are at a much higher level? In this instance, other objectives and the conditions prevailing in an economy might help us to evaluate alternative approaches. Administrative costs involved in lengthy regulatory procedures have become an important reason why governments have sought out other alternatives.

Equity objectives

These have a number of dimensions: for example, who should pay for pollution control – governments, the polluters or consumers? If a government decides to take on the duty of imposing pollution control and to impose a tax, it must decide which sector of the economy is to be taxed – this could be an industry, commerce or a residential sector. Much will depend on which creates the greatest quantity of pollution. The next question is: at what stage should the tax be imposed, consumption or production? Decisions like this will be guided by considerations of where the approach makes the greatest impact. The proposed carbon tax would clearly increase the price of fossil fuels initially, and subsequently this would mean higher energy prices for consumers. One current equity concern here is that it would impact more on lower-income groups, especially the elderly. This could be overcome by offering compensations to certain people, such as pensioners. Clearly, any approach adopted must take into consideration the conflict between efficiency and equity. Equity considerations cannot be captured in one simple rule, they must take into account the circumstances of every situation.

Government intervention

How can government overcome the problems of externalities and imperfect information? A wide range of approaches or instruments can be used, and these can be analysed in terms of the following:

- Provision.
- Regulation.
- Taxes and subsidies.

Provision

This means that the government would take over the activity which actually produces the pollution. For example, a government could nationalize or directly control the activities of the relevant energy industries. The problem with this approach is that a lot of information is required about the relationship between output and pollution, and the form of intervention relies on governments being committed to the objective.

Regulation

This is the most common form of air pollution control. It refers to a standard being set on emission levels by government or a regulatory authority. The polluter is then free to decide how to reach these minimum standards. In the UK this has been done through legislation. There two broad types of regulation. There is regulation of the total levels of CO_2 emissions, and there is regulation of the inputs: for example, energy conversion industries which produce large quantities of CO_2. Decisions need to be made about the socially efficient level, the type of regulation and the monitoring of actual emission levels. In addition, there is the question of which sectors or types of end-user to target. The larger the user the easier it is to use regulation. Regulation is unsuitable for a small number of diverse users such as households. Regulation is a more appropriate approach when it is important that a certain level must not be exceeded and when a large amount of environmental damage results. In this case, the high regulatory costs involved are justified. On the other hand, if emission levels exceed the threshold level, but do not cause a lot more damage, it may be more appropriate to use a less costly approach.

Other forms of regulation are voluntary agreements and directives. These are called non-market-based approaches. Voluntary agreements (VAs) were traditionally used to encourage energy efficiency and conservation in the 1970s. Typically, there is a contract between the authorities and a trade association or an individual company. The contract is a formal document signed by the parties to the agreement and is enforceable by law. Contracts state negotiated targets, with commitments and time schedules on the part of all participating parties. Voluntary agreements fall into two types: formal ones with contracts, and voluntary initiatives. The latter are more informal contracts, initiated by the industry rather than government, and they are often not binding. There is widespread use of voluntary agreements in Europe, although the degree of usage varies considerably among nations. Figure 11.1 shows that as yet voluntary agreements play a smaller role than other regulatory measures across all sectors, but in certain sectors such as industrial processes they are more significant.

Voluntary agreements generally supplement and help the implementation of existing regulations. For example, in France in the 1970s, the Ministry of the Environment agreed with trade associations to try and carry out certain programmes to reduce pollution in return for financial assistance. The advantage of VAs is that they are very flexible: they can be adapted to local conditions and

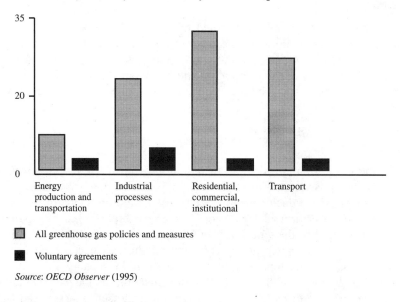

All greenhouse gas policies and measures

Voluntary agreements

Source: OECD Observer (1995)

Figure 11.1 Voluntary approaches by sector, 1994 (%)

applied to a variety of administrative arrangements. Their principal disadvantage is that they do not necessarily involve companies including the external costs they have created.

Directives are a variation on voluntary agreements and refer to general guidance rather than penalties and rewards. For example, in the UK there is the Non-Fossil Fuel Obligation, which is imposed on electricity companies. It requires them to purchase a specific amount of electricity from non-fossil fuel sources.

A different type of regulation which might help overcome the global nature of this externality is international cooperation, and efforts have been made at the EU level to encourage this approach. The current concern, as we saw in the first section, is the impact of regulation on international competitiveness. Taxes become a more attractive proposition when there is an international agreement, as all countries can in principle agree to set similar taxes. However, there are many problems with this approach: for example, what happens if parties do not agree? Countries differ in their CO_2 emission levels and there is much cross-country pollution. The costs of curbing emissions will differ between countries and this should be reflected in differing tax arrangements.

Taxes and subsidies

These are a form of intervention which, like regulation, can help reach the socially efficient emission level, and they require less information than regulation. Starting with taxes, as we saw in Chapter 3, the conventional approach comes from the work of Pigou. A system of taxes or subsidies can be devised to correct for the social costs not included in private decision making. A tax is imposed which brings the cost of the company into line with the social costs of production. Conversely, a subsidy can be applied to compensate the victims of pollution.

There are a number of advantages of taxes. They give companies freedom to decide on how and when pollution is curbed. There is an incentive to install new equipment that will allow companies to reduce emissions even further. Taxes, in theory, tend to be cost effective: as we saw in Chapter 2, if there are two companies with different abilities to reduce pollution, it makes sense to make the more efficient reducer of pollution reduce by more than the less efficient producer. This ensures that pollution is cut where it is cheapest to do so. The problem is that, in practice, companies often do not spot the cost-saving opportunities. Taxes can also act by discouraging new entrants into a market, especially if they are relatively large polluters. Furthermore, they can have relatively low administrative costs associated with them if the existing tax collection system can be used. Finally, taxes mean that governments earn a revenue, and this can be used in a number of positive ways. It can even out inequalities in the tax system, say between large and small companies, or the revenue can be used to help those sectors where international competition is very important.

The shortcomings of conventional environmental taxes are very relevant to the current concerns at national and EU levels. One problem is the amount of information assumed to be present in the Pigouvian solution. It is assumed that the costs of polluting are known and that this information will be available to the regulator: this is a very demanding assumption in reality. However, it can be claimed that the amount of information needed for tax purposes will also vary with the objective and how it will be achieved. Another problem is that taxes impose high costs, but may yield small or even perverse environmental effects from a global point of view. This is especially so in the energy industries.

Subsidies are also used, but more often in combination with other approaches. Subsidies have the advantage of interfering less with international trade. They encourage producers to seek out cleaner production processes, but they also help to keep the prices of energy-intensive goods lower.

Options for reform

The challenges facing governments were discussed in the first section of this chapter. Countries in western Europe must ensure that they encourage approaches which will help meet the CO_2 targets set in 1992. In addition, governments must ensure that their approaches are the most cost effective and appropriate for their domestic conditions. New approaches being adopted can be discussed in relation to the following objectives:

- Meeting pollution targets using market-based approaches.
- Meeting pollution targets using non-market-based approaches.

The policy options can be divided into two broad groups: market-based and non-market-based policy instruments. The former use indicators like price or profits, and incentives which alter behaviour, while non-market-based policy instruments, such as regulation and directives, might modify, but do not necessarily radically alter behaviour.

Meeting pollution targets using market-based approaches

Common examples of market-based instruments used to curb air pollution are environmental taxes and the marketing of pollution rights or tradable permits. The recent EU-wide carbon tax proposal is an example of an environmental tax. It is distinctive in that it proposes to tax not outputs, but inputs. The proposal is that the tax would be imposed on the particular energy industries which burn fossil fuels. (The burning of fossil fuels produces carbon dioxide.) The tax would vary depending on the amount of carbon produced with each energy source: gas produces the least carbon and coal the most. The proposed tax would have two parts, one relating to the carbon content and one to the energy content. So, for example, with the latter, the nuclear power industry would be taxed in relation to the energy it uses, but not the carbon content. The tax would be allowed to vary according to the emissions associated with each energy source. It is a market-based idea because the tax would increase fossil fuel prices, but the increases would be relative since coal prices would rise the most. This would produce incentives: consumers would reduce their energy consumption, switch their consumption to the fuel which produces the least carbon dioxide; perhaps switch to non-fossil fuel energy sources and improve energy efficiency by, for example, installing double glazing. These potential efficiency gains have to be weighed up against the costs of implementing the policy across all nations and the equity concerns raised earlier.

Marketing pollution rights is currently a buzz concept with economists, although there is opposition to such market-based approaches, in particular from environmentalists who are keen to see greater government intervention. The marketing of pollution rights is different to the approach described above because it aims to establish a price system and exchange between parties by assigning them property rights. The emphasis is on price incentives rather than quantity regulations. There are many types, such as tradable permits, switchable quotas and the use of coupons. Tradable permits are pieces of paper which state property rights.

A tradable permit scheme has a number of stages. A target level of environmental quality is determined by a regulatory authority. This quality level is then broken down into a total number of allowable emissions. Permits have property rights and are allocated to firms. Each polluting firm may be required to pay for the permit initially, or it may be given free by the regulating authority. The permit gives the owner the right to emit a specific amount of a particular type of pollution, defined over a specified period of time. If the firm succeeds in reducing its emissions below the limit on the permit, the difference becomes an emission reduction credit (ERC), and this can be traded with another firm which perhaps faces much higher emission levels. The idea is that trade takes place when the abatement costs exceed the permit levels. Companies can buy and sell permits depending on their ability to pollute and reduce pollution levels. Switchable quotas are similar to tradable permits. The UK government had plans to introduce a quota-switching system in sulphur emissions. Large emitters were to be allowed to buy and sell SO_2 quotas. One problem was that emission reduction rates were set at different levels for England and Wales, Scotland and Northern Ireland.

This type of approach has begun slowly to attract the attention of governments, but it is at an experimental stage in Europe. It is most developed in the USA, where the concept of tradable permits is not new. In California by the mid-1980s, many districts had trade schemes under way, although most of the schemes just complemented the command and control practices.

Meeting pollution targets using non-market-based approaches

These approaches do not rely on elements of the competitive process: for example, targets can be met through greater cooperation and agreement. One example is voluntary agreements (VAs). This type of approach, described earlier, has seen a revival in use for a number of reasons. First, VAs have been encouraged by developments taking place at the EU level. Second, they work particularly well when there are good relations between government and industry. This has not always been the case for many countries in the past; confrontation and resistance were commonplace in the 1970s. More recently, it has been argued that many industries have begun to adopt more responsible attitudes towards the environment. Maybe this is because they realize that this is a problem which is not going to go away or because they see potential new markets emerging in environmental technology. Finally, voluntary agreements increase the involvement, responsibility and motivation of companies in reducing greenhouse gases. They can be expected to provide more flexible and tailored solutions, which can be matched to the technical and economic conditions of individual sectors. For these reasons there is a case for more intense use of VAs. The case studies will describe some of the drawbacks in implementation.

The key feature of VAs is that there are no market forces or signals: the emphasis is on change through persuasion and agreement. It is an approach based on trust. In addition to good working relations between government and industry, voluntary agreements work best if trade associations exist and are well established in a country, and if there are large, well-organized industrial units. In other words, VAs are more difficult to implement in a country which has a high proportion of small to medium-sized businesses and few trade associations.

Institutional arrangements

Institutional arrangements refer to agreements reached with national governments and other institutions. So, for example, under the UN Framework Convention on Climate Change in Rio de Janeiro in 1992, the member countries of the International Energy Agency (IEA) have committed themselves to restraining global climate changes. At the same time, the EU has agreed an overall target for CO_2 emission levels and has proposed the carbon tax. The problem here is that this is a unilateral proposal. What happens if other countries and other trading blocs do not take similar action? It could mean that EU industry becomes less competitive in international markets. What is required is a 'level playing field', where the tax is adopted by all countries. The USA in particular is very sceptical about evidence on the impact of CO_2 and is unlikely to see the need for a carbon tax. The problem is trying to reach agreement and hence achieve global action, and this is a challenge because there are both different perceptions of the state of the problem and incentives for states to free ride.

Q1 Our environment is an asset. Explain why it is very different to other types of asset. Carbon dioxide is a global externality: it has an external cost. What is the impact of this on resource allocation?

Q2 Private solutions can be applied to some externalities. List the problems with these in relation to curbing CO_2 emissions.

Q3 Governments can intervene in many ways. What reasons can you give for governments emphasizing a system of regulation over a system of environmental taxes?

Q4 New pressures have forced governments to seek out new approaches. What are the distinctions between market-based and non-market-based approaches?

The following case studies consider the different emphasis given to two approaches to control CO_2 emissions. One is a market-based approach and the other a non-market-based approach. The strengths and weaknesses of both approaches are highlighted.

Case study Germany: The use of market-based instruments

Objectives

A 25 per cent reduction of CO_2 and a higher reduction in eastern Germany, taking 1987 as the base year and 2005 as the target year. To create market incentives for technological innovation.

Objectives for the EU

To stabilize emissions of global-warming pollutants by 2005.

New approaches

- Approaches to increase efficiency through market forces.

The background

Germany is a country dedicated to improving the environment. First, it is regarded as having one of the strictest set of environmental regulations in the industrialized world. It has an extensive array of regulatory controls, including taxes, subsidies and voluntary agreements. Second, it is a country at the forefront of environmental technologies: its turnover is ranked third in the world and German companies supply more than 20 per cent of the world market. Finally, expenditure on the environment as a proportion of GDP was 1.7 per cent in 1995. This was the third largest of the European nations, with Denmark and Austria spending 1.9 per cent and 1.8 per cent respectively.

Approaches to increase efficiency through market forces

Germany is very interested in using market-based approaches to curb CO_2 and other air pollutants. The German Ministry of Economics recently commissioned a

---

study on the feasibility of tradable emission permits for controlling CO_2 and other greenhouse gases. The idea of using tradable permits has been introduced, tentatively, through legislation. The Federal Emission Control Act 1985 provided the legal framework for the marketing of property rights and specifically for an emissions-crediting system. The focus of the legislation has been encouraged by independent groups, particular by the German Institute of Environmental Management. This is a body which brings together policy-makers, academics and industrialists to discuss environmental issues and instruments. It is very critical of the command and control model of regulation. What it does not like about this approach is that it tends to set out taxation regimes and regulation standards with little regard to the varying circumstances that every company faces. It claims that this leads to confrontation and not very productive outcomes. The Institute also argues that the command and control model does not bring out incentives which make companies innovate and seek more environmentally friendly technology.

The 1985 Act attempted to incorporate such incentives. It introduced the Compensation Rule which set a level. If a company manages to reduce its pollution below this level, it in effect creates 'brownie points' for itself. These have a value and are called emission credits. These can be transferred or traded within a company and between companies. Trade only occurs because there are differences among companies in their ability to reduce pollution. If all companies had the same ability to abate, then tradable permits would not work. When an emission credit is traded with another company, this means that the company with emissions above the official level is buying the permit and is in effect paying for another company to reduce emissions where it is cheaper for them to do this. The company which buys an emission credit has effectively increased its permit level. Emission credits can only be traded within a specific geographical area and for roughly similar pollutants. The Compensation Rule was incorporated for practical application through the Technical Instruction on Air Quality.

The legislation is only a beginning; it is not meant to provide a comprehensive solution to air pollution. There are a number of advantages: trading in permits goes some way to overcoming the inflexibility and inertia of the old heavy regulatory system, which is largely administrative in nature; the legislation goes some way to creating incentives for technological innovation; the emphasis is on a more sustainable prevention, focused on the sources rather than the output of air pollution; and the principle of the Compensation Rule is much less confrontational than enforcement.

The disadvantage of the trading permit initiative in Germany is quite simply that very little trading has taken place. There may be a number of reasons for this: the small number of trades actually occurring may be a product of restrictions in the legislation; there have been problems with companies' perception of these ideas, with many companies seeing them as only experimental; companies fear that traditional regulatory instruments might be brought back again and that, even if emission levels are reduced, the regulators will only increase the levels once more; and finally, transaction costs may be high for companies because they have to locate other trading companies and negotiate a price for the permit.

shows the extent of contracts between industry and government since 1990. Agreements are planned to be signed with 31 sectors accounting for 90 per cent of industrial energy consumption, and so far 22 have signed up. The second interesting fact is that the voluntary agreements are instigated by the government and are legally binding. What does this mean? The industries are obliged to set binding sectoral energy efficiency targets to enable the Dutch to meet their CO_2 emission reduction aims. This means that they are formal agreements based around a contract between government and industry. The third fact is that the Dutch voluntary agreements are very ambitious. The aim is for 20 per cent energy efficiency improvements by 2000. The voluntary agreements assist in three broad areas: in energy efficiency and conservation, in fuel switching and cleaner energy, and in renewable sources. In the first of these, the Industry Agreements on Energy Conservation specify energy-efficiency targets for 22 industrial sectors including iron, steel, chemicals, glass and cement, covering more than 70 per cent of industrial energy use.

It is important to remember that voluntary agreements are not intended to provide a comprehensive solution to the problems of air pollution control; they are typically only one of many instruments used in policy intervention, and generally supplement and strengthen existing regulations. However, they offer a number of strengths in relation to the particular pressures facing governments. Manufacturers are able to anticipate regulations because they have been involved with the agreements themselves, and this means that they have more time to plan and decide how they will keep to their commitments. In order to appreciate the advantages of VAs to industry, it is important to remember that companies dislike surprises and prefer to be assured of the regulatory environment. A VA therefore gives industry more regulatory security and stability because such agreements usually run for a period of time.

In the Netherlands, the system has worked well as it has laid the foundation for the pooling of innovative work at sectoral level. This is supported by the government's Environmental Technology Programme. In other words, companies in an industry can combine their resources to research new production techniques which will help them all meet their agreements. On the important issue of how this approach affects international competitiveness, there are two arguments. On the one hand, VAs are no different from regulations, since the adoption of a standard (on a voluntary basis) will initially increase production costs just like regulations. On the other hand, a company will be able to recoup these costs if it can generate more sales through marketing itself as being more environmentally friendly. The main benefit to the Dutch government of using VAs extensively is that there is no longer the need to draft complex regulatory legislation, hence administrative savings are made. Also there is a transfer of responsibility: it is now up to the industries to devise their own measures to meet their targets, and it is often up to the trade associations to monitor whether the environmental protection measures are being implemented. This also saves the government money. This approach particularly suits the Netherlands because it has a high proportion of companies which belong to a trade association.

The main disadvantage of voluntary agreements in the Netherlands is that the relatively high targets do affect the international competitiveness of some of the companies: in other words, the cost disadvantage is large and not likely to be easily recouped. Moreover VAs typically involve large companies, and there is a free-rider problem with small companies. Generally, the Dutch targets appear too high, and this raises the question of whether industry will be able to comply with them. The latest review of the VA programme in 1993 found that, while twelve sectors had signed up, only an 8 per cent average improvement had been made in energy efficiency. Finally, there is the question of whether VAs allow companies to do less than they actually could do under alternative approaches.

Approaches to meet targets through the use of planning

The Dutch are very good at making plans, and environmental policy is divided between many departments and bodies. This planning regime has facilitated the use of voluntary agreements. The Netherlands has had three National Environment Policy Plans (NEPPs), in 1989, 1990 and 1993, and voluntary agreements are highly integrated into the overall environmental policy plans. Specific national programmes have multisectoral reporting of greenhouse gas emissions. In the Netherlands this instrument has a particularly prominent support role for the implementation and enforcement of very strict regulatory standards. Environmental problems are scientifically analysed, targets are then set and government policies are shaped around them. A key approach in the Netherlands is the Target Group. This uses voluntary agreements to get a basis of consensus and support between the government and industry on new regulations in the NEPPs.

Industrial diversity means that plans have to be decoded for specific sectors. These plans are contained in the Memorandum on the Implementation of Target Group. The strategy is to integrate environmental objectives with each sector. Declarations of Intent state the targets for each industry and contain individual company environmental plans. The Industry Target Group feeds down to and discusses targets with the relevant industrial or trade associations. However, despite the planning efforts, there is evidence to suggest that many NEPP targets have not been met.

Two final points are worth bearing in mind. The Netherlands has aimed at energy conservation. However, if the aim is to reduce CO_2 emission levels, improvements in energy efficiency may not necessarily reduce pollution; other instruments may be needed. Second, the advantages of VAs have to be considered alongside the disadvantages of alternative policies. The Netherlands, like many other EU countries, is a very open economy (trade accounts for a relatively large proportion of GDP). This means that if it imposed a unilateral tax on energy-intensive companies that are subject to international competition this might damage their competitive position. Also it might impact on other parts of the Dutch economy which are dependent on energy-intensive industries. The costs of an approach which emphasizes a unilateral tax therefore might outweigh the benefits.

Old arrangements

Relations between government and industry were characterized by confrontation. Previous arrangements had less scope for cooperation and consensus.

New arrangements

The onus of responsibility has altered: the government has asked the private sector to police itself. The role of voluntary agreements is a supporting one for enforcing standards, and these agreements are legally binding.

Change of relationships

The trade associations are playing a leading role in negotiating target plans and publishing results for the government and the public. The role of government has altered from one of direct regulator to one of initiator and setter of targets. Industry self-regulation is beginning to grow.

Q7 *How do voluntary agreements differ from the old command and control models of environmental control? What are the advantages of emphasizing an agreements-based system rather than a penalties-based one? What are the disadvantages of voluntary agreements to the government?*

Q8 *Voluntary agreements work well under a particular set of conditions. List what these are and state why you think the Netherlands has/has not emphasized the right approach.*

Discussion

This section discusses the two approaches in terms of how efficiency has been enhanced. In Germany there have been some tentative efforts to encourage market-based approaches and although it is too early to say yet how successful trading permits will become, it is possible to evaluate some of the emerging strengths and weaknesses. The approaches can be viewed in terms of their costs and benefits and in terms of the alternatives. There are benefits to both companies and government. The benefits to companies of the trading permit initiative are that production costs should be lowered as credits can, in theory, be traded for cash with companies which emit at above their specified level. The trading permit scheme means that the previous heavy hand of the German government can be reduced, and in effect the companies do all the work, while the distribution of pollution is determined by market forces. The government's role is to design and set up the system and to determine the overall emission level. The costs to companies of this approach appear to be related to imperfect information and uncertainty. In the first case, companies need to know of other potential traders and negotiate prices. In economics we call the costs incurred in finding this information transaction costs. Under the present legislation, there is clearly some need to support information-gathering systems. In the second case, uncertainty could be overcome in time, with the government indicating a greater commitment to the initiative and moving away from the perceived experimental image it has at present. The costs to the government include designing and monitoring the scheme. These are important because if permits are not enforced and sanctions are insufficient, the market will fail as companies see no incentive to purchase credits. Trading permits is an exciting idea, but it must be weighed up against existing and other new approaches. Remember that the government wishes to devise approaches which move away from heavy regulations and do not distort the international competitiveness of its companies. Trading permits go some way to meeting these objectives, but at present there is no significant evidence that they will be easier or cheaper to implement.

The Dutch adopt a more cooperative approach, implemented through an extensive set of regional and national environmental plans. Although voluntary agreements typically supplement the existing regulations, there are some clear strengths of using this particular approach more intensively in the Netherlands. The benefits to industry are that VAs are relatively easy to implement because the Dutch have a strong trade association movement and there are mutual relations between government and industry. Also, this is a small open country where international competitiveness is important, and VAs hurt the export position of energy-intensive industries less than other approaches, such as taxes. VAs lend themselves to a wide range of sectors and are very flexible in their form and content. Among the costs of using VAs is the fact that they must be monitored via each sector so that non-compliant companies are identified. Also, there is clearly a skill in setting targets which are within the realistic reach of the industries concerned. So far, on recent evidence, this has not been mastered. There may be a case for the Dutch to intensify their use of subsidies in conjunction with VAs. This would assist companies in shifting to cleaner production processes without damaging their competitive position.

In comparing the two approaches, there appears to be some logic behind the Dutch emphasizing VAs because the Netherlands has a climate of mutual trust between industry and government. It is undeniable that, the market-creating benefits of a tradable permit system are theoretically very appealing. However, as we saw from the German experience, there remain considerable practical problems in implementation, and this approach has some way to go before it can be fully adopted.

Further reading

Introductory level

Begg, D., Fischer, S. and Dornbusch, R. (1994) *Economics*, 4th edn, Maidenhead: McGraw-Hill, ch.15.

Griffiths, A. and Wall, S. (eds) (1995) *Applied Economics: An Introductory Course*, 6th edn, Harlow, Longman: ch.10.

Gwartney, J. (1976) *Microeconomics: Public and Private Choice*, New York: Academic Press, ch.17.

Hardwick, P., Khan, B. and Langmead, J. (1994) *An Introduction to Modern Economics*, 4th edn, Harlow, Longman: chs. 12 and 13.

Lipsey, R. and Chrystal, K. (1995) *An Introduction to Positive Economics*, 8th edn, Oxford: Oxford University Press, chs. 23 and 24.

Sloman, J. (1994) *Economics*, 2nd edn, Hemel Hempstead: Harvester Wheatsheaf, chs.11 and 12.

Intermediate level

DeSerpa, A. (1988) *Microeconomic Theory: Issues and Applications*, 2nd edn, Boston, MA: Allyn and Bacon, ch. 19.

Griffiths, A. and Wall, S. (1996) *Intermediate Microeconomics: Theory and Applications*, Harlow: Longman, ch. 11.

Jenkinson, T. (ed.) (1996) *Readings in Microeconomics*, Oxford: Oxford University Press, ch. 11.

Pindyck, R. and Rubinfeld, D. (1992) *Microeconomics*, 2nd edn, Basingstoke, Macmillan: chs. 4, 17 and 18.

Other sources

Bennett, G. (1980) 'Netherlands: pollution control', *Environmental Policy Law*, vol. 6, no. 4.

Bouwer, K. (1994) 'The integration of regional environmental planning and physical planning in the Netherlands', *Journal of Environmental Planning Management*, vol. 37, no. 1.

Bovenberg, A. Lans (1993), 'Policy instruments for curbing CO_2 emissions: the case of the Netherlands', *Environmental and Resource Economics*, vol 3, no. 3.

Coase, R. (1960) 'The problem of social cost', *Journal of Law and Economics*, 3, pp. 1–44.

Douglas, W. (1995) 'Market-based instruments in Germany and the Netherlands: a case of competition versus co-operation?' *European Environment*, vol. 5, no. 1.

'The economics of limiting CO_2 emissions', *European Economy*, special edition, no. 1, 1992.

'The environment survey', *The Economist*, 30 May 1992.

'German industries follow Dutch in volunteering CO_2 reductions', *ENDS Report*, no. 244, 1995.

'Environmental technologies', *German Brief*, July, 1994.

Mohr, E. (1992) 'Tradeable permits for controlling greenhouse gases and complementary policies', in OECD, *Climate Change: Designing a Tradeable Permit System*, Kiel Institute of World Economics, Germany.

Park, P. (1996) 'The marketable permit programme in California', *Environmental Law and Management*, February.

Potier, M. (1994) 'Agreement on the environment', *OECD Observer*, no. 189.

225

Solsbery, L. and Wiederkehr, P. (1995) 'Voluntary approaches for energy-related CO_2 abatement', *OECD Observer*, no. 196.

Swift, S. (1995) 'The carbon tax', *British Economic Survey*, vol. 24, no. 2.

Verbruggen, H. (1991) 'Political economy aspects of environmental policy instruments', paper to the conference on Environmental Policy and the Economy.

Webb, A. (1995) 'The future of EU environmental policy', *EIU European Trends*, 4th quarter, Economist Intelligence Unit.

Chapter 12

Waste disposal

> Key words used: externality, market failure, free-rider, polluter-pays principle, recycling

Have you noticed how much packaging comes with any new purchase these days? Ironically, one of the functions of packaging and parcelling is to attract attention, but no one wishes to look at packaging once it becomes used. Economic prosperity means abundance, and unlike the period of the Second World War when people 'never threw things away', the modern blight is that we needlessly accumulate and discard more packaging than ever before. New environmental concerns which emerged in the 1980s came from public concerns about environmental damage. One aspect of this was that waste is a major source of pollution and damage. So waste disposal has become an area of concern and interest in its own right. Many issues have been raised about new technologies, recycling, the location of landfill sites and environmental responsibility. Governments are involved in waste disposal, and this involvement takes many forms. This chapter will review the role of governments and how economics can contribute to questions about the more efficient handling of waste disposal and the role of markets in this process.

Background to the problem

Waste material is something which we all generate, but few of us know what actually happens to waste once we throw it away, or the impact it has on the environment. Waste disposal is the desirable and necessary activity which handles waste once it has been discarded by us, and this chapter is about the pressures to reduce waste and handle it more efficiently. In an ideal world, what we want to see is a reduction in the amount of waste produced and better ways of handling waste disposal. During the 1980s, the impact of waste disposal both on public health and on the environment became an important political issue. People became concerned about the discharge of toxic chemicals and the consequences on water supply and air. This led to increasing attention to the management of wastes and its relationship with the reduction of pollution. Public concern expressed itself in political statements both nationally and at EU level.

Governments expressed their concern about atmospheric pollution and the Green Party reached its peak of electoral popularity in 1989. Concerns about waste and environmental issues placed pressure on governments, which had to respond by seeking out new approaches to controlling the generation of waste and the management of its disposal.

Waste is the end product of consumption or production, and every economic agent generates waste. As waste is a wide subject, this chapter will focus only on household and packaging waste and the incentives to reduce, reuse and recycle it. Packaging waste includes materials like paper, cardboard, glass and plastics. It accounts for 30 per cent by weight of total household waste. Packaging has come under much criticism as many people think that there is too much packaging on goods. Why study this activity? The collection and disposal of waste has been predominantly undertaken by local authorities, but various pressures have forced them to come up with innovative ways of managing waste. Many of these innovative arrangements provide examples of the use and limitations of economic instruments.

The pressures which have been exerted on governments are a combination of the growth of environmental concerns, the rapid growth in waste, and problems with traditional methods of waste disposal. Waste, in all categories, has grown rapidly since the Second World War. We must put this in its proper context. Not all waste is bad; in fact, packaging serves a valuable economic function. It protects the product, provides sales appeal and gives information on the product. The problem is that it is an increasing function of economic growth and prosperity. The per-person waste generation rate in western Europe has been growing at 3 to 5 per cent a year. Today, 345 million people within the EU generate more than 100 million tonnes of household waste a year. It is estimated that the average household generates 1 tonne of waste per year, and in the UK, 22 million tonnes of domestic waste are produced annually.

The second influence on waste disposal has been that of the European Commission. There have been two broad aspects to this influence: targets have been laid down for waste management approaches; and incentives have been introduced for recycling. In May 1990 the Commission introduced a Strategy for Waste Management, which stressed that efforts should be made to minimize waste first and foremost, and then to consider ways of reusing and recycling material. The Commission then focused its attention on packaging and set maximum recovery and recycling targets. Specifically, the Commission has been instrumental in trying to get packaging waste used more for recycling, and it has also set new duties for waste regulators and other authorities. Recycling means regenerating materials so that they can be used for their original purpose or other purposes. Recovery is a slightly broader term, meaning to recycle, regenerate or to take the energy from the waste product.

The European Commission's directive on packaging and packaging waste in 1994, which replaced an earlier directive in 1985, set targets for packaging recycling and recovery. The original target was that, within ten years of its being implemented, 90 per cent of packaging waste was to be recovered, 60 per cent as materials to be used again and only 10 per cent to go into landfills. The targets set were very high and have since been revised to an overall recovery rate of 60 per cent, a recycling rate of between 25 and 45 per cent, and a minimum recycling rate for individual materials. All member states are now collectively bound by several pieces of legislation on waste management. These directives require each country to meet certain standards by specific dates, although in most cases they do not detail how to arrive at those standards. These framework directives, which are detailed in a later section, make it possible for each country to pursue markedly different policies.

There have been problems with traditional ways of disposing of waste, which have led to pressures to rethink the whole process. Waste can be disposed of through incineration, in landfills and, less commonly, by composting. Incineration is the most common form of treatment in western Europe. This is where waste is combusted or compacted, often producing heat. This heat can produce energy which can be further used to provide steam or as a heat source. Not all household waste can be incinerated and this must go somewhere else. Usage rates are terms used to describe the percentage of total waste that goes to a particular destination. So, for example, the usage rate for incineration in Germany is 70 per cent and in France 54 per cent. There are problems with this form of disposal. One is the toxic fumes released during burning. New technology has overcome this to some extent by reducing noxious effects, but there can be other side effects, notably sludge and carbon dioxide. In 1995 tougher standards on the level of emissions were introduced, reflecting these concerns at a national level. There is still much public concern about waste incineration and the impact on health.

Landfill is the most common form of waste disposal in the UK. It is cheaper than incineration and has generally been more widely available. It accounts for the greatest proportion of hazardous waste disposal. It too has some problems. If sites are located too close to water systems, water supplies can become contaminated. Site selection is now a carefully engineered exercise, but the problem facing environmentalists is uncertainty about the impact of older, less regulated sites. Landfill can produce a landfill gas, a combination of carbon dioxide and methane, which is unpleasant and can seep out, so there is a problem with landfill gas control. When it is controlled, it can be captured and used for fuel. Preparation costs for the use of landfills are rising with all the new regulations, and it is becoming a less attractive form of waste disposal. Additionally, landfill can be an eyesore on the landscape, and it typically has high transport costs because landfill sites are often located miles away from populated areas. The European Commission has a draft directive on landfill performances and standards which will eventually increase the cost of landfill. Some countries have little landfill capacity left; others, like the UK, have plenty. However, despite its capacity, the UK introduced a landfill levy in October 1996. France is closing all its landfill sites by the year 2002. It is estimated that landfill prices will increase fivefold before the end of the 1990s.

Pressures on traditional waste disposal methods have led both to increases in legislation on standards and to incentives to develop other forms of disposal. An example of the latter is greater reuse and recycling. It is important to note that these are methods which will not overcome the waste disposal problem totally; they are only a part of the process of waste disposal and can only assist in certain areas. Household waste is one area which lends itself to greater recycling, in theory. However, there are practical problems with this activity: for example, when packaging material becomes soiled and mixed up with other materials.

There are also financial constraints. Recycling is an expensive activity because the waste products are handled so many times. It involves collection, sorting into recyclable/non-recyclable material, and sending different materials to different recycling companies. Clearly, not all materials can be recycled, but there is more scope for recycling household materials. The challenge for governments is how to meet the EU-wide targets for national recycling. Each government has to decide how to set incentives to encourage this activity and, most importantly, the best way to organize and pay for it. This problem arises because the costs of collection are relatively high and someone needs to pay for them.

There are strong economic arguments for recycling: it reduces our need for raw materials; it can produce energy savings; and it reduces the amount of waste that needs to be disposed of. If we continue to generate waste at the current rate, it will become increasingly important that producers begin to think about how the end product will be used. It is clear that the recycling activity will not occur on its own, but that government targets and incentives can go a long way to encouraging it. As recycling is uneconomic at present, and appears to require significant subsidy (although some glass and metal schemes which require people to bring in the goods are often independently viable), governments have a role in trying to encourage this activity.

It is important to point out that recycling is only one part of the process of waste management. There are other ways of handling waste, such as energy recovery. This is where the energy in the waste material is taken out and used for other purposes. Reuse refers to using packaging, such as containers, over and over again. For recycling to be promoted ahead of these other methods, there have to be strong arguments in its favour.

In summary, a combination of factors have given rise to the need to rethink and improve upon waste reduction and waste disposal management. The challenge for governments and economists, in relation to paper and packaging waste, is how to encourage socially efficient activities which are expensive to undertake.

Current system of allocation

This section examines why the generation and management of waste cannot be left up to markets alone, and why there is a need for government intervention.

The market

Waste disposal is a special type of activity. For most households and producers it is not something that we stop and think about; we know we produce it, but its disposal is really the responsibility of someone else. Chapter 2 outlined the general nature of market failure, and in relation to waste, the principal one is as following:

* The presence of externalities.

The presence of externalities

These arise because producers and consumers can discard packaging waste easily. Materials can be dumped into common property resources, such as rivers, seas and the countryside: this is called fly tipping. Common property resources are where access is unlimited, or where property rights are non-existent or poorly enforced, and there are few incentives to use the resource wisely. This gives rise to free riding. People do not perceive the costs that they individually impose on the common property. Waste, therefore, creates a negative externality. It can also create inter-generational externalities. These refer to the fact that spill-over effects may impact on future generations of people. In the absence of perfect knowledge, we may not even know what effect current waste disposal methods will have on the soil, water and air. It is undesirable to have a situation where the needs of the present generation compromise the ability of future generations to meet their needs. But markets are unlikely to take these considerations into account.

Interestingly, waste can also be said to have a positive externality. Waste can be used further down the line: it can be reused, used to make energy to produce other goods (through processes like energy incineration), or recycled. In other words, there is the potential for further economic use. In an ideal world, what we want is for these types of activity to be maximized, because they act by reducing the amount of waste to be disposed of. But it is unlikely that free markets would take into consideration the external benefits from these activities and hence an inefficient allocation of resources would probably result. The properties of waste suggest that private economic behaviour will not yield socially optimal outcomes in this area: in other words, benefits will not equal costs. Government intervention may be needed to promote the social good and protect the common resource.

Government objectives

Most local governments take responsibility for the collection and removal of household waste, and in doing this they have a number of objectives to meet. These can be divided into the following:

* Economic efficiency objectives.
* Administrative efficiency objectives.
* Equity objectives.

231

Economic efficiency objectives

These might refer to getting a system which produces the minimum amount of waste in the first instance, then employing the different methods, such as reuse, recycling and energy recovery, in a combination which maximizes the benefits for each material type. There are many ways of handling waste, and the costs and benefits of recycling, for example, would have to be weighed up against the costs and benefits of alternative methods, such as energy recovery. In an ideal situation, we wish to see the best method used to the maximum in those activities which it is best at handling. At present recycling is a relatively expensive activity, but if the overall benefits of recycling outweigh its costs and outweigh the costs of alternatives, then there is an economic argument for its greater use. The problem for economists is to find a way to value the overall benefits of recycling. To do this the benefits need to be reflected in the prices of products and there needs to be a market for recycled materials.

Administrative efficiency objectives

These refer to minimizing the costs of setting up, designing and implementing different waste management approaches. Administrative costs are relatively high in recycling in relation to alternatives. Administering a local recycling scheme might involve those costs above plus the costs of educating the public on the importance of sorting out household waste, providing suitable containers for disposal, arranging collection and having a system of contracts with recycling companies.

Equity objectives

In relation to waste, these refer to ensuring that any scheme is fair. A popular phrase at present is the polluter-pays principle. This is difficult to apply with waste. Household waste is a product which involves many parties: the producer of the product, the packager and the end user. Fairness in terms of the producer-pays principle refers to getting those who initially generate the waste to be more responsible for its disposal: this would be the producers and packaging companies. Alternatively, fairness might involve the holder of packaging waste – perhaps the consumers or retailers – being made more responsible for waste disposal. Clearly, equity considerations in waste are not easy to define.

The recycling of waste has important economic functions. Since it reduces our need to use as much raw materials, it can reduce the costs of producing that good again: for example, it is much cheaper to make certain types of glass from old glass than it is from raw materials. Recycling reduces the amount of waste that is actually disposed of, but many materials cannot be recycled, so it is only one element of waste management. If manufacturers could be encouraged to make a product that would be easy to recycle at the end of its life, then the recycling activity could be expanded.

Government intervention

The government can intervene in a number of ways in waste generation and management to overcome various externality problems. These are as follows:

- Provision.
- Regulation.
- Taxes and subsidies.

Provision

Governments can directly provide the service of disposing of waste. This may involve taking over the duty to ensure that waste disposal arrangements are in place. Conferring a duty to organize waste on, for example, a local authority overcomes the externality problem. Also, the nature of waste collection gives rise to economies of scale and there are advantages to having one centrally organized activity. It would be uneconomic to have many waste collection companies. In many cases, governments contract out the actual provision to a private company. There are a number of separate activities involved, including waste collection, disposal and regulation. In the UK, waste collection authorities (WCAs) put the household waste collection out to tender every five to seven years. These authorities also have a duty to draw up a recycling plan for their area. Waste disposal authorities have a duty to ensure the provision of appropriate waste disposal facilities. In the UK, this has been executed through the setting up of a local authority waste disposal company or through joint ventures with private companies. The involvement of the private sector in both these activities has increased substantially in the UK.

Regulation

The government intervenes by regulation. In the UK, waste regulation authorities (WRAs) are responsible for licensing the use of landfill sites, the operations, monitoring, regulation enforcement and waste planning. In April 1996, waste regulation became the responsibility of the Environment Agency. In addition, every WRA has to produce a recycling plan, in consultation with the WCAs. As well as regulating, governments can legislate: for example, they can set national and local targets to ensure that a certain amount of waste is recycled, reused and disposed by a variety of methods. The European Commission has introduced directives for standards in waste management, but has left it up to each country to decide how to meet those standards.

Taxes and subsidies

There are two roles of taxes in waste disposal: to alter the prices of undertaking certain activities; and to finance a waste management scheme. In the first case,

233

many countries have increased the cost of certain waste disposal methods. In the UK, a landfill levy has been introduced, taxing those waste products which are considered active at £7 per tonne and inactive waste at £2 per tonne. Also, there is a tax exemption if wastes have been landfilled but satisfy a reuse, incineration or recycling condition. In other words, if the waste can be removed for these purposes, there will be a tax credit. Subsidies can be used to encourage a particular activity. For example in Italy, people bringing in paper to city centre depots are paid £33 per tonne.

Waste management schemes may be financed through local taxes, or the community charge in the case of the UK. Part of this tax pays for individual refuse collection, irrespective of the amount generated. In other parts of Europe, households are charged directly for the amount of waste collected and disposed. This type of system encourages waste minimization and recycling on the one hand, but it also encourages households to dump their waste in common ground so as to avoid paying the charge.

Countries vary in their national and local arrangements. France, Germany and the Netherlands have introduced new laws, standards, objectives and priorities to encourage the growth of recycling. In the Netherlands, landfill is very expensive and recycling is therefore much more developed. It is the only country which has set a target for the reduction of packaging. Agreements between industry and government have led to an arrangement whereby the industry has set up an organization to collect and dispose of waste, and to educate the public on waste disposal.

Options for reform

The first section outlined some of the constraints facing governments in their existing waste disposal methods. This section discusses the opportunities for improving waste management, which will be discussed in relation to the following approaches:

- Approaches to increase efficiency in waste management.
- Approaches to expand the recycling activity.

Approaches to increase efficiency in waste management

These approaches refer to ways in which the handling of waste can be improved at all levels of activity. What we wish for in an ideal world is a minimization of waste, materials reused and recycled, and energy recovered from materials. What we do not wish to see is a growing proportion of materials going to waste in landfill operations. There has been progress with the first objective. Producers have been given incentives to design packaging so that it uses a minimum of resources and when it is discarded the minimum waste is generated. Minimum can mean that there is lighter packaging weight. For example, the weights of glass milk bottles, tin cans and plastic yoghurt pots have all been reduced since the 1950s.

Educating consumers about reducing their waste is another option. In Germany, this approach has had some success. National advertising campaigns and promotional literature on actual products can encourage waste minimization. Surveys have shown that when consumers are faced with overpackaged products, they are gradually beginning to choose products with less packaging. But there are difficulties with this approach. At present, particularly in the UK, there are no penalties for producing more waste. Householders do not pay for waste collection and disposal in relation to the amount of waste produced. A possibility is to levy a charge on waste quantities generated. The problem with this, mentioned earlier, is that it may encourage fly tipping.

Material reuse involves packaging material being made in a way which allows it to be used over and over again. The problem with this option is that there are resource costs involved in making, for example, thicker and stronger containers. There are further costs involved in sterilizing and preparing these containers. These costs have to be weighed up against the benefits of this activity and the costs of alternatives.

A final option is to make the costs of alternative waste disposal methods reflect the costs to society. If we wish to encourage a particular activity, such as waste minimization or recycling, and discourage others, such as landfilling, taxes can be used to 'level the playing field'. In the UK, recycling does not make sense because there is abundant landfill capacity and tipping fees are very low. However, both France and the UK have landfill levies. In France a 20 franc per tonne tax on waste going to landfill is hoped to reduce landfilling as a practice. In the UK, the 1996 landfill levy has been introduced to bring landfill costs in to line with the rest of Europe, and it will generate an annual revenue of £450 million. It is clear that this will not be sufficient in itself to encourage recycling and other activities. What is also needed are new laws, regulations and support strategies. These are considered below.

Approaches to expand the recycling activity

Recycling is an activity which needs to be supported by governments, and this can be done in a number of ways:

- Legislation and the setting of recycling targets.
- Banning some products.
- A disposal tax on specific products.
- The introduction of local recycling schemes.
- Grants and loans to promote recycling.

Disposal bans and the setting of national targets are typical of much of the new legislation in the EU. The Netherlands target is aimed at ensuring that only 10 per cent of the waste stream ends up in landfills by 2010. In Denmark, the aluminium tin has been banned and no biodegradable waste will be allowed in landfills by 1997. The UK has set a 25 per cent recycling target.

235

Local recycling schemes are being implemented in many countries. One of the challenges for local authorities is to change their procurement laws so that there is a price preference for recycled products. This can be done by providing incentives and setting local purchasing goals for recycled material.

There have been a number of failed recycling programmes. This is because there are many steps involved in recycling and there must be capacity at every stage to be able to handle waste products. Companies must have a production facility to handle recycled waste. There must also be appropriate methods to sort out different qualities of waste. Recycling fails if there are too many contaminated materials. Moreover, recycling is a volume business: if capital costs have been spent on installing the production equipment, the right amount of recyclable material must be collected in the first place.

There are other challenges involved in ensuring that there are markets for recycled material. The establishment of markets, as we shall see from the case study, is an important part of recycling. There is no point in creating a market for a material unless there is a demand for it. In the UK, the reprocessing industries either convert the material into a recycled product or it becomes part of an input into making a final recycled product. There is a strong demand in the UK for metal cans, glass and textiles. A market demand exists for paper, but it is limited by production capabilities of recycled paper users. There is an emerging demand for plastics and compost. If the volume of recycled material increased rapidly, there is no guarantee that there would be markets for these materials. Prices and revenues earned may fall, defeating the purpose of the exercise.

In summary, approaches to encourage greater efficiency in waste management are currently being developed in western European countries. There are strong economic reasons for the greater use of recycling in household waste, but there are equally strong economic forces which make it a potentially unprofitable activity. There is clearly a role for governments to change the economics of recycling, but this requires a number of conditions to be present. These can be summarized as: a way of valuing recycled waste to reflect its overall benefits to society; political willpower and legislation; the necessary technological incentives for development; economic restructuring forced by large-scale recycling; legislation which addresses not just collection, but incentives for manufacturers to use recycled materials; market stimulation and the sharpening of demand; targets aligned with present capacity and assistance given to develop capacity; and a subsidy because not all waste products have a commercial use. For these conditions to be met there is a dual role for governments and for markets.

Institutional arrangements

In 1994 the European Commission directive declared what should be done with used packaging. Its targets are not as ambitious, as those of Germany: within five years EU countries must recover at least half of their waste packaging and recycle a quarter of it, with a minimum of 15 per cent for each material. The directive tries to balance the environment with economy, so Greece, Ireland and Portugal have lower targets and countries wishing to recycle more than 65 per cent can do so only if they have the facilities to use the recycled material. Further legislation on waste is planned for the end of the decade.

Q1 List the reasons why governments are involved in waste disposal markets.

Q2 What pressures have led governments to consider how waste disposal can be better managed?

Q3 What function does the European Commission play in waste disposal management?

Q4 Recycling is one possible activity which can be encouraged to increase efficiency in household waste management. What other approaches can be adopted?

The following case studies illustrate different approaches adopted to encourage the recycling activity. They demonstrate the financial and operational difficulties involved, and the function of both governments and markets.

Case study Germany: Recycling waste

Objectives

To reduce drastically the flood of packaging waste, by first avoiding waste and then by reusing it and making manufacturers and distributors more responsible for the waste they create.

Objectives for the EU

The 1994 directive states that by the end of the century all EU countries must recover at least half of their waste packaging and recycle one-quarter of it, with a minimum of 15 per cent for each material type.

New approaches

Germany's landfill capacity is being reduced, and by 2000 half of all landfills in operation will be full. In a further five years, the number will shrink by 80 per cent. There are pressures, therefore, to increase the number of incineration plants and to introduce more composting and recycling. The German government has taken steps to encourage the last option, and this will be examined in relation to packaging and packaging waste:

- Approaches to increase efficiency in waste disposal.
- Approaches which encourage self-regulation.

The background

Germany is only one of a handful of countries which have taken steps on packaging. The government has set recovery of packaging waste targets which are considerably higher than those set by the European Commission. Energy incineration of household waste is not allowed, and the business sector has been given the opportunity to take back its packaging waste.

Approaches to increase efficiency in waste disposal

The government has adopted the role of formulating the aims of waste disposal and setting up the framework conditions, but the operational activity is to come from the business sector. The aims are contained in a piece of legislation called the Packaging Ordinance, introduced in 1991. The ordinance makes manufacturers more responsible for the waste they create, reduces local authorities' responsibility for waste disposal, and encourages multiple-use packaging (e.g. bottles which can be reused rather than cans which cannot) and the reuse/recycling of materials. The rules of the ordinance specify that:

- Manufacturers and distributors are obliged to take back all packaging material used in transport (e.g. barrels, cartons, boxes, sacks, cans and palettes) for reuse or recycling.
- Distributors, mainly retailers, are obliged to take back, inside the shops, all packaging material generated in self-service shopping, for reuse or recycling.

Consumers have the right to leave packaging with the retailer: for example, to leave packaging in the supermarkets. But retailers do not have to take packaging back if it is soiled. In addition to these rules, the German government has set ambitious recycling quotas: Table 12.1 shows the targets for the different materials.

The legislation has no interest in what will be done with the recycled material or who will buy it up – this has been left to the market. Leaving the operation up to the market has created problems. For one thing, consumers are not sorting out their waste properly: up to 40 per cent is soiled and cannot be used for recycling purposes. There is a case for urging the population to sort out their waste more carefully. Also, the recycling targets have not been met. It has been argued that they were set too high in the first place. The Federal Environment Ministry has had to extend the deadlines for meeting the recycling quotas. Now the highest recycling rates will not be obligatory until 1998. This has been done in order to allow sufficient time for recycling equipment to be purchased and installed. The waste management industry has responded to these government-imposed quotas by investing more than DM7 billion. The problem is that recycling requires capital-intensive technology and this can only be financed by large companies. It can be argued that the policy has been unfair to the smaller companies.

Table 12.1 DSD recycling quotas (%)

Material	By end 1992			By end 1995		
	Collection[a]	Sorting	Re-cycling	Collection	Sorting	Re-cycling
Glass	60	70	42	80	90	72
Tinplate steel	40	65	26	80	90	72
Aluminium	30	60	18	80	90	72
Cardboard	30	60	18	80	80	64
Paper	30	60	18	80	80	64
Plastic	20	30	9	80	80	64
Composites[b]	20	30	6	80	80	64

[a]The targets will be deemed met if 50 per cent of the total packaging material has been collected for recycling.
[b]For example, drinks cartons.
Source: Waite (1995).

Approaches which encourage self-regulation

The government, through legislation, changed the obligations on retailers and manufacturers, disallowed incineration and at the same time set recycling targets. The industry responded to these challenges by forming an independent organization. Called the Duales System Deutschland (DSD), it began operations in 1993 with the slogan 'Don't let packaging go to waste'. The DSD is called a dual system to reflect the fact that a second private sector system collects, sorts and recycles waste alongside the public waste disposal system. It is a private, non-profit-making company formed by 600 private companies from the retail trade, consumer goods trade and the packaging industry, and membership is voluntary. It takes responsibility for every stage of the packaging process: it organizes and funds the collection, processing and reprocessing of waste packaging.

The change in obligations means that costs will rise for manufacturers because they now have to add in an extra activity, that of taking back their packaging waste. This cost has to be met and the activity funded. Those who take part decide on a disposal company and DSD then underwrites the contract with that company. DSD pays for the collection and separation of the waste, and the recycling cost is absorbed by the packaging company. The system is funded by licensing the use of 'Der Grüne Punkt' (the green dot). In order to use the green dot, manufacturers or importers apply for a DSD licence, which verifies to consumers that the materials are recycled. DSD collects a fee according to the number of items sold per year and the packaging volume. This fee is between 1 and 20 pfennigs an item, based on the rates shown in Table 12.2. This is a guarantee that the packaging material is recycled and not just recyclable. The fee effectively becomes part of the production costs and creates incentives for manufacturers to use more easily recyclable materials.

Waste packaging collection operates a household-orientated system. House-holders are given bins in which to put aluminium, tinplate, plastic and packaging material for collection. Private and municipal waste disposal companies collect and sort these sacks, which are forwarded to recycling companies for processing and the production of new packages.

There is a neutral inspection agency which looks at recycling plants and submits reports on incoming and outgoing material. Among its aims is to ensure that the material stipulated in the Packaging Ordinance is being recycled.

There are a number of strengths and weaknesses with this self-regulatory approach. On the positive side, targets have had a valuable role in stimulating change. The tough new laws on recycling waste have both reduced packaging and changed the type of packaging used. Waste packaging fell from 12.79 million tonnes in 1991 to 11.86 million tonnes in 1993. Households and small firms are responsible for more than half of the reduction, and in some sectors, growth in recovery rates has been exceeded: the percentage of returnable packaging in the beverage sector increased from 7 to 75 per cent (the Packaging Ordinance only required 72 per cent). The type of packaging used for products has changed, and compound materials are on the retreat: for example, packaging which used to be made up of plastic, aluminium and paper is slowly becoming packaging which is made from one material, and this improves the possibility of recycling. Manufacturers have been made responsible for recycling. Recycling costs are passed on to packaging manufacturers, which provides an incentive for them to use fewer, more easily recyclable materials. Ecology has become a sales argument: consumers are being urged to buy the green dot product in the knowledge that they are making environmentally friendly decisions. In the medium term, what should happen is that products with packaging which is easier to dismantle will have lower costs than those which require more pre-sorting. Consumers will be faced with a more environmentally friendly product which is also cheaper. There have been additional spin-offs, such as a 7 per cent growth in the private waste disposal industry.

There have, however been operational and financial problems with this system. Large-scale national policies were set with little regard to how small and medium-sized firms would cope. This has caused cash flow problems by increasing the

Table 12.2 DSD packaging levy rates

Material	Levy (Pfennigs per kg)
Glass	16
Paper and board	33
Steel cans	56
Aluminium cans	100
Plastics	300
Composites	166

Source: Waite (1995).

capital requirements and risk to firms. The targets were too high in relation to the existing capacity of the processing industry and, as we saw earlier, these had to be amended. DSD was nearly made bankrupt in 1993 due to escalating costs. There were opportunities for free riding, in that packaging companies could understate the amount of packaging used and avoid paying the fee. DSD ended up being in debt to its contractors. The system has also had high administrative costs. For example, DSD spent DM3.5 million in 1991 on a large-scale advertising campaign and total costs have mounted to DM7 billion over five years. The system is said to have added just over half a penny on average to the cost of every supermarket product.

The system inevitably benefits the recycling industry and hurts the scrap markets. So far, it has caused a boom in the waste disposal market, but there have been competition pitfalls. The arrangements encourage horizontal collaboration between competitors at all levels of the packaging chain. If market-support activities emerge, restrictive practices may follow, and this poses a danger to EU competition policy. Hence, the system has come under criticism from other countries and from the EU. Certain aspects of the law, like refillable bottles, tend to discriminate against other nations' products, and some retailers are reluctant to take Germany's products. The laws have created a crisis for collection and recycling infrastructures in other countries. They have also led to huge surpluses in plastics, paper and board, for which there was no market, and their prices consequently collapsed in 1994. The problem with the system is that the legislation showed no interest in what the recycled materials would be used for or who would buy them. This was left up to market forces.

Old arrangements

Packaging material was typically disposed of in landfills, incinerated or incinerated for energy purposes. Companies had to make their own arrangements for waste packaging disposal and no separate organization existed.

New arrangements

Existing collection systems in towns or cities are now integrated into the DSD system. The collection of waste is covered by contracts between DSD and municipal or private waste disposal firms. Overseas companies can use the green dot.

Change of relationships

The responsibility which lay on local authorities or municipal organizations for waste disposal has now been shifted to manufacturers, distributors and consumers. The government's role in this situation is one of creating a change in obligations, plus setting tough new targets on recovery, to which industry was forced to respond. The second role of the government has been one of monitoring the achievement of the targets, but it has allowed the operational side of things to be undertaken by a private organization.

Q5   *Under the DSD system, who are the gainers and who are the losers?*

Q6   *What has been the economic function of increasing production costs by insisting on take back for recycling? Given the various problems, in what ways do you think improvements could be made to the present system?*

Case study   France: Waste recycling system

Objectives

The French government wishes to actively encourage and support the greater recycling of packaging waste.

Objectives for the EU

The 1994 directive states that by the end of the century all countries must recover at least half of their waste packaging and recycle one-quarter of it, with a minimum of 15 per cent for each material type.

New approaches

France has a high landfill usage rate, but the government wishes to close many of its landfill sites by the year 2000. It is looking at other ways of reducing and disposing of waste, including the following:

*   Approaches to increase efficiency in waste disposal.
*   Approaches to encourage a recycling scheme.

The background

The French government, like Germany, has adopted the approach of an industry-wide organization to work alongside the waste materials handling industry. However, the French system allows for household waste to go to incineration for energy (unlike Germany), and does not duplicate the collection and sorting activities of local authorities. The approach is one of system support, through the promotion of local schemes, and it aims at maintaining a balanced market to avoid surpluses.

Approaches to increase efficiency in waste disposal

France has undertaken a number of combined steps. It has set recovery targets of 75 per cent of all packaging waste by the year 2000. France is to introduce a 20 franc per tonne landfill levy, which will be collected by the French Environmental Protection Agency (ADEM). The money raised, estimated at FF500 million each year, is to be used to support recycling infrastructure developments. In relation to supporting waste disposal, the government introduced a *décret* (a decree or order) in April 1992 on the collection and disposal of household waste. This allows incineration where the packaging can be used for energy use. France has separate laws for household and for commercial packaging waste. The *décret* on the former is based on the idea of 'producer responsibility' which is placed on the packaging company. The *décret* has a number of elements:

- The local authorities remain responsible for waste collection.
- The packaging industry has to levy itself to fund the costs of waste packaging recovery.
- Only companies taking back their own packaging will be excluded from paying the levy.

The establishment of a recycling scheme

The 1992 *décret* gives packaging companies a choice. They can either use a private company to recover their packaging waste or use the state-approved organization. The latter has the aim of encouraging local collection and separation systems. It charges a fee, which allows the companies to use the German 'green dot' on packaging. This guarantees collection for reuse, recycling or energy incineration. Targets are set at every stage in relation to how much will be demanded and supplied. For household packaging waste, the approved organization is the Eco emballages (EE). The system is being introduced very gradually, with pilot projects, to allow time for adjustment.

The system works by the local authorities collecting all the household waste. They then agree amounts and content of the waste with the EE, and sell it to the organization. The local authorities use these revenues to develop their collection and sorting systems. The EE then arranges to supply this waste to material handling companies. There are different companies for different types of waste (glass, paper, etc.) These companies then take the waste and decide what will be put to reuse, recycling or energy recovery purposes. There is a network of contractual guarantees. For example, the EE enters into a contract with the material companies under which it provides a guarantee to take back a certain amount of separated waste. The material organizations then contract with recycling and incineration companies.

The financing arrangements operate by the local authorities receiving a financial payment from the EE. It pays them a fixed price, but this is not a sale. The EE is acting on behalf of the manufacturers, which produced the packaging in the first place, so it does not own the packaging waste. In essence, the EE is acting for a third party, and makes a financial contribution to ensure that the manufacturers are meeting their obligations to take back/recycle. The manufacturers then pay EE a fee which gives them a guarantee of take back and allows them to use the green dot.

Among the advantages of this system are that the green dot is used, as in Germany, which indicates to consumers that the packaging will be reused or recycled. The system relies heavily on the use of contracts. So, for example, material will not be supplied to recycling companies unless there are contracts in existence to take specific amounts. The value of this is that it avoids stockpiling and the export of surplus waste. The EE is acting like a middle man to align the local authorities' output of sorted waste on the one hand, and the equipment and the capacity of the material companies on the other hand.

Old arrangements

Previously there was no middle man working between the local authorities collecting waste and the industries which used the sorted material. The old arrangements did not facilitate the handling of greater quantities of recycled materials.

New arrangements

The system effectively means that packaging manufacturers and packaging companies pay a levy to the EE which subsidizes the prices paid to the local authorities for the collection and sorting of waste materials.

Change of relationships

The idea is to support the activities of local authorities and to ensure that packaging companies meet their recycling obligations. The government is intervening through the provision of subsidies.

Q7 *What effect is raising landfill levies likely to have on waste disposal methods and management?*

Q8 *Why does recycling have to be subsidized? What is the role of the Eco emballages?*

Discussion

The aim of this section is to describe and contrast different approaches to encouraging alternative forms of waste handling and disposal. In the case of Germany, the approach adopted compels manufacturers to take back packaging. This requirement is coupled with a prohibition on sending packaging to landfill sites or for energy incineration, and high national recovery targets. There are strengths and weaknesses with this approach. The benefits are that recycling as an activity has increased, the recyclability of packaging materials has improved and there has been an increased awareness of the benefits of recycling to consumers. These benefits must be weighed up against the costs. The problems are of an operational, financial and market-distorting nature. The high collection targets imposed on DSD meant that it could not negotiate contracts; it had to take anything it was offered. Retailers were forced to use contractors. These contractors had a captive market and they collected waste which had no relationship to market demand, often supplying it free of charge or at negative prices to paper mills and other recyclers. German reprocessing companies could not handle the quantities of packaging waste and, as a consequence, waste packaging was dumped in neighbouring countries. This had a spill-over impact on other markets.

Financial problems arose because there was scope to free ride. Packaging companies could understate the amount of packaging used and hence avoid paying the green dot fee. The Ministry of the Environment has intervened by adjusting the quotas and paying off some of the debt accumulated. Clearly, setting incentives to encourage this activity and leaving the rest up to markets was an insufficient approach, as it ignored the current state of technology and the capacity of companies to handle the quantities of waste materials.

In the case of France, the experience has been slightly more successful. The approach adopted has been more gradual, to allow for the current state of technology and processing capacity of companies. It has been more contracts-based than the German system because the EE has the function of aligning supply with demand through specific contracts. The quotas set have been less demanding than in Germany, and energy incineration has not been ruled out. There has been no duplication of activities: the public authorities collect and sort household waste material. The French system has introduced a landfill levy to try and level the playing field between alternative waste disposal methods. Revenues collected are to be used to support and build recycling capacities. The benefit of this particular approach is that a greater reliance on a system of contracts, coupled with feasible targets, has avoided the exporting of surpluses and stockpiling, experienced in Germany.

Further reading

Introductory level

Griffiths, A. and Wall, S. (eds) (1997) *Applied Economics: An Introductory Course*, Harlow: Longman, ch. 10.

Intermediate level

Griffiths, A. and Wall, S. (1997) *Intermediate Microeconomics: Theory and Applications*, Harlow: Longman, ch. 11.

Other sources

Billingmann, F. (1994) 'The dual system: the why and the wherefore', *Wastes Management*, March.

Clark, M., Smith, D. and Blowers, A. (eds) (1992) *Waste Location*, London: Routledge, ch. 6.

Cooper, J. (1994) 'Recovering waste paper: an international perspective', *Wastes Management*, November.

Coste, A. (1993) 'Accelerated mineralisation of domestic refuse', *Wastes Management*, July.

Department of the Environment (1995) *Digest of Environment Statistics*, no. 17.

'Recycling in Germany: a wall of waste', *The Economist*, November, 1991.

'European rubbish: tied up in knots', *The Economist*, January, 1995.

'The new challenge of waste management licensing', *ENDS Report*, no. 231, 1994.

'New EC waste strategy finalised', *ENDS Report*, no. 258, 1996.

'Waste disposal law – economic instruments', *Environmental Law and Management*, May/June, 1993.

Fairbank, K. (1994) 'Recycling – the inevitable reality', *International Waste Management*, July.

Rose, M. (1994) 'The PRG comes to the packaging mountain', *International Waste Management*, October.

Schypek, J. (1992) 'Germany on trial over green packaging', *Marketing*, July.

Waite, R. (1995) *Household Waste Recycling*, London: Earthscan.

Wolfe, P. (1995) 'Germany's industry must produce more recycable products', *Pollution Prevention* (European edition), April.

Chapter 13

Summary and conclusions

Key words used: intervention, deregulation, contracts, incentives, privatization

In this book we have examined the issues of government intervention in a range of areas and under a variety of pressures. We have compared different approaches adopted in selected western European countries and considered the new role of markets in public policy areas. It is my view that the fundamental issue underlying the question of the role of governments rests with what we think governments should be doing. Undoubtedly, political considerations will impose on economic ones and vice versa – the two areas will overlap. What we have seen is that economic analysis provides a starting point from which to justify government intervention in a market economy, by identifying a number of areas where markets can fail. The assertion is that government intervention will improve on these deficiencies. We have also seen that governments fail too. The challenge is therefore to combine the strengths of both systems of allocation in an effort to improve on the efficiency and equity outcomes in important public areas. Ultimately it is a political decision as to how much intervention actually takes place in practice.

We have seen that countries with different political, economic and social backgrounds have adopted different objectives and hence implemented different approaches. Some have claimed that European politico-economic systems are converging as the process of industrialization develops. We have witnessed a definite move towards the greater use of market-based approaches in this book, but the approaches still reflect different goals and this has in part prevented full convergence.

Of the future, it is clear that EU-wide directives play and will continue to play a key role in a number of areas. The European Commission has been instrumental in increasing awareness of environmental concerns and reviewing possible new approaches on an EU-wide basis. In its pursuit of the internal market, it has prompted debates on the need for greater clarity over government subsidies to the transport and energy industries, encouraged deregulation of existing monopoly structures, and lastly reviewed the case for a Community-wide universal postal price. It is likely to have a continuing role in influencing the direction of public policy.

What we have seen could be claimed to be a revival of the *laissez-faire* form of capitalism, as many countries strive to reduce inefficiencies in resource allocation. This change can be partly explained by the slowdown in economic growth, the rise of budget deficits and electorates which are becoming increasingly reluctant to accept increases in taxes. Against these efficiency pressures, there remains the question and challenge of how to bring about increases in efficiency without damaging equity outcomes. Many governments, as we have seen, have addressed this issue through separate legislation to protect the low income and less advantaged members of society.

Many of the market-based approaches described in this book are underpinned by a belief, among many, that intervention has had a damaging rather than enhancing impact on systems of allocation. In particular, it has been argued that in a world characterized by constant change, flexibility and adaptability are the more appropriate requirements of any allocation system. It is my view that the mixed economy will survive, but that the form of intervention will be modified and adjusted. Governments are likely to have a key role in the markets, whether these are internal markets or privatized ones, and there will be a role for setting standards and monitoring outcomes and behaviour. Some of the changes in the roles of governments are summarized below, along with reservations and commendations about the new directions in public policy.

Social welfare themes

Part 2 of the book examined the health care industry, social housing and higher education systems. Three common policy themes emerged: the separation of the purchaser and provider function; changes in funding mechanisms; and the introduction of a system of contracts between purchaser and provider. These are special markets in that, in some cases, consumption is free at the point of delivery, a purchasing organization makes decisions on consumers' behalf and there is a limited role for a price mechanism. In many cases, governments have retained their role as funder of the welfare services, but the function of provider has been transferred to either a government agency or a not-for-profit organization. The benefits of the internal market are that they represent a move away from the problems of government provision, monopoly provision, inflexible arrangements and loss of control over subsidies. The internal markets are supposed to enhance efficiency in provision, choice and responsiveness to demand.

In the case of health care, the use of internal markets has been introduced and extended. While there are potential benefits to be had with a system which seeks to bring greater cost consciousness, there are concerns in the area of cream skimming, information disclosure on the quality of health outcomes, and the position of consumers in making efficient and equitable choices. It is likely that individuals will be unable to overcome these problems and that the reforms will need further intervention and refinement to make the market work efficiently.

In the case of higher education, the introduction of competition for funds between the providers of higher education has sharpened the focus of many institutions, successfully expanded higher education systems and reduced costs at the same time. However, concerns lie in how the quality of the service may be affected and whether the present procedures will sufficiently deal with quality control and simultaneously provide a greater diversity of course choice for the student.

In the case of social housing, governments have withdrawn from the role of principal provider and have shifted this responsibility on to a variety of independent provider organizations. There is competition for public funds through the bidding process between the providers. At present, as in the UK, they are monitored by a single purchaser, which has to inspect and regulate a large number of diverse providers. Besides this, increases in rents towards market levels have raised some doubts over equality of access in the social housing market. The use of private funds for social purposes is as yet an undeveloped market and needs further refinement and support if it is to provide a sustained and effective role.

National industries themes

The industries chosen in Part 3 of the book are those which have national significance and form part of a nation's infrastructure, transport, communications and energy sectors. Here the new directions in policy are deregulation and privatization. Governments have intervened to free up the existing public sector and market provision. There have been varying degrees of deregulation in each industry. The emphasis has been on increasing the levels of competition and increasing the efficiency of the public subsidies.

In the case of the postal services, the challenge to governments is in dealing with the natural monopoly elements and the fact that competition is undesirable in particular areas. Privatization is not, therefore, an obvious solution. The approaches adopted have been ones of gradual deregulation: in particular, involving a specific number of steps such as the reorganization of businesses so that greater accountability can be achieved between expenditures and revenues of particular services. The separation of the different businesses into corporations has been seen as a necessary step towards greater efficiency. Finally, the liberalization of the statutory letter monopoly has been the final step in the UK. It remains an unanswered question as to how the problem of cream skimming will be avoided and through what mechanism subsidies will be allocated.

The railways industries have had a different experience, involving a shift from a rules-based organization to a system of contracting, and privatization in the case of the UK. Different policy objectives were involved in the two industries studied. The Dutch involves one of expansion and incentives for greater efficiency, without a change in ownership, while the UK privatization of train service provision may meet efficiency objectives, but may have an uncertain impact on the size of the industry. In both cases there is likely to be a significant role for governments in both the provision of a public subsidy and quality of service regulation. The high level of transaction costs involved in setting up the institutional environment for these contract-based systems must be weighed up against the benefits of a railway system with limited scope for service competition.

Electricity industries have had decades of government intervention in pricing, planning and investment decisions. This has now been substituted by the market, and in the case of the UK, the industry was privatized. This was followed by the setting up of a regulatory organization responsible for protecting the consumer and for creating conditions for greater levels of effective competition. While there are clear efficiency gains from more open markets in energy generally, as the EU is keen to encourage, these benefits will be realized only when the commercial decisions of all national industries are truly independent from their governments. Differing national objectives in France mean that the public monopoly structure is unlikely to be altered radically in the near future. This raises the interesting challenge of how to demonstrate and reconcile EU-wide benefits of open competition with national industrial and social concerns.

Environmental themes

In Part 4 we saw a wide variety of innovations on the part of governments to improve the incentives for efficiency on the one hand, and to create conditions which support the private sector making more environmentally friendly decisions on the other. Market-based approaches have been used in a range of ways to overcome pressures on governments to meet expenditure constraints and achieve internationally agreed pollution targets.

In the case of roads, the need to provide additional funds for the construction and maintenance of national road systems has been paramount in terms of addressing demand-side pressures. This appears to have been met with some success. Governments have creatively provided incentives for greater private sector investment, which has accelerated road-building programmes and thereby reduced the social costs of provision. However, while greater accountability has been achieved through earmarked funding in both countries studied and the successful adoption of user charges in Sweden, there are some concerns about policies which have tended to ignore the environmental impacts of the use of shadow pricing in the UK. There is likely to be a continued role for governments as the principal funders and planners of road networks, with the construction and maintenance of specific roads being left to the private sector. Governments will have a more interactive role with private companies.

In the case of air pollution, amid pressures at EU level and from pressure groups and world organizations, governments are seeking new ways of ensuring that nationally agreed targets are met. Chapter 11 looked at two distinct approaches, one which sought to focus on cooperative and self-regulatory methods, through the more intensive use of voluntary agreements, and one which experimented with market creation incentives. Both approaches faced a set of implementation problems. In the Netherlands, the problem of setting feasible targets has been exposed, while in Germany, perception and credibility problems have hindered the successful implementation of a tradable permit scheme. Clearly, there is a further role for governments in both cases to modify and reinforce the existing systems.

Waste management is an area which has seen many local government initiatives taking place. A strong EU-wide presence in the setting of targets over specified periods has left open the option for governments to experiment with different approaches. The German case is an example of where the industry responded to the government's ambitious targets for waste disposal, by creating its own waste management system, and with good economic justification, set in place incentives for the recycling of paper products. The success of this initiative has been hampered by the oversight of its impact on international trade and on waste markets. Government has a further role in supporting and modifying this innovation. In the case of France, incentives have been aimed at 'levelling the playing field' between the various waste disposal options, by placing a hefty levy on landfills. This approach has had greater effectiveness and less impact on international markets.

Glossary

Access Legal entitlement for a potential competitor to use something which was once used by a monopoly: for example, rail tracks.

Adverse selection Where a high-risk individual is more likely to buy insurance than a low-risk individual. If insurance companies have imperfect information and cannot identify the individuals, then it becomes unprofitable to sell insurance.

Allocation of resources How factors are used, how the goods are produced and how the goods are distributed to consumers.

Asymmetric information Where a buyer and a seller have different information about a transaction.

Command and control approach Where an authority lays down what will be done and how it will be enforced. Often this is a blanket approach and little consideration is given to the specific circumstances of a company.

Commercialization Making a business unit run on commercial lines, or provide a profit and loss account. This is not a substitute for competition.

Common property resource Property that can be used by all citizens as intensively as they like; no one has the right to exclude another from using such property.

Competitive markets Where individual buyers and sellers have little or no ability to affect prices.

Cross-subsidy Where some users or usages are charged below average costs while others are charged above average costs in a way which ensures that total costs are covered.

Deadweight loss A measure of efficiency loss.

Deregulation of housing finance Freeing up the amount of financial dependence on the government.

Distribution The transfer of electricity from distribution points to end users.

Earmarked finance The designation of funds to a particular end use.

Economic efficiency When applied to society as a whole, this means that the sum of the benefits of a particular allocation of resources exceeds the costs.

Economies of scale Where the average cost of producing an item falls as the production of it increases.

Economies of scope Many companies produce more than one service. There are cost advantages from when two or more services are produced: for example, from common production facilities.

Energy incineration Incinerating waste material in order to extract its energy content.

Equilibrium A balance of offsetting economic forces so that there is no tendency for change.

External costs An action of an individual or group that harms the welfare of another individual or group.

Externality A cost or benefit imposed on people other than the consumers and producers of a good or service.

252

Free-rider One who receives the benefit of a good without contributing to its cost.

Generation Any plant or apparatus which produces electricity.

Guild choice Where there is measured competition and organizations are choosing between a number of independent organizations, but not on the basis of prices or the content of a basic package of services.

Housing finance Finance raised by the public sector to fund the building, maintenance and development of social housing programmes.

Incentives Economic rewards and penalties.

Landfill site A site at which waste is deposited for permanent disposal.

Market-based approaches Any arrangement in which buyers and sellers interact. There may be a role for a 'price' mechanism and some form of trading. Typically, this approach takes into consideration the specific circumstances of a company.

Market choice Where choice is on the basis of prices and the quality of services.

Market equilibrium A price and quantity such that quantity demanded equals quantity supplied.

Model An abstract representation of a situation or problem, designed to simplify and describe the essential features.

Monopoly A market structure characterized by a single seller, a unique product and impossible entry into the market.

Moral hazard Where an insured person can affect the liability without the knowledge of the company.

Natural monopoly An industry in which the average cost of production declines throughout the entire market. As a result, a single firm can supply the whole market at a lower cost than two or more smaller firms.

Opportunity cost The value of the best alternative forgone when choices are made under conditions of scarcity.

Pareto efficiency Where an allocation of resources makes one person better off without making someone worse off.

Performance indicators These capture an attribute which is considered desirable, but which could not usually be judged by the naked eye, such as cost per student, the student experience or the quality of teaching.

Policy approach A method or instrument of intervention which seeks to achieve a policy objective.

Policy objective A government aim, target or aspiration.

Polluter-pays principle Where those who created the pollution are penalized for it. The victim-pays principle is where the non-consenting party has to pay the polluter not to pollute.

Pollution abatement Reduction in pollution.

Property rights Legal rules or restrictions that govern the way in which resources or goods may be used by their owner.

Provider An organization, public, private or a mixture of the two, which provides a good or service: for example, universities, hospitals and housing associations.

Public funding Money raised from general taxation to fund a particular welfare service.

Public good A good or service which, once produced, has two properties: users collectively consume its benefits and there is no way of excluding people who do not pay from consuming such a good or service.

Public service obligation A broad term referring to the requirement of an industry to provide a minimum level of service.

Purchaser (health) This may be a health insurance company, a health purchasing organization or a GP practice. It decides on the health needs of a population and buys treatments through a contract, from a provider.

Purchaser (higher education) An organization which purchases higher education places on behalf of the student: an example in the UK is the Higher Education Funding Council.

Purchaser (housing) An organization which purchases housing on behalf of the consumer, or tenant. It might set down rent levels, quality and size of housing in a contract or through regulation.

Quality regulation In the case of teaching, ensuring that both the teaching standards and the procedures to ensure teaching quality do not fall.

Rail infrastructure Non-moving assets, such as bridges, tracks, signalling, crossings and tunnels.

Recovery To recycle, compost, regenerate or take the energy from the material.

Recycled materials Materials which have been recycled either by combining them with another product or in the form of a secondary raw material.

Recycling rate The tonnage of waste recycled as a percentage of total waste.

Reprocessing industry A stage of recycling which takes the material and changes its physical form.

Restructuring Changing the structure of an industry: for example, breaking up a monopoly structure into smaller sized units.

Reuse Using a product more than once without changing its physical form.

Road finance Investment needed to plan, design and build roads. This also includes road subsidies.

Road infrastructure Assets like road foundations, surfaces, road banks and verges, and signposts. This is different to the operation of a road, which is about traffic management.

Selective contracting In the health care market, this refers to a more formal type of exchange between health purchaser and provider. The former selects providers and forms contracts with them on the basis of amenities, access, quality and costs for contracts.

Semi-public good A good which has elements of non-excludability and non-rivalry in consumption.

Shadow pricing Where a public authority pays a fixed sum for each vehicle using the privately financed and open-access road.

Social costs The sum of the private costs of a decision-maker plus any external costs of the action imposed on non-consenting individuals or communities.

Statutory monopoly A monopoly created by statute, which usually gives exclusive rights to one supplier, such as the postal authority.

Technological innovation The body of knowledge and skills applied to how goods are produced where the body of knowledge is brand new.

Third party access In the case of electricity supply companies, being able to use another nation's national transmission grid.

Tolls A form of user charge, not principally used to manage traffic congestion.

Transmission The bulk transfer of electricity from individual generating stations to distribution system entry points.

Universal access This refers to everyone being able to receive a good or service, irrespective of income, social status, location or state of health.

Universal service obligation A principle conferred on an organization to provide a specified service, often on a national basis, to all those willing to pay for it.

User charges (roads) These are levied on road users and can raise finance or reduce traffic. They are based on the idea that users are willing to pay for improvements in roads or for their time savings.

Utility The level of satisfaction that a person gets from consuming a good or service.

Vouchers Substitutes for cash, these have a value which covers part of the costs of education.

Index

Note: Bold page numbers refer to the glossary.